ULTRA-MARATHONING

ULTRA-MARATHONING

The Next Challenge

Tom Osler
and Ed Dodd

WORLD

World Publications, Inc.
Mountain View, California

Library of Congress Cataloging in Publication Data

Osler, Tom, 1940-
Ultramarathoning, the next challenge.

1. Marathon running. I. Dodd, Ed, 1946-
joint author. II. Title.
GV1065.08. 796.4'26 78-68612
ISBN 0-89037-169-5

World Publications, Inc.
Mountain View, CA

To my wife, Denise,
and my children, Ed, Michael, and Jennifer

To my father and mother,
Joseph and Rose Osler

Contents

Foreword

For two decades we have been enthusiastic participants in road and track races at the shorter distances. The chance discovery of an old scrapbook, containing what appeared to us as nearly unbelievable accounts of foot races of the past century, sparked our interest in the history of this sport. As we researched the performances of the old-timers, we wondered how it was possible for men to cover distances of 500 miles on foot without enduring complete physical breakdown. Spurred on by the colorful descriptions of reports from old newspapers, we decided to try similar efforts ourselves, and thus we joined that tiny fringe element of track athletes known as ultramarathoners.

We approached World Publications with a proposal to write a book on the history of the great six-day pedestrian races of the past century. Joe Henderson suggested that we also include information on how to train and race for the longest runs as well. At first we saw this as an unlikely marriage of two different subjects – one history, the other technical advice for modern athletes. As we gave the project more thought we realized that, like ourselves, others might find the story of the great pedestrians to be an inspiration to try ultramarathoning and explore new dimensions in their physical and psychological potential. Thus the present volume was born.

We thought it best to divide the writing into two distinct parts and to view the result as two separate books bound by one cover. In this way, each author was free to express his view without the necessity of constantly consulting the other for approval. However, while we each wrote our own part separately, the reader should know that the contents are largely a joint effort. Both of us spent years researching old newspapers and journals and constructing the present history of a decade in pedestrianism. Likewise, both of us spent hundreds of hours discussing our training and racing techniques for competition on the road and track.

It is our hope that this book will stimulate the reader to experience for himself or herself the great joy of the long journey on foot.

Tom Osler
Ed Dodd

Acknowledgments

The historical portion of this book would not exist if it had not been for the quick and friendly help we received from many sources. I wish to thank the staffs of the Library of Congress, Free Library of Philadelphia, St. Joseph's University Library (Philadelphia), New York Public Library, Mutter Museum and Historical Section of the College of Physicians in Philadelphia, Queensborough Public Library, Chicago Public Library, Chicago Historical Society, Los Angeles Public Library and the Library Company of Philadelphia.

Several people went far out of their way to fulfill our requests. Special thanks to Rosemary Hsieh of the St. Joseph's University Library in Philadelphia, and Pat Connors of the College of Physicians in Philadelphia.

Two individuals, whom I have never met, were of invaluable assistance. John Lucas unselfishly shared numerous references with us and even sent us original copies of three very useful publications: *The American Championship Record, Weston and His Walks–Souvenir Program of His Walk from New York to Minneapolis, and Souvenir Program of his Great Transcontinental Walk.*

Andy Milroy of Wiltshire, England, spent hours answering the many questions I put to him in my long letters. I waited with anticipation for each of Andy's replies, which always included new and exciting information.

I thank my parents for their constant encouragement. When I

felt that there was no way I would finish on time, this encouragement helped greatly. Thanks also go to Terry Dougherty for reading the original manuscript and offering suggestions for improvement.

The initial motivation for the book came from my long-time friend and running companion, Tom Osler. But he supplied far more than just that. He helped with the research and, more importantly, we spent hour after hour discussing the incredible achievements of the pedestrians. From these talks came a feel for and an understanding of what it was to be a pedestrian, and a desire to share this knowledge.

It is impossible to give my wife, Denise, enough praise and thanks for her contribution to the completion of this book. Right from the very beginning she has been untiring in her efforts to uncover long-forgotten accounts and publications of the pedestrian era. She spent endless hours with a phone in one hand and a baby in the other, scouring the country for this or that reference. Ninety percent of the material we now have is a direct result of her labor. Beyond this she photocopied, cut and pasted, and organized the material, proofread and typed the manuscript, and even helped me in the darkroom. Her endurance was that of a true pedestrian.

I thank my children Ed, Michael, and Jennifer for understanding why I spent so much time in my room with the door closed.

Finally, I would like to thank Bob Anderson and the staff of World Publications.

Ed Dodd

While I have been racing for twenty-five years, my interest in ultramarathons became intense only during the past five. For this reason I am indebted to all the runners who trained and raced with me during this period, when the ideas offered in this book grew. In particular, I am grateful to Bob Zazzali, with whom I so frequently trained. When we met a few years ago Bob was a lunchtime jogger. Shortly thereafter he was entering races of twenty-six miles, fifty miles, and twenty-four hours. His willingness to experiment and his countless hours of reflection forged the ideas which I now present.

Special thanks go to Joe Henderson and Dr. Joanne Trimble who made valuable comments on the manuscript; to my wife, Kathy, and my sons, Eric and Billy, who tolerate my frequent absence on long runs; and to Bob Anderson and his staff at World Publications for their patience with this procrastinating author.

Tom Osler

Introduction

In 1958, Vernon Ordiway, a young medical student at Temple University Hospital in Philadelphia, was given a dusty scrapbook by an aged and dying patient. The man had no family or friends except for Vern, who would sit and talk to the man whenever he had the chance. The old man had been a professional runner at the turn of the century and the scrapbook was filled with clippings from local newspapers and the *National Police Gazette* magazine from the years 1899 to 1903.

Vern took the scrapbook and gave it to Browning Ross, who was then writer, editor, and publisher of *Long Distance Log.* Browning in turn gave the book to Tom Osler. Tom was amazed at the detailed accounts of a group of athletes called the "pedestrians," who competed professionally in races up to six days long. Tom said it was like reading "science fiction." In the late '50s the marathon was considered the ultimate test of one's endurance. To discover that men had covered more than 500 miles within six consecutive days was indeed incredible. Tom read through the scrapbook and then put it away, occasionally bringing it out to show fellow marathoners.

Ten years passed. Tom won three national championships and in 1968 was invited to Dr. David Costill's Human Performance Lab at Ball State University. Costill showed Tom an article, written by Professor John A. Lucas of Penn State University, about a series of five six-day races called the Astley Belt Races that were held in 1878 and 1879. Tom was surprised to see that these crazy six-day affairs had existed almost thirty years prior to the scrapbook.

Seven more years passed. Tom had run in several fifty-mile races and I was beginning to give them serious consideration. One day in 1975 Tom recalled Lucas' article, made a copy, and showed it to me. The time was right and our enthusiasm for ultra-running was high. We reread the article and the scrapbook. I showed the scrapbook to my wife, Denise, who has library experience. She started a search for all possible material on pedestrianism, led in the beginning by the references in John Lucas' article. This search is not yet ended. In fact, I see no end in the immediate future. We have, however, accumulated, with the help of scores of friendly people, notebook after notebook of information on the history of distance running in general and ultramarathoning in particular.

We have concentrated our study on one phase of this history—the incredible six-day go-as-you-please contests of the late 19th and very early 20th centuries. Since the beginning of recorded history there have been stories and legends of men who could travel long distances on foot. The legend of Pheidippides, for instance, is well known. In the late 18th century in England two men, Foster Powell and Captain Barclay, won fame and fortune with their pedestrian ventures. Powell covered 100 miles in twenty-two hours in 1788, and Barclay walked 100 miles in nineteen hours in 1806. Later, in 1809, Barclay won a huge wager when he became the first man to walk one mile in each and every one of 1,000 consecutive hours.

In 1777, a young boy of nineteen by the name of Jonas Cattel ran ten miles through the night from Haddonfield to Fort Mercer, New Jersey, to warn the American troops of an impending attack by the British. He became known as the "Paul Revere of South Jersey." At the age of fifty-five, in 1813, Cattel won a wager by running from Woodbury, New Jersey, to Cape May, New Jersey, a distance of eighty miles, in one day. He then turned around and ran back to Woodbury the next day.

Still, there is no more astounding record of man's endurance and tenacity than found in the exploits of the six-day pedestrians. When I first read through the scrapbook I was filled with wonder and amazement. How could they do it? How could they circle a dusty eight-lap-to-the-mile (sometimes as small as sixteen-laps-to-the-mile) track in smoke-filled arenas, living in small tents, competing in inadequate shoes, without the great knowledge of diet and training that we runners of the 1970s have had?

After four years of research and nine ultramarathons of my own, I remain in awe of their ability and pluck. In the chapters that follow I have detailed the birth, growth, decline, and death of the pedestrian mania that swept the United States and Great Britain in the latter part of the 19th century. I have attempted to convey to the reader what it must have been like to witness or participate in a six-day go-as-you-please event. Who knows? In the future we may have the opportunity to experience such an event ourselves.

Ed Dodd

Introduction to Part Two

Most runners who enter races of fifty miles and longer have had extensive experience in shorter races. They have found from this experience that the major difference between, say, racing five miles and the twenty-six mile, 385 yard marathon* is the need to put in greater training mileage before the race, and run at a slower pace during it. It might seem natural, then, to assume that ultramarathons will be simple, linear extension of the runner's experience with shorter distances. Nothing could be further from the truth.

To run ultramarathons with the same intensity with which the standard marathon is successfully approached will invite physical breakdown of startling proportions for all but the most gifted athletes. Ultramarathoning is less like marathoning and more like hiking. It is best viewed as a totally new sport in which a trained marathoner is but a novice.

Wait you say! What about those marathoners who were remarkably successful in their very first fifty-mile race? Jim Pearson entered the National AAU fifty-mile Championship in Seattle in

*In Part II "marathon" or "standard marathon" will be used for the twenty-six mile, 385 yard distance. "Ultra" is used for ultramarathon throughout.

1975 and won, setting the American road record in his initial try beyond the marathon. In 1977, the great Nina Kuscsik, pioneer woman marathoner established the women's fifty-mile record on her first outing at the distance. Even these examples don't contradict my position that ultramarathoning is best approached as a different sport from marathoning, however. This author was also one of those who claimed victory in his first fifty-miler, and the experience showed clearly just how little I knew about this difference.

1967 was my best year as a competitive runner. I had been racing the marathon and shorter distances for thirteen consecutive years. The National AAU fifty-miler was scheduled for Poughkeepsie, New York, on Thanksgiving Day. Having won the National AAU Thirty Kilometer Championship in the spring and placing fourth in the AAU Marathon, I decided to run the fifty-miler, even though I had never gone beyond thirty miles in training.

Race day brought a freezing rain; I set to work with the competitive abandon that had brought success at the shorter distances. I won, missing the American record by a few seconds, but the post-race recovery was a nightmare. Never before had I known such fatigue. I was lethargic and weary for three weeks. I frequently fell while training, because I was unable to lift my feet in the accustomed manner. Not only did I fall, but my reactions were so slow that I would fail to throw out my arms to break the impact. (Hitting concrete, chest first, has no training value whatsoever.)

I was now hailed in running journals as an "ultramarathoning" specialist, but as far as I was concerned I never wanted to enter another fifty-miler again. Ted Corbitt, my close friend and America's premier ultramarathoner, said I was "gun shy." It took seven more years before I found the courage to enter my second ultra. Since then I have learned how to cover great mileage without such extensive abuse.

Once the proper methods are mastered, great distances can be covered on foot with surprising ease. Since 1974 I have run in numerous fifty-milers, three twenty-four hour runs, two hundred-milers as well as one 200-mile effort in seventy hours. At first glance these distances appear most intimidating. After all, the marathon can be very fatiguing, but, when properly executed, ultras can be far less tiring than standard marathons. This apparent contradiction is resolved when the runner learns the art of mixing gently-paced running with walking, the major new skill that the marathoner must acquire.

My career as a runner began twenty-five years ago. I have run more than 800 races at all distances up to and including the standard marathon. In contrast, I have run fewer than two dozen ultras. Even though I attained some success at the shorter distances (AAU championships at twenty-five and thirty kilometers), it is the ultras that have brought me the greatest fulfillment.

Part One

The Great Six Day Races

by Ed Dodd

1

Weston's Walk in Newark

Outside the Washington Street Rink the weather was cloudy, windy, and cold. Inside it was damp and warm. A haze of tobacco smoke hovered over the arena. As night approached, the Saturday crowd became denser. Before seven o'clock that evening the central space of the vast amphitheatre began to fill up and the galleries and aisles "swarmed with an excited throng."

This scene was far different than it had been earlier in the week. At that time the attendance was sparse and there seemed to be little interest in the event taking place. Perhaps it was the *Newark Daily Advertiser*'s comment on Wednesday that "from this evening on until the end of the walk the pedestrian may be seen at his best," or ex-mayor Ricord's pleading in Thursday's paper that "Newarkers should show their appreciation of the athlete's effort," that finally had the people pouring off the Broad Street horse cars and walking the short but chilly distance to Washington Street. The 6,000 spectators composed all classes of society. A group of city and state dignitaries gathered at the judges' stand and the enclosed space in front of it that was reserved for the walker's attendants.

Mayor Perry and the Chief of Police, Captain Dwyer, were in attendance. The day before, the mayor had threatened to mobilize the entire Newark police force and the militia if necessary to guard against any attempt to hinder the success of the historic pedestrian

Washington St. rink–the scene of Weston's 500-mile, six day performance, 1874 (Newark Library)

feat being attempted by the well-known Edward Payson Weston. Since Weston had failed in three previous tries that same year to walk 500 miles in six consecutive days, there were large sums of money bet on his failure this time also.

Rumors had spread rapidly early in the week that some type of disruption was planned. In fact, Captain Dwyer had received telegrams from New York City to the effect that Joe Coburn (a New York City gambler) and a gang of roughs intended to visit the rink and stop Weston from finishing. The rink was surrounded by the police to guard against any intrusion and warrants were issued for the arrest of Joe Coburn and his entire "gang."

By eight o'clock it was clear that Weston would succeed. Waves of contagious excitement swept through the crowd. They were about to witness the conclusion of an extraordinary feat of human endurance never before accomplished. Many of the best pedestrians in the United States and England had attempted to cover 500 miles in six days but they had all failed.

Edward Payson Weston

Edward Payson Weston was born in Providence, Rhode Island, March 15, 1839. His father was a merchant and later a school teacher in Rhode Island and California. His mother was well known for her poetry and romance stories that appeared in the leading journals and magazines.

Weston showed no special athletic ability while growing up in New England. His capacity as a pedestrian first became apparent while he was an office boy at the *New York Herald* in 1858. As the story is told, Mrs. Bennett, the wife of the Scottish owner of the paper, was about to leave on a European vacation when it was discovered that an important package had been left behind. The nineteen-year-old Weston volunteered to run the twelve miles round trip to Bloomingdale's to retrieve the package. He surprised everyone by returning on time and the *Herald*'s owner was so impressed that he doubled Weston's wages on the spot to the envied sum of six dollars a week.

Weston became a reporter for the *Herald* a few months later. In this era before rapid transportation and telephones his ability to cover ground swiftly on foot won for him many journalistic scoops.

His first attempt at a long walk was in the winter of 1861 to attend the inauguration of Abraham Lincoln. He started at the State House in Boston on February 22 and reached the nation's capital on March 4, traveling 453 miles in 208 hours. He missed the inauguration by half a day.

Weston's career as a professional pedestrian really began in 1867. From October 29 to November 28, a period of twenty-five days (Weston never walked on Sundays), he walked from Portland, Maine to Chicago, Illinois, a distance of 1,326 miles, winning a $10,000 wager for his effort. His tenacity won him recognition from crowds and whole towns. The newspapers of the day gave long, detailed reports of the walk. "This walk," said *Harper's Weekly*, "made Weston's name a household word."

In 1868, at White Plains, New York, he did 100 miles in 22:19:10, a world record. In January and February of 1869 he walked from Bangor, Maine, through New Hampshire and Vermont, passing over the Green Mountains and through northern and central New York to Buffalo, New York, covering a distance of

Edward Weston, c. 1862 (Library of Congress)

1,058 miles in thirty days. All but the first eight miles were over snow. In 1871 he walked 400 miles in four days, twenty-three hours, and thirty-two minutes at the Empire Rink in New York City. This walk included 112 miles in 23:44:00 in one day.

In addition to these accomplishments, however, there were numerous failures. It was reported that he unsuccessfully attempted to cover 100 miles in twenty-four hours forty-seven times before finally succeeding. Three times during 1874 he failed in attempts to cover 500 miles in six days. But even in failure he achieved a measure of success. His first failure took place at the American Institute Hall in New York City. The *New York Times* of May 17, 1874, reported his failure on page one:

> Greeted by the cheers of several thousand spectators and amid a scene of excitement not often witnessed, Edward Payson Weston, last evening, within a few seconds of midnight, completed the 430th mile of his great journey. It will thus be seen that he fell short by seventy miles of accomplishing the task he had undertaken, but nevertheless he has found himself the champion pedestrian of the world, and his feat of walking 115 miles in twenty-four hours, the first day, stands without parallel . . . .
>
> As the pedestrian crossed the score on the completion of the last round of the 430th mile, he was greeted with the wildest applause, and an eager throng of spectators rushed towards the judge's stand to congratulate him. Weston himself was so overcome that he could do no more than bow an acknowledgment of the applause, and by the advice of the doctors he was removed from the room. Despite the wonderful pluck and spirit he displayed to the last it was but too painfully evident that he was thoroughly tired out.

Weston had duplicated his "feat without parallel" the first day of this walk. From 12:05 a.m. Monday, December 14 to 12:04 a.m. Tuesday, December 15 he covered 115 miles. The *Newark Evening Courier* had this to say:

> We have become so accustomed to his (Weston's) great pedestrian triumphs that we are apt to underestimate the remarkable endurance and pluck, not to say speed, which this great undertaking calls for. What he has done ought to be amazing.

Monday's labor (accomplished with only an hour of rest), subsequent efforts of seventy-five and eighty miles on Tuesday and Wednesday, the lack of sleep, the low attendance early in the week, and the threat of physical violence, had so affected Weston that by Thursday morning he was "approaching the highest point of nervous tension, being so susceptible to outside influence that the slightest untoward accident would be sufficient to break him down for the whole journey."

But the pride and satisfaction generated by anticipated success after an arduous struggle and the sheer exhilaration of being the focus of attention before a standing, wildly cheering crowd of 6,000, whose shouts of "bravo" and "well-done" reverberated off the wooden walls of the arena, drove Weston on. The adrenalin surged through his body. His nervousness was gone. He accelerated his pace.

A touch of comic relief was added when, at 8:30 p.m., the mayor set out to walk a bit with Weston. Two laps of the 331-foot track left the poor mayor red-faced and panting much to the delight of the spectators, who roared with laughter.

The *Newark Daily Advertiser* captured the spirit and mood of the final hours in their edition the following Monday, December 21, 1874.

> The closing scene at the Rink was the most extraordinary occasion within the memory of Newark audiences. The appearance of the pedestrian, who was dressed in his usual black velvet knee-breeches, with ruffled white shirt and black leather leggings reaching to the knee, doubtless suggested extreme fatigue and lameness. His hollow cheeks, disordered hair and unmistakable limp seemed to betray the extent of the physical strain and the immensity of the task. Yet to those familiar with the man, these signs conveyed no hint of the real condition. They knew he was absolutely free from consciousness of fatigue, cheerful in spirits and full of indomitable will.
>
> Ladies and sedate elderly gentlemen distinguished themselves by their extravagant display of enthusiasm and extreme anxiety for the result, vying successfully with the boys in the noisy and ostentatious methods of getting rid of superabundant feelings. By nine o'clock the scene had grown stupendous. Between the divided mass of noisy humanity that choked the ground floor of the building lay the narrow path of the pedestrian, kept sacred from the intrusion by a police guard forming a cordon around the entire parallelogram.
>
> Round about the galleries was packed an army of gentility and respectability, six rows deep, hooting, gesticulating, and otherwise manifesting the intensity of its interest in the feat so soon to be decided. Between the divided phalanx below, the white-garbed central figure spun on his everlasting round, pale, earnest, eager, adding circuit to circuit and mile to mile. As each mile was called from the timekeeper's

desk, the general enthusiasm bubbled over into cheers and at times the noise of the band was lost for whole minutes amid the uproar.

Still the walker walked on while the time drew on to eleven. His pace had increased with the growing excitement, and was fast and strong. At his side marched, or rather trotted, the chief of police and a martial-looking captain, while close behind followed two policemen and a detective. In this order the walk was continued for the next two miles amid the thunder of applause and such notes from the band as survived the general uproar.

The progress of the pedestrian was measured by the motion of the mass of faces in the galleries as they followed his course. When the last sixteen laps, comprising the last mile, was begun the enthusiasm that had been working frantically towards its climax rose higher and higher with each successive circuit of the walker.

Twenty minutes to twelve. This is the last circuit. As the six days' trial was narrowed to the last strides, the crowd at the judge's stand condensed, and the final step that measured off the greatest feat of physical endurance on record, was made into the arms of friends who bore the hero in triumph to the stand.

This was the climax and the scene was indescribable. Hats and handkerchiefs waved and danced in the air while the yelling crowd overcame

Edward Weston completes 100 miles in twenty-two hours (Frank Leslie's Illustrated Newspaper)

the police guard in an effort to surround the place where Weston stood, pale, panting, but smiling as he stood supported by the arms of friends.

Mayor Perry then made a short speech that was completely drowned by the roaring crowd. The bedlam did not stop until Weston was carried from the track to his room, where he was undressed, his feet soaked in salt water, and put to bed. Weston woke at six a.m. Snow had just started to fall. He dressed and walked over to his hotel, the Mansion House on Broad Street. There he ate his first leisurely meal in a week. Later he attended church services at Association Hall, where the minister Dr. Nicholson preached an appropriate sermon from the text "And Enoch walked with God" and the choir sang Weston's favorite hymn, "Nearer my God to Thee." He walked to and from church through what had now become a raging blizzard that would eventually drop seventeen inches of snow on Newark that Sunday. The brief sleep had revived him completely. Perhaps the one quality of Weston that amazed people as much as his physical endurance was his incredible recuperative powers.

Weston had done it. The impossible. Not even the legendary English pedestrians of the late 18th and early 19th century, Foster Powell and Captain Barclay, had ever accomplished 500 miles within six days. Now, however, the barrier was broken. Others would follow. One was waiting in Chicago.

2

The Challenge to Supremacy

Daniel O'Leary was born on a small farm in the village of Carrigroe near Clonakilty, County Cork, Ireland on June 29, 1846, at a time of widespread famine and desolation in Ireland. O'Leary worked on his father's farm until he was twenty, then emigrated to the United States. Finding no work in New York City, he quickly settled in Chicago, and found a job in a lumberyard.

He stayed at the lumberyard only seven months and, with the coming of the winter of 1866, headed south to the fields of Boliver County, Mississippi. Here, he picked cotton for a year and a half before he went back to Chicago in the spring of 1868. He became a book and picture agent selling door-to-door on the installment plan. John E. Tansey, in his 1878 biography of O'Leary, gives us a description of a book canvasser's life.

> In order to obtain the three square meals necessary to supply the wants of the inner man, a book agent must rise with the sun, toil hard all day, climb numerous stairways (often descending much quicker than he ascends), and not unfrequently is bamboozled in the end out of at least four-fifths of the money for which he sells a book, owing to the "moving system" so much in vogue among the monthly-paying purchasers.

O'Leary was moderately successful at this venture until the great fire in October 1871. The fire scattered his customers and he lost more than $3,000 in stock and unpaid bills. After the fire, financially crippled, he started out in business again, but money being scarce and books being considered a luxury to the burned out and homeless Chicagoans, O'Leary was forced to sell his books in the surrounding villages. This often meant an early morning walk of ten to fifteen miles and a similar trek home in the evening. For two years he continued his daily rambles about the Chicago suburbs, laying the foundation for the great things to come.

Then, as Tansey recounts, one day in the fall of 1873 business brought O'Leary into one of the large dry goods stores on Wabash Avenue. There, he found three or four men busily engaged in discussing the merits of Edward Payson Weston, who was then attempting to walk 500 miles in six days. The prevailing opinion was that if Weston failed no one else could possibly accomplish such a task.

"None but a Yankee can place on record such a gigantic performance," said one of the men.

"Hold on, not so fast," said O'Leary, "perhaps a foreigner could do it."

"He won't be an Irishman, though," chimed in another of the party.

"Ireland has sent forth good men," O'Leary suggested calmly.

"Yes, wonderful fellows, indeed. They can accomplish almost anything with their tongues," was the sarcastic response.

"But the tongue is no mean member of the human frame," said O'Leary.

"Bully fellow, hire a hall, and get your name up," remarked another as they all burst out in a fit of laughter.

From that moment on, the story goes, O'Leary left nothing undone by way of training for a twenty-four-hour race against time.

O'Leary Becomes a Pedestrian

On July 7, 1874, O'Leary rented the West Side Rink in Chicago and announced that one week later he would walk 100 miles inside twenty-four hours. At half-past eight on the evening of July 14 he began his first public exhibition and a career that would span more than half a century. He succeeded in covering the 100 miles in 23:17:00.

One month later, August 12, in the same building, he walked 105 miles in 23:38:00. This performance gave him the confidence to challenge Weston, who, even at this early date, was acknowledged "The Champion Pedestrian of the World." Weston, however,

Weston vs. Daniel O'Leary, London, 1877 (Illustrated London News)

refused on the grounds that O'Leary was not sufficiently established as a pedestrian to warrant the challenge. He told O'Leary, "make a good record first and meet me after."

Determined to force Weston into a showdown, O'Leary traveled east in March of 1875 to begin his full-time professional pedestrian career. On April 9 he walked 100 miles in 23:38:18 at the American Institute Building in New York City. Two weeks later he surpassed Weston's best twenty-four-hour effort by completing 116 miles in 23:12:53 at the Chestnut Street Rink in Philadelphia. This clearly established O'Leary as a first-class long-distance walker. He again challenged Weston, who once more refused to meet him. While O'Leary excelled at twenty-four hours, he was untested over six days. So back to Chicago he went to prove that he was worthy of a race with the "father of modern pedestrianism."

Within two weeks, O'Leary had made arrangements to rent the West Side Rink for an attempt to walk 500 miles in six and a half days. When O'Leary and his handlers arrived at the rink early Sunday afternoon, May 16, 1875, they found the walking surface in horrible condition. The Rink was used for skating during the winter and the flooring rested on a bed of mud and water, which splashed up between the boards at every step. It would have been impossible to walk on such a course. O'Leary and his friends went to work, and obtaining some boards placed them around the circumference of the track and then covered these with large quantities of sawdust and shavings. This caused a three and a half hour delay in the scheduled 1 p.m. start.

Finally at 4:30 p.m. with Mayor Colwin and Senator Miles Kehoe in attendance, O'Leary set out, accompanied by an Officer Conners, who had agreed to do fifty miles with him. The *Chicago Tribune* describes the start:

> The ambitious peeler (Officer Connors) dropped out before the third mile was made, and though he started off again in the sixth, will probably make fifty miles sometime next week.

While Officer Connors added a touch of slapstick to the scene, O'Leary was all business. With his arms held high, elbows far back and head erect, his short, quick hip-step carried through ten miles in ninety-six minutes, fifty miles in 8:56:00, and 100 miles in 23:01:00. This was far faster than his time in New York City one month before, and here he had five days of walking left.

O'Leary had scheduled a three-hour rest every evening from about 11 p.m. to 2 a.m. The excitement of the trial had made him so nervous, however, that he rarely slept the three hours.

By Thursday he was thirteen miles ahead of schedule and moving ahead "tireless as a locomotive." Most of the mud and water had drained off, and fresh sawdust made the track quite adequate for the task. Enthusiasm had been gradually building all week and on Thursday night the Rink was packed. Hundreds of gas jets brilliantly illuminated the scene and a band played lively music constantly. O'Leary seemed to derive inspiration from this, and would time and again put on a spurt for the benefit of the crowd. As this was his first walk for a great distance, he had made up his mind that his condition at the end must be regarded with care. He was not concerned with achieving an unheard-of performance; rather, he wished to finish well within himself.

Saturday evening at 6:10 p.m. O'Leary finished his 470th mile and went off the track for his last rest. During this pause Dr. Dunn, his physican, rubbed him down with alcohol and bandaged a blister on his left heel. This was the only sign of discomfort exhibited by the pedestrian.

O'Leary went back onto the track at 7:30 to finish his last thirty miles. He walked with "astonishing vigor." Shortly after he was presented with an elegant easy-chair by A. L. Hale and Company and with a beautiful gold medal by his friends, bearing the inscription "champion pedestrian of the world." From the *Chicago Tribune* we read,

> The great walker during these grateful performances paused for a moment. The medal was pinned to his breast amid tumultous cheers, and then he started forward again. About twelve o'clock he finished 490 miles, and again was detained an instant, to accept a purse containing $1,000, which was made up by his admirers, the Hon. A. L. Morrison making an enthusiastic presentation speech. He walked thenceforward without a pause, except to stop occasionally for an instant to partake of beef-tea, which was generously supplied to him.
>
> The crowd during the latter part of the walk was simply immense. The police, of whom there was a large number in attendance, had all they could do to keep the track clean. Everybody was determined to stay till the finish.

O'Leary completed his 500th mile amidst the "wildest cheers," three hours within the allotted 156 hours. He appeared in no distress and had walked the last ten miles "at a speed that would be considered rapid under any circumstances."

At the conclusion, O'Leary was hurried to his carriage by the police to avoid being trampled by the crush of the overenthusiastic well-wishers. He was driven to his home on the corner of Robey and Lake streets, where he took a short nap and then a light meal. As most athletes have experienced after an outstanding performance, O'Leary was full of life. He felt so elated, in fact, that he took a walk over to the South Side to see and astonish some friends that very day. He was greeted by numerous cheers and hearty congratulations all along his stroll that Sunday afternoon.

The *Chicago Tribune* was not so full of praise for the infant sport of pedestrianism. On May 24, the day after O'Leary finished his walk, the paper had this to say:

> We have no disposition to deprecate Mr. O'Leary's feat or feet, although we fail to see where the *cui bono* comes in, but it does seem a little inconsistant that, while this pedestrian has been walking and receiving his handsome rewards, thousands of people have been walking on errands of mercy, and charity, and despair, traveling the hardest and the

most flinty roads, and have never been interrupted to receive even a penny or a good wish.

At the same time that O'Leary was succeeding in his attempt, Weston was in New York City failing not once but twice more. He set out to cover 118 miles in twenty-four hours and 515 miles in six days at the Rink on Monday, May 10. He was immediately in trouble. At twenty-two miles he stopped to have his shoes cleaned of pebbles and it was discovered that his left foot was badly cut just below the ankle, where it had come in contact with the raised portion of the track. On advice from his doctor, Weston rested four and a half hours and all chances of his success were gone. He managed only 370 miles by the end of the sixth day. Undaunted, the following Monday, with only one day's rest, he began his second attempt at 515 miles. Once more he failed.

Weston could no longer claim that O'Leary was "not sufficiently established as a pedestrian." O'Leary's walk in Chicago had been his baptism. Not only was he swift over the shorter distances of fifty and 100 miles, but he had now demonstrated that he could keep moving, and moving well, for six days. Weston finally agreed to travel to Chicago in November. He certainly needed the five-and-a-half months to prepare.

O'Leary warmed up for his confrontation with Weston by walking 100 miles against John Ennis for a purse of $500 on October 16. He won easily, with Ennis retiring at 68 miles. O'Leary went on to a time of 18:53:40, an American record. O'Leary was ready.

What about Weston? It had been a year since his brilliant triumph in Newark. Since then he had failed miserably three times in six-day trials. The prevailing opinion was that he was hopelessly outclassed by O'Leary. Everyone in Chicago certainly thought this way, but not Weston. He came into Chicago full of confidence, ready to take on O'Leary and have fun at the same time. It is in this performance that we see, for the first time, the showman in Weston.

Weston Takes On O'Leary

The site was changed from the West Side Rink to the larger Exposition Building, downtown. Each athlete walked on a separate track; Weston on the inside, one-seventh mile track, and O'Leary

O'Leary and Hughes–Second Astley Belt, 1878 (Frank Leslie's Illustrated Newspaper)

on the outside, one-sixth mile track. The race began at 12:05 a.m. November 15, 1875, before a sparse crowd of 300 to 400. From the outset Weston was playing a waiting game. He was sitting back taking his time, watching O'Leary and expecting him to walk himself to a standstill. O'Leary did move out at a fast pace; 100 miles in 20:48:00, with a total of only two hours' rest made up of four short stops. He finished 110 miles on the first day and went to his room for a few hours' sleep. At this point Weston was already twenty miles behind.

As the crowd increased in size and vitality during the evening of the second day, Weston also livened up. After a two-hour rest he returned to the track at 7:20 p.m. in the best of spirits. "His gestures, scraps of song, mimicry of actors, and other recreations were greatly enjoyed by the audience, and seemingly by the actor." O'Leary went to bed at 10:30 p.m. the second night with 190 miles completed. Weston walked on in his casual manner, entertaining the spectators until 2:30 a.m., at which time he had covered only 168 miles.

The remaining days went much the same way. Weston never even attempted to close the gap on O'Leary that was opening wider every hour. Each man would take several fifteen- to forty-minute breaks to eat, change clothes, bathe, and be rubbed down during their "walking" day and retire for three to four hours' sleep somewhere around midnight.

The Newark papers had described the crowd during Weston's solo walk as "comprising all levels of society." The *Chicago Tribune* gives us a far more detailed description of the spectators who filled the Exposition Building to capacity the final two days of the match.

> The crowd was dense, sweeping hither and thither, shouting, yelling, or cheering. The crowd was motley, but largely respectable. It represented wealth, standing, and brains, and thieves, gamblers, and roughs. Ladies were there in large numbers, some with husbands, some with lovers, but all had a terribly hard time of it in the ceaselessly moving and noisy throng . . . . In front of the judges' stand the crowd assumed the character of a mob, and was largely composed of the bummer, political, and gambling elements, scattered through which was a still greater portion of thieves, rowdies, and pick pockets, etc., who, no doubt, by pretended crowding on many occasions, plied their nefarious vocations. The police had trouble with the crowd, and were several times overwhelmed, the mob taking possession of the tracks . . . . The greater portion by far of the mass was orderly, and consisted largely of working men, many of whom brought their wives and children . . . .
>
> . . . A large crowd of urchins had taken possession of the mammoth flywheel at the north end of the building, which by some means began to turn, and in a short time, a dozen or more were sprawling in the pit . . . . The great elevator, the town-clock, and the pagodas, all had their crowds on top of them, but up in the galleries the loftiest perches presented themselves. Numerous boys and men climbed up the trusses and squatted on the iron supports, near the roof, and held their positions calmly, coolly, and deliberately.
>
> Near the elevator some boys sat down on the planking laid on the iron roof supports, but the planks began to sag, and a fall of over 100 feet was threatened to those upon them, which resulted in a quick retreat and a very bad scare to some.
>
> Though the crowd made a great deal of noise, it was very good-natured, and though it felt pleased with O'Leary's feat, it did not forget to heartily cheer the New York lad.

O'Leary finished with 503-1/3 miles in just under the six-day, 144-hour time limit. Weston completed 451-4/7 miles. Both Weston and O'Leary concluded the walk without suffering any undue fatigue. Weston had waited all week for O'Leary to collapse and had lost the race because of this overconfidence. If he was upset at losing it was not evident. He had covered a respectable distance, had avoided damaging exhaustion, and had had a good time. It seemed as though Weston was not overly concerned with the title "Champion Pedestrian of the World," which he had just surrendered to Daniel O'Leary. Weston had, in fact, a number of years before expressed his actual disdain for the title "champion" in a letter he wrote to the *New York Times*.

> I do not aspire to wear the title "champion" . . . . I repudiate the word, since it is associated with every feat characterized by brutality and with every species of humbug. If there is one thing I claim not to be, it is that of "champion." I undertake feats requiring physical endurance to prove to the capers of the Old World that the prize ring does not embrace all the physical manhood in America; to demonstrate that our climate is not averse to muscular development and to stimulate our youth to the practice of walking, which I regard as one of the most beneficial branches of athletics. This is my ambition, and if it is not a laudable one, I am content to bear whatever odium may be attached to it. Assuredly, as a people, we do not walk enough to meet the requirements of health.

Whether Weston "repudiated" the word or not, he was no longer the champion pedestrian in the United States. He had, in the eyes of the sporting world, failed once more. Daniel O'Leary had vanquished the "father of pedestrianism," and now wore the crown.

The *Chicago Tribune* again editorialized on the day after the conclusion, November 14:

> The race being over, there is now no good reason why the city should not settle down again to its customary pursuits. The members of the Board of Trade can return to their betting on oats, peas, beans, and barley. His honor the mayor will not have to make any more speeches nor be aroused at midnight for pedestrian purposes. The race decided nothing except that Mr. O'Leary can walk faster than Mr. Weston. If the two "walkists" want to try again, we entreat Mr. O'Leary to take his gold medals and laurels, and Mr. Weston his ruffled shirt, and go to some other locality. We are satisfied with the fact that Chicago is once more ahead, even in the leg business. The most grateful thing that O'Leary and Weston can do is to walk to St. Louis. The people there need amusement.

3

Two Americans Storm Britain

The English sporting press refused to believe the accomplishments of O'Leary and Weston. In fact, many were willing to wager large sums of money that neither O'Leary nor Weston could duplicate their performances when watched by English scorers. Weston, aware that he was now a dethroned king and considered by many in the United States as an over-the-hill failure at age thirty-six, sailed for England in January of 1876. While he had been soundly defeated by O'Leary, he knew that there were, at present, no English walkers or even runners who could match him over an extended trial.

Weston arrived in England in possession of an astounding but suspect reputation. The sporting elite in England were absolutely convinced that no man, especially an American, could fairly cover 500 miles in six days. The British contempt for the athletic prowess of Americans shouts from the pages of *Lancet* (a British medical journal):

> But with characteristic go-a-headness it has been reserved for the Americans to develop conditions far beyond other nations in their hygienic unwholesomeness. Living habitually in their close, stove-heated rooms, bolting their food at railway speed . . . year by year Americans grow thinner, lighter, and shorter lived. Rowing and other athletics, with the exception of skating and baseball, are both despised and neglected in America.

Weston's first match in England took place in Agricultural Hall, Islington, London, February 8, 1876. It was a twenty-four-hour competition against William Perkins, "the Champion of England." Weston won with 109 miles, walking Perkins to a standstill. Then with only five days' rest, he walked 180½ miles in forty-eight hours February 15 and 16. At the conclusion there was "no evidence of distress perceptible. He appeared active, cheerful, and made an appropriately expressed speech in which his tongue moved as nimbly as his legs had previously done."

Again he was given only five days' rest before his next competition—a walk of 275 miles within seventy-five hours against a little-known Englishman, Charles Rowell. During a rest period on the second day he read some letters and transacted some urgent business. In the evening he led the band around the hall himself, accompanying them on the cornet. This was to demonstrate that he still possessed a great reserve of strength upon which he was not afraid to call. Weston went on to complete 275 miles, 3 minutes 39 seconds within the allotted time. Rowell covered a mere 176 miles. Weston had walked the first ninety miles and the last sixty miles without a rest.

This walk, though, was not as easy as the previous two. The effort left him quite exhausted. He came down with a bad cold and fever for two days. He was back, however, circling the seven-lap, gravel-and-loam track inside Agricultural Hall just ten days later. He was going to attempt to duplicate his Newark feat of 500 miles in six days. The British countered with three of their best pedestrians: Newman, Martin, and Taylor. Weston again triumphed, but walked only 450 miles. There were extenuating circumstances as the *Lancet* medical journal, (now enamored of this American) tells us.

> Mr. Weston has performed, not the feat which he proposed, but another which, we think, more remarkable. He has walked with a sprained, painful, and considerably distended knee-joint in the middle of the period. The praise is more justified, as Mr. Weston was from the outset very insufficiently recovered from a feverish cold which confined him to his house at Brighton with a 100-degree temperature.

Even with all this, "at eleven o'clock on Saturday night the pace was that of a man with whom few of us would like to walk far." Weston had now covered 1,015 miles in competition within a period of five consecutive weeks before 200,000 people.

Weston was under constant scrutiny by the British medical profession during each of these four contests. Everything that he ingested and excreted was measured and analyzed. Numerous articles were written in *Lancet, The British Medical Journal,* and even the *Journal of the Royal Society of England.* Dr. F. W. Pavy summarized the feelings of the medical men. "We have great pleasure in bearing testimony to the genial and cheerful spirit of Mr. Weston, to the entire absence of coarseness in his athleticism, and his willingness to make his walking feats subservient to scientific purposes." Weston had not duplicated his suspected performances made in the United States, but the British saw clearly that he was no ordinary pedestrian.

Weston made 450 miles in six days once more in Edinburgh, Scotland, from June 19 to June 25. He then accomplished what all Great Britain had been waiting for. From September 25 to 30 at the Toxteth Park, in Liverpool, he covered 501 miles within 144 hours.

In the eight months that Weston had been in England he had won $30,000 and a whole host of rich, influential friends. One of these was Sir John Dugdale Astley, a member of Parliament, who was known as the "Sporting Baron." Astley was the epitome of the Victorian sporting gentleman. He had a large stable of horses which he raced often and he would financially support any athletic endeavor he considered worthy. Weston's performance had so impressed Astley that he offered to back Weston for 500 pounds sterling a side against "any man breathing" in a six-day contest.

Besides stirring the hearts of thousands of spectators, Weston's achievements had stimulated the British pedestrians to realize that there was a great deal of money to be made if an Englishman could defeat him. They watched and studied him and gradually learned the intricacies of competing for protracted periods of time. How well they learned their lesson was exhibited by Peter Crossland at Manchester, September 11 and 12, as he covered 120 miles 1,500 yards in twenty-four hours, a world-record performance that caused quite a sensation.

Since Weston had left the U.S., O'Leary had dominated the pedestrian scene. His popularity spread from Chicago throughout the United States. In April 1876 he covered 500 miles in 139½ hours at the Mechanic's Pavilion in San Francisco. In August, at the American Institute Building in New York City, O'Leary walked 500 miles within six days for the third time. His friends, in order to show their appreciation of O'Leary's accomplishments, entertained him at a banquet at the Union Square

Hotel on August 28 and presented him with a gold watch.

The reports of the furor created by Weston in England and the success he had met with in the U.S. induced O'Leary to look across the Atlantic. There was also a more personal motive that drove O'Leary 4,000 miles to compete. Weston had stated to the London press that he received "foul play" in his match with O'Leary. He claimed that the people in Chicago had thrown pepper in his face and threatened to shoot him. O'Leary was determined to show that he had won fairly and to remove all doubt as to who was the best six-day walker in the world.

Immediately upon his arrival in England in October an exhibition was arranged to attempt to better Weston's performance of the previous month. The British were still reeling from Weston's walk when O'Leary became the second American in a month to demonstrate the superiority of American pedestrianism as he walked 502 miles in 143 hours. O'Leary now challenged Weston. However, Weston thought it best to avoid a direct confrontation at this time and refused.

O'Leary had to be content racing the best British pedestrians. They were a far more experienced and toughened set of athletes than Weston had first met nine months before. While O'Leary won his first match with Peter Crossland at 300 miles in November, he was defeated at the same distance by William Howes in December and then by Crossland in February of 1877.

Weston and O'Leary's Rematch

Negotiations for a Weston-O'Leary rematch had been going on for several weeks when the articles of agreement were finally signed January 3, 1877. They would walk six days for 500 pounds a side, with the winner also receiving two-thirds of the gate money and the loser the balance. The editor of *Sporting Life* held the stakes. Weston was backed by Astley and O'Leary by Sam Hague, the American minstrel manager. The showdown was scheduled for April 2 through April 7 at Agricultural Hall. The two parties would appoint five judges and if they could not agree, the editor of *Sporting Life* would make the final decision. Two bands, which were hired to play from 5 a.m. to 12 a.m., would be under the direction of both men at alternate hours and discontinued while either man was sleeping. The prospect of these two rival champions meeting once again created much excitement on both sides of the Atlantic.

Weston was convinced that anyone making 506 miles would win, and he was also confident that he would be that person. He wrote out an elaborate time schedule, detailing how far he would travel each day and the exact amount, and time, of each rest period. Weston led the first day with 116 miles 753 yards to O'Leary's 113 miles 135 yards. The excitement got the better of O'Leary and he could not sleep the first night, taking only a one hour and twenty-four minute rest. Weston took twice as long and surrendered the lead.

When O'Leary began building up a sizable lead early on the second day, Astley urged Weston to keep up with the Irishman. Weston refused, and, as the self-assured champion he was, told Astley he was certain O'Leary would go to pieces and come back to him. But O'Leary was the "gamest of the game," according to Astley, and maintained his lead throughout the week.

On Friday, the fifth day of the competition, Weston was getting very leg weary and attempted to relieve the stiffness by "all sorts of styles in his walk," and when the band began at 5 a.m. he started off in a "most suspicious manner, which finally resulted in Mr. Watson, the New York judge, objecting to the tallying of a lap." A second judge, Mr. Conquest of *Sporting Life,* declared the walk fair. This left the ultimate decision up to Captain Webb. He was the popular long-distance swimmer who had recently crossed the English Channel in twenty-one hours. He stated, "It wasn't much worse than he has been doing since he started." After delivery of this "Solomon-like" opinion, the protest was withdrawn, and the lap tallied as Weston continued with his very peculiar gait.

Though he was completely used up on the morning of the last day, O'Leary still led Weston by ten miles and was increasing his lead as Weston slept in his tent. Astley was sure that all Weston had to do was get back on the track and the race would be his. He implored Weston to leave his bed. But, as Astley recounts in his autobiography, "He (Weston) went soft, and on my telling him I should chuck some cold water over him, he burst out crying, and that settled the matter; for you can do nothing at any game with a party who pipes his eyes."

O'Leary struggled on and at 2:05 p.m. he finished his 500th mile. The *Chicago Tribune* described the scene.

> Ladies waved their handkerchiefs and gentlemen threw their hats in the air, while the cheering was perfectly deafening. Bouquets began to arrive and soon the front of the O'Leary's tent looked more like a florist's shop than anything else. The ladies who presented these would walk quietly past the barriers and hand them to O'Leary, each gift being the occasion of more vociferous cheering.

At 8:03 p.m. Astley conceded the defeat of Weston and told O'Leary's backers they could take him from the track. O'Leary continued until he had covered 519 miles 1,585 yards a minute before 9 p.m.

Astley recalls, "I helped Dan off the track, to his four-wheel cab at the private exit and he was so stiff he could not raise his foot to get into the cab. In fact, I lifted one foot and then the other the few inches required to land him in the conveyance. And when I got back into the Hall, there was my man (Weston) running around the track, pushing a roller in front of him, and keeping time to the music of the band." Weston finally completed 510 miles shortly before 10 p.m.

Weston had accomplished what he set out to do. He had bettered the existing world record without totally exhausting himself. He had essentially ignored O'Leary during the competition and had run his own race. He was not disturbed by being defeated for he knew there would be other days and other races. He wanted to be around to participate.

Throughout the week, 70,000 people paid to witness the contest and vast sums of money were won and lost on the race. Astley himself was covering all bets against Weston fifty pounds to thirty and lost a reported 20,000 pounds or $100,000. But true sportsman that he was, Astley gave Weston a large purse of money for exceeding by four miles the distance he had agreed to do.

The Astley Belt Races Are Born

Astley was so taken with this long-distance business (he said that he was never more excited over any performance) that he decided to inaugurate a series of six-day races for the "Long Distance Challenge Championship of the World." These would not be merely walking races but "go-as-you-please." The pedestrian could walk and/or run in any fashion he chose. There are two conflicting reasons given for the advent of the go-as-you-please concept. Astley says he proposed this because of the peculiar "wobbling gait" of Weston that was open to objection as not being a fair heel-and-toe walk. O'Leary gave a different reason. He claimed that since the American pedestrians were so much superior to the English walkers that "it was deemed necessary to invent a style of progression which would place the legitimate champions at a decided disadvantage."

The conditions of the races, which became known as the "Astley Belt Races," were originally laid out as follows. The winner would receive a championship belt valued at 100 pounds and a purse of 500 pounds, second place 100 pounds, third place 50 pounds, and other prizes to those who succeeded in finishing 450 miles. In addition, a certain percentage of the gate money would be divided up among those over 450 miles. The champion would be required to defend the belt against any legitimate challenger (as decided by Astley) within three months of the challenge, but would not have to compete more than once every six months. If he won the belt three times in a row it would become the permanent possession of that athlete.

The championship belt was made of solid silver and gold. Five plates of silver, plain in the center, with rustic border close around the edges, made up the greater portion of the belt. One gold plate in the center, with the words, "Long Distance Champion of the World," in raised letters, was flanked by a silver plate on each side, similar in shape and border to the others, but bearing, in the center, figures of walking and running, in high relief. The plates were each about two and a half inches in width by three inches in length.

All was now prepared for what was to be one of the most incredible series of athletic contests that have ever taken place in the arena of sport. The Astley Belt competitions would become the "Golden Age" of pedestrianism.

4

The First and Second Astley Belt Races

Monday, March 18, 1878—Agricultural Hall, Islington, London, England. The clock struck 1 a.m. The scorers and judges were in their places. Sir John Astley stood before eighteen of the world's best pedestrians. Some were nervous and fidgety, making last minute adjustments to their trunks, hats, or shoes. Some stood quiet and serene, almost bored. And a few stood motionless with a look of terror upon their faces, pondering, no doubt, the suffering and pain that was inevitably to come to them by the end of the week.

The vast (500 foot x 300 foot) steel and glass building, lighted only by three chandeliers, looked anything but festive. Two tracks, a seven-lap-to-the-mile one for Englishmen and an eight-lap-to-the-mile one for foreigners, marked the oval center of the building. The scorers and clerks were alert and ready near the judges stand. The press, trainers, handlers, and the friends of Sir John (there by special invitation), filled the enclosure in the middle, around which the track was laid. No other observers were present. A *New York Times* reporter described the surroundings.

> The great wide space of benches, set apart for spectators, looked chill and dirty. The light of a charcoal fire in a brazier fell mysteriously upon the small encampment of the pedestrians near the entrance doors. One tent stood alone near the foreigners' track. Among the group of onlookers, the soft hats of Transatlantic visitors were conspicuous.

Sir John Astley addressed the pedestrians.

"You are about to enter on a trying match, in which running

and walking and physical pluck and endurance are necessary to compete. Every possible arrangement has been made to have a fair, straight fight, and I hope the best man will win. I appeal to you to second our efforts, for the best man to win, no matter what his nationality or where he comes from . . . . Now lads are you ready? A fair, honest, manly race, and the best man wins. Ready? Then away you go."

And so the first contest for the Astley Belt began. It had been eleven months since Sir John Astley had proposed a six-day, go-as-you-please world championship competition. The English pedestrians had used the time well. There were now several well-trained men capable of defeating the single foreign entry, Daniel O'Leary of the United States. Two in particular had conditioned themselves to not only walk but to run also. They planned to take full advantage of the go-as-you-please provision.

William "Corkey" Gentleman of London, forty-six years old, a twenty-five-year veteran of the pedestrian track, was small in stature (five feet four inches, 114 pounds) and had a stooping, awkward gait. He trotted "ungracefully and with a sad look on his face." Henry "Blower" Brown, in contrast, was six feet six inches, the tallest man in the field, but weighed only 138 pounds. Brown had early distinguished himself by the swift manner he carried his barrow of bricks to the kiln and back again.

Before the race, both of the men were even favorites for second place with O'Leary. The bookmakers choice for first place went to Henry Vaughan of Chester, a carpenter by trade and called by Astley "a real clean-made and thoroughly respectable man." He was admired by all, even by his fellow competitors, for his "long-striding giant-like" step and the steady pacing of his races.

Vaughan had been one of the first Englishmen to turn in a notable performance as a result of Weston's competition in 1876. In the latter part of that year he turned in 100 miles in 18:51:35, and 120 miles in 23:45:00. Both were world records at that time.

Another hometown favorite was the novice William Lewis, twenty-one years old, of Islington. Just three weeks before, he was second to William Howes in a twenty-six-hour contest in the same building. In that race he walked 100 miles in 18:37:35 and covered 125 miles 990 yards in twenty-four hours. Both of these were the best on record except for Howes' performances, in the same race, of 18:08:35 and 127 miles 1,395 yards, respectively. Lewis, however, was young, inexperienced and untried at six days.

Weston Sits Out First Astley

Conspicuous in his absence was Edward Payson Weston. After his defeat by O'Leary in April of the previous year, he remained in England and had been quite active. In June of 1877 he walked 400 miles in five consecutive days in the Skating Rink at Bradford, and then repeated the performance in July at Bristol, in August at Newcastle-on-Tyne, and in September at Hull. From December 26, 1877, to January 11, 1878, he walked 1000 miles in 400 consecutive hours at the Northumberland Cricket Grounds, Newcastle-on-Tyne (without walking on Sundays). In February he performed the unparalleled feat of walking 1,500 miles in 625 hours (twenty-six days) at the Denistown Skating Rink, Glasgow, Scotland, and in the Skating Rink, Bradford, Yorkshire, England. Weston was in excellent condition and was expected by all to be a challenger for the Astley Belt.

Weston had submitted his entry within the specified time period. O'Leary's, however, had been late and there was some question as to whether he would be permitted to compete. As soon as Astley decided in O'Leary's favor, Weston withdrew, presenting a medical certificate that was regarded by many as "too thin." O'Leary had defeated Weston both times they had met and the prevailing opinion was that "O'Leary had made him ill."

It was indeed a strange sight as the eighteen men set about their awesome task. Some walked, some trotted, some ran. One reporter described them as going "round and round something like a school of herrings in the Brighton Aquarium, round and round, in groups, in twos and threes, in ones and twos, in threes and fours, round, and round and round."

Brown and Gentleman went immediately to the front, with Vaughan and O'Leary following. An incident during the first three hours illustrates some of the brash tactics used during these events. George Hazael of London began staying right up with O'Leary, "haunting him on the English track like his shadow." Hazael was not, at this time, a well-known pedestrian. His style was described as "hangdog and crouching" in contrast to the "straight, upright, graceful" form of O'Leary.

The athletes were permitted to walk in either the clockwise or counterclockwise direction around the track as long as they switched at the conclusion of a lap. Hazael was walking in the opposite direction of O'Leary. When he passed the Irishman on each curve, he would verbally challenge O'Leary, attempting to get him upset. On one turn Hazael said, "I'll kill this wonderful man before I've done with him."

At the time Hazael was gradually pulling away from O'Leary. Hazael's constant harassment and increasing lead combined to do just as Hazael had hoped. O'Leary became worried and agitated and began to run, much to the dismay of his handlers. During a short rest period his handlers begged O'Leary to stop running. O'Leary responded, "leave me alone. I know what I am about," and set off again at a run to cut down Hazael's lead.

Hazael had been threatened with disqualification several times for his conduct. This, and the fact that he soon needed all his breath to continue moving all but silenced the insolent pedestrian. O'Leary, walking and running, relentlessly ran Hazael down and in the third hour passed him. Hazael quickly fell to the rear and eventually dropped out of the race. O'Leary, a bit nauseous and dizzy from his unfamiliar running, finally agreed with his handlers to stop running and he resumed his standard walking form.

By 5 p.m. Monday, Gentleman held onto a slight lead of eighty-seven miles to O'Leary's eighty-three miles. Brown was third with seventy-eight miles, and Vaughan fourth with seventy-seven miles. The attendance slowly grew during the day so that by 6 p.m. there were 5,000 spectators encouraging the pedestrians on. At 11 p.m. each night the building was closed to all people except the press and a few favored friends. This was usually the time when the pedestrians took the only real rest they allowed themselves. Generally, it amounted to two to four hours in their individual tents that were erected inside the two concentric oval tracks. On this, the first night, Gentleman, Vaughan, and Brown all retired around 11 p.m. But O'Leary, who possessed a kind of "morbid dread" of anyone being ahead of him, walked on until 2:44 a.m., at which time he had taken over the lead and accumulated 124 miles.

Through the second day Gentleman's rapid walking and occasional trotting had overtaken O'Leary, and once more placed "the thin little figure" in front. But by mid-afternoon the running began to tell on Gentleman, and by 7 p.m. O'Leary drew even at

Agricultural Hall, London (Illustrated London News)

174 miles. Brown wrestled third from Vaughan and led him by a mere mile, 170 to 169. Gentleman then went in for a short rest. His everpresent wife, who attended to him day and night, was at the door of the tent to meet him with a steaming bowl of ellbroth, his favorite drink. His legs were very painful and his short rest turned into one of several hours. By the time he came back onto the track he had not only lost his lead but second place as well. At 6 a.m. Wednesday the score stood as follows: O'Leary 211 miles, Brown 206 miles, Gentleman 196 miles, and Vaughan 191 miles. There were still sixteen men walking, but from fifth on back they were far in the rears.

The bookmakers had moved O'Leary into the favorite roll laying 5 to 3 odds against him. The odds stood at 5 to 2 against Vaughan, 3 to 1 against Gentleman, and 5 to 1 against Brown. O'Leary's backer, Al Smith, the sportsman from Chicago, had wagered several thousand pounds on the Irishman's victory, while Astley and Captain Wyndham were backing Vaughan against all takers.

Throughout the day O'Leary extended his lead and Gentleman slipped farther and farther behind. At 1 a.m. Thursday, after three days, it was O'Leary first with 288 miles, Vaughan and Brown next with 270 miles, and Gentleman, all but used up, with 256 miles.

Public Interest Increases

Interest in the international pedestrian contest kept increasing day by day throughout London. All classes were present from the "titled dukes and lords to the Cheapside hackmen." The various editions of the newspapers were brought up as fast as they were printed in order to read the hourly bulletins from the Hall. Inside the building the excitement was intense. The cheers often drowned out the music from the band with men dancing and waving their hats.

Vaughan kept within striking distance of O'Leary throughout Thursday and Friday (thirteen to sixteen miles behind). Late Friday afternoon O'Leary finally showed the first signs of weakening. His left leg started to swell and a slight limp was noticeable. This was Vaughan's chance. But he, too, was suffering. Both feet had been blistering badly since Wednesday and they were now swathed in cotton wool. The hope in the Vaughan camp was that he could continue all Friday night, especially when O'Leary went in to rest. As the damp night air seeped into the vast arena, O'Leary occasionally staggered and his knees would tremble. Vaughan pressed on. Spurred by O'Leary's deteriorating condition, he started to run. For a short time he was able to keep up lap-for-lap with O'Leary even though he was on the seven-lap track and O'Leary was on the eight-lap track. At 7 p.m. Vaughan got within twelve and a half miles of O'Leary, 438½ to 426 miles.

O'Leary rested from 11:30 p.m. until 3 a.m. Saturday morning. Vaughan, sticking to his plan, rested only at intervals throughout the early morning hours. When O'Leary returned to the track, legs stiff and sore, feet in pain, he still managed to walk at a steady pace. He was cheered on by those present, especially by the Irish members of Parliament and their wives. O'Leary was able to increase his lead on Vaughan, who never again was a challenge. At 3:30 p.m. O'Leary completed his 497th mile with Vaughan twenty-four miles behind. The closing hours were depicted by the *New York Times*' London correspondent.

> It was a sorry sight the last few hours of the week's walk. Haggard, dazed, staggering O'Leary, his arms no longer knitted in pedestrian form and braced with muscular strength, were limp and almost helpless. His legs were swollen. He went his miserable round in evident pain, though 15,000 cheered him on. Vaughan went on until 7:30 Saturday night, and retired at the solicitation of his friends when he had scored 500 miles. O'Leary at this time was nineteen miles ahead, and he was determined to make his record in round numbers, 520 miles, beating, it is said, all his achievements on both sides of the Atlantic. His pluck is undeniable, and the vast crowd acknowledged it in hearty demonstrations, the band played "See the Conquering Hero Comes." (O'Leary conducted himself with modesty, and he walked in a style equaled only by Vaughan.)

At the close the figures were: O'Leary 520¼ miles, Vaughan 500 miles, Brown 477-2/7 miles. There were no others walking at the end.

O'Leary Earns the Astley Belt

O'Leary came away with the Astley Belt and a total of $3,750 in prize and gate money. He took the belt to America and declared he would not part with it "till some better man came and fetched it." Vaughan received $1,300 and Brown $525. It was estimated that a total of $500,000 was wagered during the race.

The *Chicago Tribune*, as it had done after O'Leary's other two triumphs, editorialized the following day. The tone, however, is the complete antithesis of the previous two editorials.

> Chicago is ahead again. Chicago is always ahead. The splendid record that O'Leary has made in his walk in London is something of which every Chicagoan has a right to be proud. It has been a great time for the United States and for Chicago and "a great day for Ireland." Daniel O'Leary went over to England without any blowing of trumpets or waving of flags. He has not made a public exhibition of himself after the style of Weston. He left us quietly to take part in a walking-match in which a score or more of the best pedestrians in the United Kingdom were his competitors, trusting to his legs rather than his tongue for success. And he has used them to such good advantage that today the one name that is blown over the world through the trumpet of fame is O'Leary. The international wrangle over Turkey pales before the international contest of legs. All London throngs to the arena as the great

struggle draws to it's close. Even members of Parliament leave their tiresome debates on the Eastern question to watch O'Leary and greet him with applause and inspire him to renewed efforts with their enthusiasm. Ireland is in a very sunburst of excitement over the achievements of her favorite son, who has returned from America to beat the "blarsted Britisher" on his own soil and now that he has won, will probably elevate him to the peerage by virtue of his descent from some early Irish king and "the legs he has under him." The Eastern question halts until the match is decided, and Bismarck, Andrassy, Gortschakoff, Schouvaloff, Derby, Disraeli, and Stolberg-Wernigerode have ceased their squabble over the Congressional conditions because their governments cannot pay attention to minor matters until this all-absorbing question, in which the whole world is interested, is settled.

How sudden are the changes of fortune! Five little years ago no one knew O'Leary except the servant-maids on his postal route in this city, to whom he brought every morning good or bad tidings from absent swains. Little they dreamed that O'Leary was to be one of the heroes of the world, the first question in the morning and the last at night, the burden of every newsboy's yell, and the theme of discussion in every social gathering. Little they thought of the fame those legs that went plodding along from house to house would achieve. Little he thought, perhaps, that the time would come when his name would go flashing along the oozy bed of the ocean day after day, and that two Continents would hang upon that one word O'Leary. There is no one who will question his right to his fame. He has earned it honestly and legitimately. It is useless to attempt to decry his achievement with the sneer that this is a mere question of legs, and that the achievements of his femur, tibia, fibula, tarsus, metatarsus, phalanges, and the muscular fibers are of that low order that pertain to the brutes. The remarkable victory of O'Leary will not alone be a triumph of legs, but of brain. It will not alone be the result of physical endurance, but of mental and moral endurance also. It requires courage, patience, will, and intellect—a mighty concentration of will-power upon a certain object to be attained. If, further, it is thrown out that all these qualities were exerted for money, it may be answered that all efforts are made for money, and that without the spur of money the world would stand still, stagnate, and rot. It is all very well to glorify the victories of the intellect; but, if the dollar of our fathers were removed as an inciting cause for effort, intellect would be about as strong an incentive to action as a horned frog bottled in alcohol. Money makes the mare go, and O'Leary go, and the minister, philosopher, poet, and sculptor go. The dollar is the hub on which the world revolves and will continue to revolve until the last man reaches that blessed country were money is everlastingly demonetized, and the peaceful saints are not distracted with legaltenders, bullion certificates, outstanding debts, or the balance of trade. We are inclined, therefore, to congratulate our wiry little O'Leary upon the splendid exhibition of

Chicago brawn and brain that he has made, and that he has beaten the Briton in the very class of exercise for which the latter has always been famous; and Chicago will congratulate herself that she is ahead again as usual, however much it may add to the discomfort of St. Louis and her other suburbs. At the same time, the tension has been so great that we are glad it is removed, and that we can once more know the exact status of the Eastern question and of the great war which England is now waging against the bold, bad Caffres, as well as have time to clear up the Pacific Railroad muddle and unsnarl our municipal finances, which have been held in abeyance pending the result of the great contest in Islington.

Even the *New York Times* got into the act and praised O'Leary's accomplishment in an editorial:

The pride of the Americans in the success of Daniel O'Leary of Chicago, in the ped match in London for the "Championship of the World" may be tempered by the fact O'Leary is an Irishman, and that Weston, the pure-blooded Yankee, was unable to start because of illness. But the feat accomplished by O'Leary is the greatest on record, and one in which every lover of manly exercise may take satisfaction. To the ordinary New Yorker who seeks relief in a crowded horse car rather than occupy an hour in walking two or three miles from his home to his business or vice versa, this labor must seem nearly fabulous. It involves not only natural strength, but patient training, indomitable pluck, and mental endurance and long practice of temperance and energy. These are qualities which it is well to have developed.

O'Leary sailed home, with a stopover in Ireland, and returned to Chicago May 19, 1878. Below is an interview with O'Leary that appeared that day in the *Chicago Tribune.*

"What kind of a time did you have?" said a *Tribune* reporter to Dan O'Leary, the pedestrian, last evening.

"A good time," was the reply.

He reached home yesterday morning, bringing the champion medal, but leaving in the New York Custom-House a magnificent clock, which was presented to him by admirers in Cork. He looks well, and is in excellent condition, having fully recovered from the effects of his great London walk—the greatest ever accomplished.

"How did the Englishmen treat you?"

"Oh, pretty well—about as an Englishman would be treated if he walked in America. They didn't like to see the belt leave England, and did all they could to keep it there."

"You had to talk for it?"

"Yes, for over a week, but we had justice on our side. They encouraged men to go there from all over the world, and claimed, after I was fortunate enough to win the belt, that it was not to go out of the country. There was no such stipulation in the agreement."

"Was there any trouble over the stake?"

"No, that was given up freely. Let me say that Mr. Astley is a gentleman, and a lover of fair play."

"Did anything unpleasant occur during the walk?"

"O no; I was treated fairly well, but Englishmen don't admire Irishmen. That is sure. They were very quiet on the last two days—didn't have much to say."

"Did you enjoy your trip to Ireland?"

"Yes, but it cost me 300 pounds to see Dublin."

"How is that?"

"I walked there, and it was very unprofitable. There are five Englishmen in Dublin to one Irishman; but the hall in which I walked was the finest I ever saw. If I had been an Italian or a Bohemian I would have done better."

"Why didn't you try Cork?"

"Because I thought Dublin was Ireland, and when I found out my mistake I had enough."

Mr. O'Leary then got the belt, and exhibited it in a glass case to the reporter. The trophy has a red morocco base, to which are attached seven oblong squares, 3x2 inches, of solid silver with embossed edges, the centre piece, however, which is oblong, being of solid gold. On the latter is the following, in raised letters:

"Long distance champion of the world."

On the left adjoining silver plate is the figure of a runner in bas relief, and on the right one is that of a walker.

"They put the runner ahead," said Mrs. O'Leary, "because they wanted him to win."

The "buckle" plate contains this inscription:

"Presented by Sir L.D. Astley, Bart., M.P., March 1878."

"Won by Daniel O'Leary, of Chicago, U.S.A., March 18 to 23, 1878: distance 520¼ miles in 138 hours 48 minutes, beating M. Vaughan, Chester, 500 miles, H. Brown (blower) of Pulham, 473 miles, and fifteen others."

"Why is Brown called 'Blower'?" said the reporter.

"Because he blows more than the other Browns," was the reply.

"How does Vaughan walk?"

"He is the best pedestrian I ever saw, and a very decent fellow, but he is not a stayer."

"Were you sociable with your competitors during the journey?"

"Yes, we had a laugh once in a while. Some one in the crowd would present a contestant with a bouquet made of cabbage and water-cresses, and that would enliven us."

"How was your appetite during the week?"

"Appetite? Why, I didn't eat anything for six days."

"Not eat anything?"

"No, sir, except an orange now and then. I lived on tea, coffee, and milk."

"Were you tired when you finished?"

"Pretty tired. I couldn't get into the carriage when I left the track, but if I had stayed on I could have walked several miles more. Stopping was what used me up."

"How much longer could you have kept going?"

"I couldn't tell. It pleased me greatly when I saw the others drop out."

"Why was it you refused to accept any of the challenges when the match was over?"

"Because the challengers wanted to walk in London. Having won the belt, I had the say where the walking should be done. I wouldn't walk in London again, but offered to walk in France, Italy, Germany, or Spain. They don't know where America is, and of course wouldn't come here."

"You will hold the belt?"

"I'll try to. It is mine if I hold it for eighteen months. Under the conditions, I must accept any challenge within three months after its issue. Only two matches can be walked in a year. Any one who wins it must walk 600 miles. There will be at least one corpse on the track."

" 'Oh! don't Dan,' said Mrs. O'Leary. "

"Have you anything in hand just now?"

"No. I tried to get the Hippodrome in New York, but Theodore Thomas had engaged it, and that is the only place I would walk."

"Then you will keep quiet for a while?"

"Yes, I shall stay at home for a few months and look after the babies."

O'Leary Is Challenged

When Weston set the world record in 1876, O'Leary was quick to challenge him. So now, several challenges came to O'Leary in rapid succession. Vaughan, Gentleman, and Brown all wanted another chance at O'Leary in London. O'Leary refused, saying that he would walk for the Belt only in the United States.

Soon after arriving home, O'Leary was challenged by John Hughes, another Irishman, from New York City. Hughes was prompted not only by a desire to be the champion but also by an intense personal antipathy for O'Leary. When O'Leary first went east in 1875, Hughes wanted to compete with him but could find no one to back him. He continually boasted to all who would listen that if he only had the money he could easily defeat O'Leary at any distance. This constant harangue of Hughes' greatly annoyed O'Leary. When he returned to the East in 1878 to sail for the Astley Belt competition, Hughes told O'Leary he would come to

England and beat him but he had no money. O'Leary replied sarcastically, "I'll build you a bridge." This nettled Hughes so that whenever he talked of O'Leary after this he would always say bitterly, "the rapscallion told me he'd build me a bridge!"

As soon as word arrived of O'Leary's performance in England, Hughes eagerly sought someone to back an attempt to surpass O'Leary's. He finally found Harry Hill, who wagered $1,000 against Pargh Davis, a former 100-yard champion. A trial against time was set up for April 21 to 27 at the Central Park Garden. The track was almost oval in shape and partly in the hall of the Garden and partly outside in the garden. Fifteen laps would leave the pedestrian 205 feet short of one mile.

Hughes' confidence in his ability far outstripped his actual ability. He set out at a suicidal pace covering the first mile in 6:22. He covered the first five miles in 36:25, twenty-five miles in 3:05:10, and thirty miles in 3:41:45. Then, as would be expected, he crashed. He did finish 100 miles for the day, but he had destroyed all chances of success in the first hours. Somehow he managed to last out the six days and eventually finished 389 miles 3485 feet. His handlers said that this was accomplished with no real training and that he would now begin professional training for another attempt at O'Leary's record. This he did, and was reported to have completed 500 miles in Newark later that year. The result was doubted by the sporting press.

Hughes now formally challenged O'Leary under the Astley Belt rules. O'Leary considered Hughes a mere "speculator" and not worthy of a contest. Hughes persisted and Sir John Astley finally decreed that O'Leary must meet Hughes or forfeit the Belt. The match was set for Gilmore's Garden at Madison Square from September 30 to October 5, 1878.

At the start O'Leary struck out on a long, body-swinging walk, while Hughes, having learned little from his failure at Central Park, dashed off on a run, making five miles in 35:41 to O'Leary's 53:14. O'Leary was on the outer one-eighth mile track; Hughes on the inner one-ninth mile track. Members of the Harlem Athletic Club kept the scores in three separate notebooks, each lap being called out distinctly to both men. Hughes was handled by his family, trainer, and backers, and occupied a tent at one end of the Garden. O'Leary used one of the rooms in the main building. It was clear early on in the competition that O'Leary was working simply to beat Hughes and had no concern for records; O'Leary, refusing to believe Hughes, had fairly covered 500 miles in Newark. The match had little excitement and was concluded at 11 p.m. Saturday. O'Leary won easily with 310 miles.

O'Leary had now won two matches. If he won one more challenge match he would become the permanent owner of the Astley Belt. The English pedestrians anxiously inquired among themselves as to who should be the man fortunate enough to regain the coveted prize. Vaughan was considered by many as the obvious choice. Had it not been for his badly blistered feet, he may have beaten O'Leary in the first Belt race. Others thought either Gentleman or Brown would be better selections since they were still convinced it would take a runner to beat O'Leary.

This opinion was strengthened when Astley sponsored a race for the "Astley Belt and Long Distance Championship of England," go-as-you-please at the end of October 1878. This race was won by the "runner" William "Corkey" Gentleman. He equalled O'Leary's distance of 520 miles 440 yeards in 138 hours–one hour less than O'Leary. Henry "Blower" Brown, another runner, was second with 505 miles 754 yeards. This was only the third time that two men had both surpassed 500 miles in the same race.

The problem of regaining the "World" Astley Belt intensified for the English when it was learned that two Americans, John Ennis of Chicago and Charles Harriman of Massachusettes had already challenged O'Leary. Preliminary arrangements were, in fact, already being made. A competent English challenger had to be found.

In addition to the two Astley Belt races, O'Leary had walked in seven other races or exhibitions in 1878 for a total of 3,110 miles. He was "raced out." His advisors suggested a long rest. O'Leary, seeing the wisdom of their advice, left the north and went to the hot springs of Arkansas. His rest was cut short, however, by Sir John Astley's call to defend the Championship Belt.

5

The Third Astley Belt Race

Round and round the gravel walks of the kitchen-garden he went. The morning mist, which had left the path wet, was just beginning to rise. The sun had yet to break through. He had been covering every mile in seven and one-half minutes. Sir John Astley was watching intently. Today would decide if this was the man to send to America to win back the Championship Belt.

For several weeks Astley had conferred with his associates at the Guard's Club of Maidenhead. Lord Balfour had suggested Charles Rowell, the five foot six inch, 137 pound former boat-boy at the club. The Prince of Wales seconded this suggestion. Rowell had competed against Weston back in 1876 and most recently had finished third with 471 miles in the English Astley Belt Race. Astley remembered recognizing him there and being impressed with the manner in which he conducted himself both on and off the track. Rowell really seemed to enjoy the competition. Astley described the scene in his biography:

> He ran the first sixteen miles with such ease in two hours that I went away, telling one of the gardeners to score up the laps with a bit of chalk on the garden wall. In about an hour I returned, and he seemed to be going easier than when he started; so I let him continue another hour, and when he had covered thirty-two miles–just under four hours –he had not turned a hair. I stopped him and advised him to have a good rubdown between the blankets, but he ran off to the stables, and stripping, got two of the helpers to chuck three or four buckets of the coldest spring water over him. He was then rubbed dry in the warm

stables, put his things on, and asked me to let him go and shoot some rabbits, and away he went.

This convinced Astley that Rowell was the man all England was looking for. He paid the $500 entry fee and gave an additional $1,250 to cover expenses for Rowell and two handlers.

Arrangements for the third Astley Belt Race were soon completed. It would be a four-man race at Gilmore's Madison Square Garden, March 10 to 15, 1879. Daniel O'Leary, the defending champion, would attempt to win sole possession of the Belt. Charles A. Harriman of Haverhill, Massachusetts and John Ennis of Chicago, Illinois would be the American challengers, and Charles Rowell would be the lone representative of Great Britain.

John Ennis was, like O'Leary, an Irish emigrant, coming to Chicago in 1869. He was thirty-seven years old, five foot eight inches tall, and 156 pounds. He had competed against O'Leary twice before in handicap 100-mile races, losing both times. At Buffalo in July of 1878 he walked 108 miles in twenty-two hours. His only previous six-day effort came in the English Astley Belt, where he finished fifth with 410 miles.

Charles Harriman had no experience in six-day contests. He was well-known, however, for his victory in a thirty-six hour championship race held in New York the previous year. He covered 160-1/8 miles in thirty-four hours and twenty-nine minutes, taking only seventeen minutes of rest during the time. He made 100 miles in 19:36:52 without a single rest. He was twenty-five years old, stood six foot one-half inches tall and weighed 170 pounds.

The duty of keeping score was placed in the hands of the well-known sporting gentleman of New York City, Mr. William B. Curtis. Each of the twenty-four hours were divided into four tours of six hours each.

The judges were: G. W. Atkinson, *London Sporting Life;* Charles Colwell, *New York Clipper;* Captain Bruce, *Turf, Field and Farm;* E. Plummer, *The Sportsman;* W. B. Curtis, New York Athletic Club; George W. Carr, Manhattan Athletic Club; James Taylor, Brooklyn Athletic Club; W. J. Kendrick, Harlem Athletic Club; Max E. More, Scottish-American Athletic Club; and John Gath, American Athletic Club.

Sunday March 9, 1879. All-day preparations were made for the contest and by nightfall they were hardly finished. The sawdust track was completed and rolled until it was hard and firm. The four houses to be used by the pedestrians were readied. The furniture, gas stoves, lights, cooking utensils, cots, and so forth were brought in during the afternoon. The giant blackboard at the lower end of the enclosure was painted with the competitors' names.

Gilmore's Garden was arranged better for this than any former race. The entire space within the track was boarded over. This was an attempt to cut down on the dust that had greatly hindered the walkers in previous matches. The eight-lap, 10-foot-wide track was surrounded by a strong wooden railing. The area reserved for the press and scorers was protected by a high picket fence. The long bar was placed under the southern tier of seats and was gaily decorated. Thomas Gallagher paid $2,525 for the privilege of selling the liquor.

Long before 10 p.m. when the tickets were to go on sale, a large crowd had gathered in front of the Madison Avenue entrance. When the gates were opened there was a tremendous rush. It was impossible for the ticket sellers to keep up with the demand and the crowd extended down Twenty-sixth and Twenty-seventh streets to Fourth Avenue. As the eager spectators poured into the building, the band began to play, and the bartenders at once began to do a lively business. The long tiers of seats filled rapidly and by 11:30 there wasn't a vacant seat left.

The oval area inside the track was filled next. The bookmakers and betting centers set up were scenes of mass confusion. People pushing, shoving, and hollering to place bets on their favorite pedestrian.

Shortly before 12:00 a.m. Peter Van Ness, the celebrated pedestrian who had recently completed 2,000 half-miles in 2,000 consecutive half-hours, entered the hall and was given a standing ovation. It was with the greatest difficulty that he was escorted through the crowd to his private box near the starting line. The four contestants were smuggled in a side entrance without any notice.

Half an hour before the 1:00 a.m. starting time, Rowell came out of his cabin and, accompanied by one of his trainers, walked once around the track amid mild applause. As soon as Rowell returned to his cabin, Ennis left his and walked slowly around the track with his wife at his side. The applause was far greater than that given Rowell. Next to O'Leary, Ennis was the favorite of the crowd.

At 12:45 the crowd seeking admission had become so uncontrollable that Captain Williams of the 29th precinct ordered the sale of tickets stopped and the doors closed without warning. Hundreds of people were still rushing up to purchase their tickets in hope of seeing the start. Unaware that the doors were closed they began to press in on those in front. The crush of humanity was becoming unbearable on those being hemmed in against the doors. Amidst curses and yells of pain, everyone began to push and shove.

At 12:55 the champion O'Leary made his appearance. The 10,000 people now jammed into the Garden gave him a resounding welcome. He was presented with a "token of luck" in the shape of a silver horseshoe by a lady admirer. Mr. Curtis called them to the line. O'Leary, dressed in white shirt and pantaloons, black velvet trunks, with a silk handkerchief around his neck, was on the inside. John Ennis stood beside O'Leary. He was wearing white tights, blue trunks, and a white sleeveless undershirt. Next to him stood Harriman in his white tights and shirt, purple trunks, and a ribbon across his right shoulder. He also was sporting a diamond pin on his shirt. On the far outside, Charles Rowell, the youngest of the four, waited. His costume was the most colorful: lavender tights with a blue and white striped shirt that "made him look like a little zebra."

The word was given and the four pedestrians began their incredible journey. For the first two laps they walked in a line, O'Leary leading. Then Rowell broke into a trot followed immediately by the others. The applause was constant and tremendous. Rowell finished the first mile in 9:25, O'Leary in 10:27, Harriman and Ennis in 10:40.

The shouts and cheers from inside the Garden that announced the start of the great walk "acted upon the mob outside much as the flaunting of a red flag in his face acts upon an infuriated bull." They charged through the lobby past the ticket windows and hurled themselves against the flimsy doors that blocked their entrance. Two policemen and several Garden employees made a futile attempts to reinforce the barrier with pieces of wood. But in less than a minute the first of the mob broke through and rushed toward the track. At the same time Captain Williams and twelve policemen came upon the scene. With their night sticks flailing, they tore into the crowd. "The sound of the heavy blows that rained upon the defenseless heads and bodies of the unfortunates who happened to be in the front ranks was sickening." The crowd fell back and was driven not only from the Garden but all the way up to Twenty-seventh street. There they were held in check until after 3 a.m., when they gradually dispersed.

The first twenty-four hours brought immediate surprises. After only thirty miles, Ennis became ill. He vomited freely, and was forced to stop several times during the day for up to an hour. The biggest surprise, however, was O'Leary. In the first twelve hours he covered only fifty-nine miles—seven miles behind his performance at Agricultural Hall the previous March. He suffered from colic and an upset stomach. Both men, however, seemed to revive a bit later in the evening.

O'Leary retired to bed at 11:00 p.m. Monday night with 93-3/4 miles. Rowell left the track at 11:16 with 110 miles. Harriman finished 100 miles at 11:30 and promptly went to bed. While the others rested Ennis plodded on, making up as much of the lost ground as possible. Finally at 12:30 a.m. Ennis finished his 95th mile and turned in for sleep. O'Leary now found himself in the unusual and uncomfortable position of being behind after the first day. The betting men were in a quandary. O'Leary, who looked to be a certain winner at the start, appeared to be almost out of the race.

Early the morning of the second day, O'Leary was finally able to keep down his first solid food since Sunday afternoon (a little calf foot jelly and some mutton stew). Throughout the day he then restricted himself to small doses of limewater and eggs. This appeared to perk up the champion, but the O'Leary of old showed himself, only sporadically. It was evident that O'Leary was a broken man. "His hands were allowed to droop, his chest was not held as high as usual, and his stride was far shorter than normal." He continued to lose ground.

As if to add insult to injury, Rowell continued his questionable tactics of the previous day. He would follow right in O'Leary's footsteps. If O'Leary altered his pace, so would Rowell. For a man who is accustomed to controlling a race, this was more than O'Leary could stand. He would attempt to pull away from Rowell, but that was a hopeless task in his condition. With no effort Rowell would plod right along. O'Leary would then slow to a crawl, and Rowell did likewise. When Rowell thought he had O'Leary disrupted enough, he would pull up beside the poor pedestrian and "give him a look that was a crowning act of insult" and then break into his trot once more. He would continue like this until he had gained another lap on O'Leary and then would begin his stalking technique again.

Rowell was taking no chances. He was certainly many miles ahead of O'Leary, but he realized a comeback was not impossible. He did everything he could to disturb and dishearten O'Leary. He probably felt confident of victory, if he could only break O'Leary completely. By the end of Tuesday this was just about about accomplished.

Peoples' interest in the pedestrian contact seemed to increase hour by hour. At least 2,000 people remained through the night. By 1 p.m. the crowd grew to 4,000, by 7 p.m. 6,000, and by 9 p.m. 10,000. In the evening Madison Avenue swarmed with scalpers selling fifty-cent tickets for sixty to seventy-five cents. There was no trouble as on Sunday night. As the *New York Times* noted:

> The great bulk of those present were well-dressed, respectable-looking people. In the afternoon and evening a fair proportion of the immense throng was of the fairer sex—ladies in the height of fashionable attire, wearing camel's hair shawls and other expensive wraps, and bedecked with valuable jewelry. All classes were, however, represented. The millionaire, the black-leg, the hard-working mechanic, the common laborer, the tramp, the thief, and the street-urchin were the component parts of the vast mass of human beings that framed the track and jostled each other in the excitement of a common impulse on the inner floor.

Many of the actors and actresses from the Broadway stage would stop by after their performances. William H. Vanderbilt was in attendance, as was Sir Edward Thornton, the British Minister.

As the match continued into its third day, the progress of the pedestrians became the "one theme of town talk." Hourly reports were kept on large bulletin boards in hotels, barrooms, cigar stores, barbershops, corner groceries, and every place where people gathered. Some establishments even charged a small cover charge to view their scoreboard.

Immense crowds, without a hope of gaining admittance, formed daily outside Gilmore's Garden. They lined Madison Avenue, opposite the main entrance, four and five deep. On Twenty-sixth Street, crowds of "street boys" hung around a series of low doors that were previously used to allow entrance to the animals of Barnum's Museum. They would work diligently to dig holes through the panels with their jackknives and once the holes were complete, they fought each other for a chance to look in. In addition to those outside the Garden, large crowds gathered in Madison Post Office and Printing House squares to study the large illuminated boards that had been erected to show the mile-by-mile progression of the peds. Uptown, the two main bulletin boards were at the intersection of Broadway and Fifth Avenue and Broadway and Thirty-third Street. At all of these locations the police had their hands full in keeping the streets cleared for the regular traffic. There were always shouts of excitement whenever the mileage was changed for any of the pedestrians. Light showers or a strong midday sun had no effect upon these people. They would stand in the mud for hours just watching those boards and arguing the merits of their favorite pedestrian. At the end of forty-eight hours, the score stood: Rowell, 197 miles; Harriman, 186 miles; Ennis, 173 miles; and O'Leary, 164 miles.

Daniel O'Leary struggled through Wednesday morning and on into the afternoon. His situation was hopeless. By 4 p.m. "looking sick and worn," he left the track. His physician, Dr. Robert Taylor, advised him to withdraw from the competition. Several other physicians concurred with this opinion. And so at 5:36 p.m. O'Leary said to the judges, "Gentlemen, I have finished." Later on he said, "I feel like a worn-out piece of machinery, and think I shall never be able to walk again; but I trust the public will look upon me with a lenient eye."

O'Leary expressed the despondency and despair of a defeated champion. Like many athletes who reign supreme for a time, the moment of failure seemed to be the end of his career. O'Leary would never again gain possession of the Astley Belt, but no one would ever again put together such a string of six-day victories as he did from 1875 to 1878.

With O'Leary's withdrawal came cries of "fraud" and "sell out." Friends of O'Leary would hear none of this, and came to his defense. They claimed he had been tricked into accepting one or two attendants of suspicious character. One of his best friends, John E. Tansey, in a biography published a few months after the race, gave this reason for O'Leary's failure:

> . . . a few of his attendants were disreputable individuals of the cut-throat stamp, creatures in whom neither the pedestrian nor the public could place the smallest amount of confidence–men who would consider no crime too glaring, no art too fiendish, provided a few dollars were given them to accomplish it. Such was the character of those cooking his food and preparing his drinks. Is it no wonder that Daniel O'Leary was seized with violent pains and curious sensations never before experienced by him previous to his being twelve hours on the track? . . . That he was drugged by one of his trainers I (Tansey) have no doubt. . . . It is to be deplored, that one or two men long since lost to honor were permitted to enter the champion's tent, and act in the all-important capacity of trainers.

As further evidence that O'Leary was in the best of health and spirits and confident of success, Tansey noted that prior to the race O'Leary had deposited $3,000 in the office of *Wilkes Spirit of the Times* on his ability to cover 540 miles inside 142 hours. The money was held for one week by Mr. Curtis but no one covered the bet and it was returned to O'Leary.

Third Astley Belt (Frank Leslie's Illustrated Newspaper)

O'Leary himself would not publicly admit to being drugged. He did, however, deny throwing the race in a letter dated Saturday, March 15, 1879 and published in the *Turf, Field and Farm.*

> To the Public:
> I desire to say that the statement published in a morning journal of yesterday, to the effect that I was backed to lose by a clique of gamblers, who knew that I had been drunk for weeks before the race, and therefore unfit to enter the contest, is an infamous lie. It is a well-known fact to the sporting world that gentlemen of that profession will back the favorite. From my previous record I was naturally the favorite, but the fact is that the great loss sustained has fallen entirely upon myself.
>
> Daniel O'Leary

The retirement of O'Leary did nothing to decrease the enthusiasm in the contest, as we see from the *National Police Gazette,* March 22, 1879:

> It is almost impossible for residents outside of New York City to understand the extraordinary excitement which pervades all classes of the community over the result of the pedestrian contest for the championship of the world and the position of holder of the Sir John Astley Belt . . . . This excitement permeates all classes of the community, from the staid Wall Street banker and the solemn legal dignitaries of the Supreme Court, down to the bootblacks and newsboys of the street. The crowds at the scene of contest, too, have been enormous, far exceeding those present on any occasion of a similar character in the history of the city.

The question of nationality began to play a greater part in the public's interest. O'Leary had been almost everyone's favorite. All hopes were placed on him to keep the "Belt" on this side of the Atlantic. Now support was divided. The Irish backed Ennis, an Irishman by birth. The native-born Americans gave their allegiance to the "Yankee" Harriman. But it was the little Englishman Rowell who still maintained a sizeable lead that third night.

He continued to circle the sawdust track with his incessant "dog-trot." The spectators had given him the nickname "sawed off." While he was by far the shortest of the three remaining pedestrians, he was the most solid-looking. His calves were large and out of proportion with the rest of his body. With O'Leary out of the race, Rowell began to use his stalking techniques on his next most challenging opponent–Harriman. Unlike O'Leary,

Harriman was undisturbed by Rowell following so close behind. Harriman was "tall, raw-boned, thin, hollow-cheeked," with very thin thighs and calves. His stride, however, was tremendous and his machine-like motion had obtained for him the nickname "Steamboat." It was impossible for Rowell to stay up with Harriman without breaking into a run. At times when Rowell would trot along behind Harriman he would be greeted with taunts of "There's Harriman's pup"; "Trot along, doggy"; "Get a chain for Harriman's dog"; and "Give a poor doggy a home."

While Rowell was concentrating his attention upon Harriman, John Ennis had been slowly making up ground on both of them. He had fully recovered from his upset stomach of Monday. Early Wednesday morning Cusick, the noted trainer of the professional boxer Heenan, took over the duties as trainer for Ennis. At his hut at the northwest corner of the enclosure his wife fixed all his food and drinks and watched anxiously as her husband moved lap after lap around the oval.

The following is an excerpt from the *New York Times* of Wednesday, March 13, 1879, describing the early morning hours inside the Garden:

> It is damp and chilly, and altogether dismal. There is no music, and the smell of stale cigar smoke, left by the crowd of the night before, lurks in every corner, waiting for fresh puffs to come from fresh crowds, and drive it out through the skylights. The remains of the big masquerade balls, signs in gilt and colors, do not help to make the place habitable. The people who are present look as if they had been up all night, and so they have, most of them, watching the pedestrians. Some of them, too, look as if their stay had been prolonged not so much by a desire to see the walking as by the absence of any other bed.

The evening hours were quite different. From the beginning of the race, the pedestrians had been receiving bouquets of flowers at frequent intervals. Long tables had to be placed in front of each cabin to display these many gifts. Whenever one of the pedestrians was given a bouquet it was a signal for the entire Garden to break out in loud cheering and applause.

At 8:30 p.m. a tremendous crash was heard to the right of the main entrance. Here, the previous winter, an addition was built to the gallery bringing it out over the garden. Between two and three hundred persons were in this gallery and a similar number were sitting underneath when it began to give way. Panic spread rapidly and about one half of the audience began a mad dash for the exits. Many of the spectators, however, seeing that the trouble was confined to one area kept their heads and their seats and did not add to the confusion. The panic lasted only about two minutes and the police were quick to come to the aid of those trapped by the fallen timbers. The people who had been sitting underneath were very lucky. The wood from which the gallery had been constructed was nearly new and it did not break and fall all at once. It actually took almost a minute to collapse, giving them time to escape. Only nine people sustained injuries, ranging from bruises to a broken leg.

All three pedestrians were on the track at the time of the accident. They had to leave the track to allow the police to clear the debris. Immediately after the panic subsided an eerie hush fell over the stunned crowd. It did not last long. The excitement over the match was too great to be quieted by anything short of some great calamity. From 9:30 p.m. until unseasonable hours Thursday morning the cheering, yelling, and applauding were almost continuous, going the rounds of the building as the pedestrians made their laps.

Because of the incredible crowds, the management decided to raise the admission charge to one dollar beginning at 8 a.m. Thursday.

At the halfway point in the competition, 1 a.m. Thursday, the distances were: Rowell 283½ miles, Harriman 270 miles, and Ennis 250 miles.

All three of the men took long sleeps, ranging from three and one-half to four and one-half hours. Harriman entered the track at 4 a.m. a different man. His eyes were bloodshot and his stride was stiff. The experts' opinion that he was too "fair" for the six days of walking seemed to be coming true. He had averaged ninety miles a day for the first three days, but by mid-morning it was clear to all that he was finished as a contender for the Belt. Rowell and his trainer, realizing Harriman's state, turned their attention to the only man left—John Ennis. Ennis was still more than thirty miles behind but actually looked fresher than he did on Monday.

His step was quick and sharp, his disposition pleasant, and his appetite immense. He was almost constantly munching on chunks of beef and bread, refusing to leave the track to eat in his effort to catch Rowell.

Rowell, while still in control, was not without his troubles. Both of his feet were badly blistered and the upper portion of his left thigh had a terrible chafe. He left the track several times during the morning to have the dressing on his swollen leg changed.

By 3 p.m. Ennis had cut Harriman's twenty-mile advantage down to five. Rowell now decided that he must test this Irishman for in the last days of such a contest the victory went to the pedestrian who could endure the most. Rowell suddenly accelerated his pace and flew by Harriman, who gave only a passing glance as he sailed by, and then set after Ennis, who at this time was about 100 yards ahead. As Rowell sped by, Ennis hesitated a second and then took off. The crowd roared to its feet, shouting encouragement as the two men, seemingly oblivious to the fact that they had been on their feet for almost four days, continued to increase their pace around the track. Rowell lead for two laps and then Ennis took over, slowly pulling away from Rowell. The race lasted one mile with Ennis turning an impressive 8:05 to Rowell's 8:35. Rowell now knew that Ennis was to be feared.

The worn-out Harriman took several long rests during the day. His trainer, Mr. Lathrop, revised his schedule. They now hoped just to manage 450 miles so that Harriman would win a share of the gate money. Harriman was not really sick or lame but was overcome by an overpowering drowsiness. Whenever he left the track to rest, he would throw himself on his cot and instantly be sound asleep. It was all his attendants could do just to awaken him and push him back onto the track.

At 6 p.m. Ennis caught Harriman and moved unchallenged into second place. Ennis became the center of attention. All hope for retaining the Belt was placed on his shoulders. Every minute that he was on the track he was followed by a continued barrage of cheers. The public did not, however, forget the valiant Harriman. It was impossible to find a single individual who did not sympathize with the struggling athlete. All urged him on toward the completion of his 450-mile goal. Bouquets of flowers were given to Ennis and Harriman almost hourly.

Among the notables present Thursday night were Senator Blaine, Senator Jones of Nevada, General Ewing of Ohio, and General Chester A. Arthur (who in four years would find himself President of the United States), and Mr. Edwards, the British Vice Consul.

At the end of four days, Rowell had the lead well in hand with 360 miles. Ennis was second with 335 miles and Harriman third with 325 miles.

On Friday Ennis tried desperately to close on Rowell but the plucky Englishman, with thigh swollen and feet terribly sore, kept plugging away. While he was on the track he stayed right with Ennis and allowed him no chance at making up a lap. Harriman continued to "totter" around the track. His handlers realized that the only way to keep their man moving would be to use stimulants. They fed him milk-punch, champagne, brandy, and "other stimulants." Among the "other stimulants" were most likely doses of belladonna and strychnine. The use of these two drugs was a common practice among these men who ran for money. Time after time a pedestrian would enter his tent looking, as the newspapers said, "all done-in" only to return fifteen minutes later fully recovered, eyes ablaze and ready for more pounding of the sawdust. It was no different in this race. Besides stimulants, Harriman's handlers administered electric shocks at regular intervals.

The positions remained unchanged all day Friday. The fifth day drew to a close with Rowell having 428 miles to his credit, Ennis 406 miles, and Harriman 390 miles.

Even though a Rowell victory was apparent by Friday evening, this did nothing to reduce the extraordinary public interest in the race. Saturday found Gilmore's Garden swarming with the largest and most frenzied crowds of the week. They came to urge their favorites on through the last day of their ordeal.

Just as the morning light was beginning to filter through the skylights Saturday, a drunken Irishman rushed onto the track toward Rowell. With a loud curse he raised his arm to strike the Englishman. In a flash a policeman grabbed the drunk, spun him around and threw him to the outside of the track. Several other policemen were necessary to subdue the would-be assailant.

Ennis heard the commotion and slowed his pace until Rowell had caught up to him. Then, shaking Rowell by the hand, he turned to the crowd and shouted out, "Gentlemen, I don't know if you are friends of mine or not. If you are, you can best show your friendship by respecting this man." He pointed his forefinger at Rowell as he spoke, and a loud cheer went up from the crowd. When the applause had subsided, Ennis pointed his finger at Rowell again, while his eyes flashed. "You see this man. I want you all to understand that if this man is injured I will leave the track and not walk another mile. He is an Englishman, and I'm an Irishman, but that Englishman has done the square thing ever since this walk began. If he wins it, it will be because he is the best man. Give him fair play, gentlemen. If you don't, I'll give you foul play by leaving the track." This was no idle threat. A good deal of money had been bet on Ennis finishing second.

Rowell then grasped Ennis by the hand and the crowd cheered as hand-in-hand the Englishman and the Irishman circled the track.

During the early morning hours a dense cloud of tobacco smoke hovered over the arena. At 8 p.m. the skylights were opened and the cold air mixing with the smoke tinted the air blue. While the subsequent drop in the temperature of the building was uncomfortable for most, the three pedestrians found it to be a welcome relief.

All through the day Harriman hobbled on. His eyes were sunken and his legs trembled as he went slowly on his way towards 450 miles. Earlier in the morning Rowell and Ennis, convinced that it

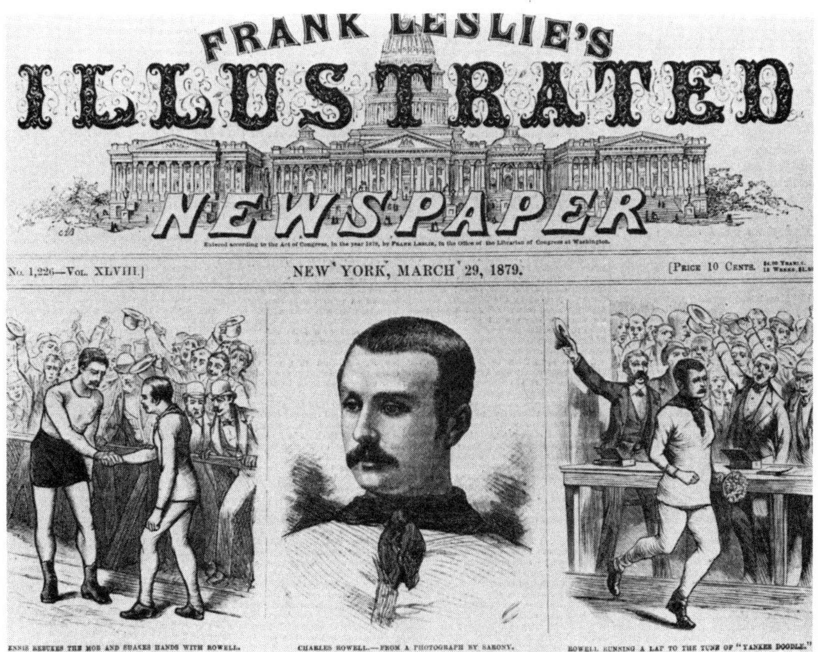

FRANK LESLIE'S ILLUSTRATED NEWSPAPER

No. 1,226—Vol. XLVIII.] NEW YORK, MARCH 29, 1879. [Price 10 Cents.

ENNIS REBUKES THE MOB AND SHAKES HANDS WITH ROWELL.

CHARLES ROWELL.—FROM A PHOTOGRAPH BY SARONY.

ROWELL RUNNING A LAP TO THE TUNE OF "YANKEE DOODLE."

Front page of Frank Leslie's Illustrated Newspaper, March 29, 1879.

was impossible for Harriman to finish 450 miles by 11 p.m., agreed to give him his share of the gate money if he would withdraw. This was no small sum. It was estimated to be about $10,000. Harriman, however, refused this charity and said that he would not accept a penny unless it was earned "squarely and honestly."

He did, however, accept the encouragement and camaraderie of Rowell and Ennis. Rowell, in particular, spent the majority of the day walking beside Harriman giving him advice and aid. Throughout the week Rowell had received little sympathy or praise. But now personal prejudices were forgotten and the crowd, recognizing his generosity, cheered him heartily.

Whenever Harriman looked especially bad or would begin to stagger the band would strike up "Yankee Doodle" or "Marching Through Georgia" and the crowd would yell "three cheers for the Yankee." This never failed to perk up the exhausted pedestrian. Harriman had been receiving bouquet after bouquet and there was no longer any room to hang the flowers on the front of his tent. All three of the long tables beside the tent were filled to overflowing. There was one large basket on the roof but the flowers were "withered and faded—as nearly used up as the pedestrian on whom they were showered."

The competitors were not the only ones feeling the strain. Everyone concerned with the organization and running of the race was showing the effects of the past six days. The scorers were complaining that they were "wearing away" and tired of eating the same type of sandwiches day in and day out. The judges were tired and irritable. Even the young man who had climbed a ladder to the blackboard at the east end of the Garden to post the number of miles looked "pale and thin."

At 6 p.m. Captain Williams entered the north door of the Garden with a squad of 110 policemen. They marched right up the track until they reached the center of the building and then every six feet a man was dropped off and left standing on the edge of the track inside the rail. The appearance of the officers was greeted with applause. Their presence was a guarantee that Rowell would be fully protected.

The *New York Times* described the last evening of the race in the March 16, 1879 edition:

The attendance was the largest of the match. Along the sides of the building the crowd was so dense that all outline of boxes and seats was extinguished. The side pens below, skirting the outer edge of the track, were fairly bursting with people. In the inner ellipse there was such a dense throng that moving about was a matter of the greatest difficulty. Every projection of the false rockwork of the grotto and every niche and crevice of the vast building into which a person could be packed was occupied. Even the remaining wing of the temporary gallery was filled. The track only was clear. That was lined by a double row of stalwart policemen and nobody was allowed to pass them. Another force of reserves was packed in the long caves under the seats near the Madison Avenue entrance. Never before was an assemblage so madly and persistently enthusiastic.

The cheers rolled in successive swells around and around the vast amphitheater, wave following wave as one man after another appeared in sight. . . . Rowell and Harriman kept close together, the little Englishman devoting all his time to coaching the poor, miserable-looking, staggering, but plucky Down-easter, in his desperate effort to encompass 450 miles.

. . . In this style the procession went—Rowell with head erect and eyes bright, but hobbling painfully on tender feet; tall Harriman, pale, hollow-eyed, thin almost to a skeleton, and looking as though every tottering step would be his last; and sturdy Ennis, stiff and tired, but plodding with determined gait.

The scene as Harriman walked his last lap was incredible. For three long days and nights the crowd had watched the broken-down pedestrian struggle. Their relief was evident. Their admiration intense. Everyone was standing, screaming, stamping, and hollering out his name, waving hats, canes, and handkerchiefs. Harriman finished at 8:44 p.m. He went immediately to his tent, but reappeared within two minutes, "his face aglow and his eyes glittering with excitement and gratification." Across his chest he wore a tri-colored silk scarf with fluttering ribbons. He circled the track three more times, "bowing and shaking hands on every side as he passed." The rafters shook with applause. He retired for good after completing 450 miles and three laps in 139:46:40.

Eleven minutes later, Rowell finished his 500th mile amidst the same cheering and waving of hats and handkerchiefs. He covered the last lap carrying a large American flag while the band played "God Save the Queen" as he retired to his tent at 8:56 p.m.

Ennis was now left to himself. The applause continued without a stop for the next hour as he closed in on his personal goal of 475 miles. With one mile to go the band played a lively tune as he spun around the track in the fastest mile recorded for the entire week, 6:55. He finished at 10:00.57 p.m., having covered the distance in 141:00:57.

When Harriman finished he was immediately carried from the track and placed into a carriage that hurried him to the St. James Hotel. There he was placed in bed in a feverish state, and he fell asleep instantly. Rowell, the effects of fatigue camouflaged by the thrill of victory, walked briskly from the Garden and down Fourth Avenue, chatting with his attendants, to the Ashland House Hotel. There he took a salt-water bath, drank some beef-tea, and went to bed for a brief two-hour nap. He was in "capital condition and spirits." He claimed that he could have made twenty more miles without any great difficulty.

Ennis was also in good condition, as evidenced by his last mile, when he finished. He walked, with apparent ease, across the street and up two flights of stairs to his room in the Putnam House. He was given a hard rubdown by his trainers and buried under several blankets in bed. In answer to a reporter's question on how he felt after tramping around a track for six days and nights, Ennis was not at a loss for words:

> I feel first class. They have given me a scrubbing, and I am fresh as a lark. I have no blisters to speak of. There are three or four little fellows on my feet, but they'll be all right by Monday morning. Rowell is a good man, a tough man, but I think I can beat him, nevertheless. He did not worry me in the slightest by keeping so closely on my heels. I returned the compliment, I believe, once or twice. He broke up O'Leary completely, however. O'Leary didn't have head enough on him to see the game that the Englishman was playing. Harriman is a good fellow, but hardly built for long walking.
>
> I'm going after the Astley Belt, and am going to challenge Rowell next week, before he returns to England. I'm positive I can beat him, and if there had been one more day to the match I think I should have carried off the Belt. Cusick didn't take charge of me until Wednesday, and I began to pick up right away. If I had him the first two days the results would have been different. I shall get a good night's rest tonight, and tomorrow will take a walk around town.

Hardly had the word of Rowell's victory been flashed over the cable to England before a dispatch returned to Sir John Astley.

"Well done, my boy. Pay O'Leary 100 pounds deposit on the Belt. Weston has challenged you. Match to take place in London, May 5th. Astley."

On Monday March 17, 1879, the *New York Times* contained an editorial that attempted to explain the fascination of the race.

> It is not easy to account for the depth of interest with which the public has regarded the walking match just concluded in this city. While it lasted, no other event on the face of the earth was so absorbing to the people who read the New York newspapers. It was a great concession to any other question of passing moment to say that it vied with the walking match in exciting public interest. During the past week, while three or four men were walking against time, and against each other, at the circus building on Madison Avenue, everything was more or less colored by the current which flowed from the match. The woes of O'Leary, the hopes and ambitions of Ennis, the patriotic endurance of Harriman, and the comic diversions of Rowell formed an inexhaustible staple in the conversation of the day, and furnished food for thought. Almost everyone within easy reach of the walking match has been to see it. Thousands who scoffed at what Charles Sumner would have called the "ridiculosity" of the affair, yielded to the strange fascination of the spectacle, and remained to watch the struggle which they went to deride as a popular craze.
>
> It is very true that many of the men most interested in the walking match belong to the worst class of New York. It is true that immoral and vulgar branch of human society which is called in this country "the sporting gentry" was completely absorbed in the contest. And it cannot be denied that the crowd which surrounded the circus building was rough and unsavory in manners and atmosphere. Notwithstanding all that, the horrible fascination of the hour spared neither age, sex, nor condition. It is idle to say that only rude sporting men or coarse women sympathized with the contestants, cheered them in their arduous task, and devoured with avidity the details of the race daily spread before the reading public by the newspaper press, which never fails to seize the fleeting fancy of the hour. Once drawn to the consideration of the fluctuating fortunes of the contestants, no man or woman could resist following thereafter the course of events as the possibilities of victory and defeat rose and fell. There was nothing about the struggle to ennoble mankind, to establish any valuable principle, to prove any dictum relating to human health or strength, or to confirm any theory concerning the physical powers of mankind. Yet it was an absorbing interest to thousands of people. This absorbing interest was ridiculous; yet it was impossible to resist.
>
> . . . It seems, however, as if one might assume that a six days' walk, covering 400 or 500 miles, is the supreme effort of a man's exertion. No man can put on his endurance such a tremendous strain as this and escape without serious consequences. And that is certainly not a healthful struggle, the effects from which the contestant does not recover for many months.

> . . . But a race is a race the world over, whether the racers be inanimate machines of wood or steel, or quivering frames of men or beasts. The element of chance which enters into such contests is a great awakener of enthusiasm. And when the end is certain, and the trial is continued only for form's sake, it is impossible to allay the tempest which has been evoked. The most trivial incident rouses a storm of applause. When, in the last, the generous rivals help along their least fortunate competitor, the human heart of the vast multitude is stirred with a touch of nature, and it hoarsely roars its distempered joy. We are glad that the race is over and that the week's craze may be succeeded by sobriety. We are glad, too, that the American love of fair play, our shining national characteristic, has been vindicated once more, and that the plucky little Englishman takes home his trophy without having won an unfair bruise in the long struggle.

Wednesday morning following the race, Rowell and Ennis visited the New York Stock Exchange and were mobbed as though they were selling gold futures for a tenth of the going price. They shook every hand in the place before they were able to make their escape.

That afternoon the pedestrians and their backers and trainers met at Kelly and Bliss's Turf Exchange to divide up the proceeds of the previous week. Rowell was accompanied by his trainers Atkinson and Busby, Ennis by his agent Hatch, Harriman by his backer Walton and O'Leary by Smith, Harding, and Aaron.

After an amicable greeting and some small talk the three pedestrians who had finished the full six days went upstairs to a small room for "consultation." There they argued back and forth for almost four hours. The major disagreement was whether or not O'Leary should receive any of the gate money. On Tuesday, during the race, a hastily drawn agreement was signed by Kelly, Hatch, Walton, and Busby. The agreement said that each man would receive $2,000 whether he finished 450 miles or not. At that time O'Leary was still considered by all to be in contention for first place. After O'Leary withdrew two of the signatures mysteriously disappeared from the document.

Rowell still seemed to be in favor of giving O'Leary the full $2,000. But Ennis and Harriman were set firmly against this idea. It was proposed then to give O'Leary $1,000. Once again Harriman and Ennis vetoed the suggestion. Finally, it was decided that O'Leary would receive no share of the gate money. O'Leary's backers were furious. They claimed that without O'Leary in the race the first three days, the crowds would have been greatly reduced. They were no doubt correct, but the argument had no effect. O'Leary received nothing. O'Leary seemed to take the disappointment rather philosophically, saying he had enough money to support himself and he did not mind the loss of $2,000 "as much as he did the feeling manifested against him by his late friends and rivals."

Charles Rowell took home, in addition to the gold and silver championship belt, the fantastic sum of $20,398. John Ennis won $11,938 and Charles Harriman was happy with his $8,679. At this time the average salary of a working man was about $500 a year. Rowell thus collected almost a lifetime's earnings for his six-day effort. Sir John Astley said later that this was "a pretty good haul for a man who seldom had two sovereigns to rub against each other."

6

The Fourth Astley Belt Race

Rowell's victory marked the end for the walker. Never again would the victor of a six-day go-as-you-please race be an athlete who walked exclusively. O'Leary, convinced that his time was up, was driven into a premature but short-lived retirement.

Rowell was quickly challenged to a rematch by John Ennis. In England, "Blower" Brown issued his own challenge to the new champion. Arrangements were rapidly completed for a match in mid-June. In May, Edward Payson Weston entered his name among the competitors.

While we have mentioned little about Weston since his defeat by O'Leary in April of 1877, he was far from inactive during this time. He took part in numerous solo exhibitions throughout 1877 and 1878. He did not, however, engage in head-to-head competition for a year and a half. During that time the English pedestrians tried again and again to get Weston onto the track. At least twice a month the sporting press carried letters of challenge. But Weston shrewdly avoided all matches. He spent his time walking throughout the British Isles cultivating the patronage of the leading ladies and gentlemen of society. His exhibitions were conducted with the utmost civility. He refused to have anything to do with the raucous, tobacco-smoking, beer-guzzling, gambling fraternity.

A Hero For The Upper Class

Whenever Weston performed he wore a frilled shirt and black leather leggings. Quite often he topped this off with a broad blue sash, and he was never without his small white walking stick. In his shining suit of black and white he gave an almost clerical appearance.

The *Turf, Field, and Farm* magazine of January 3, 1879, commented upon Weston's handling of his exhibitions.

> . . . When he pursued his weary way around the track, the best people thronged the immense buildings and applauded him earnestly. From the dainty hand of fashion he received many floral tributes, which he gallantly acknowledged, and during the pauses in his walk the profound, the cultivated, and the beautiful gathered around him. Reclining in his chair, he held his court as if he had been a sprig of royalty. He had the shrewdness to see that in order to secure the patronage of the best elements of the social world, he must cultivate the leaders of society and make public exhibitions conform to their tastes. The boisterous classes thoroughly hated him, which hate was returned with interest. He was loudly denounced as a humbug, still he never failed a draw; and it was specially remarked that generally richly attired women predominated in the gathering. Weston stimulated a love for walking in the very circles where such was most needed and where the best results followed.

He was the complete antithesis of the other pedestrians. He was refined, intelligent, and educated. He gave the upper class a hero with whom they could identify.

Weston was a colossal showman and the people loved to watch him. In the early part of 1879, from January 18 to February 28, he had attempted to walk 2,000 miles in 1,000 consecutive hours along the country roads of England. Throughout the forty-two days he was constantly mobbed in every town through which he traveled. In Brighton the crowds were so large that he was forced to take refuge in a shop for two hours. The next night in Winchester, Weston's attendant William Begley disguised himself in Weston's cloak and hat to divert the spectators so that the pedestrian could make it to the George Hotel for a temporary rest—a ruse that was carried out at least two more times during the walk.

Not only was Weston attempting an incredible feat of endurance but at least once and often two or three times a day he was delivering lectures to large audiences. His talk was a combination of the joys of walking and the benefits of temperance. His delivery was quick and energetic, even after a long day spent slogging through six inches of mud during a winter rainstorm. Whether he was speaking to a group of farmers at a local corn exchange or to a group of undergraduates at Oxford or Cambridge, the response was always the same—unbridled enthusiasm. He left them roaring with laughter from his numerous anecdotes gathered from twelve years of "wobbling" over the dirt roads and sawdust tracks in America and Great Britain.

A combination of this much too arduous lecture schedule and some bad weather left Weston 22½ miles short of his 2,000 miles when the final hour elapsed. He had "failed" once more.

Weston had only two competitive races since the O'Leary match. Both were six-day affairs. In the first All England Championship held at the end of October, 1878, he quit on the fifth day with the inglorious total of 365 miles. In this race William "Corkey" Gentleman went a near world record of 520 miles 440 yards. He was followed by "Blower" Brown with 505 miles and Charles Rowell with 467 miles. This was just five months prior to Rowell's success at Madison Square Garden. In the second All England Championship held April 21 to 26, 1879, Weston finished fifth with a mediocre 450 miles. In this race three major world records were broken. George Hazael, who had trained exceedingly hard after his embarrassment in the first Astley Belt race, blasted through the first 100 miles in 15:35:31 and covered 133 miles within the first twenty-four hours. He then faded badly, and Brown went on to set a six-day world record with an astonishing 542 miles 440 yards.

It was now quite clear to the sporting press that Weston was through. Forty years old, he was the aging ex-champion feebly attempting to win back the glories of days now lost forever. *Bell's Life* dubbed him the "game old ped" and the "weary wobbler." *Turf, Field, and Farm* commented, "As Weston is not a runner, his chances of winning the belt are not good. Rowell's most dangerous competitors in the forthcoming contest will be English blood. The Astley Belt is likely to remain in England for sometime to come."

Even Sir John Astley, Weston's close friend and most vociferous supporter in England, had given up on him. Weston went to Astley requesting a loan of 100 pounds for his entry fee. Astley's response was, "Why not let well enough alone? No walker can compete with these runners, and I'm not going to let you throw 100 pounds away that way. I'll lend you 100 pounds for anything else, but not to waste on this walk."

Undaunted, even though his best friend thought that his chances were hopeless, Weston wrote to the other entrants in the race asking for a one-week extension in the deadline for the deposit of the entry fee. The other competitors, who recognized Weston's popularity, granted the extension. Within the week, Weston had talked his wife into giving up $500 of her father's inheritance for his entrance fee.

Weston, ever confident in his ability, began to think more and more about running. In an interview after the race he said, "While I was in this country (U.S.) I never believed that running could hold out against walking; but when I saw the easy pace of some of those runners, I changed my mind. Some of them ran a ten-mile gait with less apparent exertion than a man makes walking four miles per hour." So, one month prior to the competition, Weston began to experiment with a new form of locomotion. He ran, and he liked it. "I fell accidently into an easy running pace, just as I did in walking," he said some weeks later.

Two weeks before the starting date, Rowell injured his right heel. After much consultation with his medical advisors it was decided that he should not start. He thereby forfeited the Belt and it was up for grabs.

As the time drew near it became clear that this would be a four-man race, as it had been for the third Belt Race. With Rowell injured, O'Leary in retirement, and Harriman having romantic problems back in the United States, John Ennis would be the only survivor from that race.

"Blower" Brown, the present world record holder from Turnham Green, became the odds-on favorite. Bets on Brown were taken at 6 to 4. Ennis, even though inconsistent, brought odds of 5 to 1. Even a relative unknown, William Harding of Blackwell, was given 6 to 1. Edward Payson Weston was, in the opinion of all, far outclassed and hardly a soul laid any money on the "weary wobbler," even at 10 to 1.

On Sunday June 15, the eight-lap loam and fine gravel track had been laid. The judges' stand was stationed midway on the north side of Agricultural Hall and opposite it was a large scoreboard. By 12:55 only about 500 people had gathered to witness the start of what appeared to be a foregone conclusion. The only question was whether or not Brown could better his own record.

As the four pedestrians approached the starting line all eyes turned towards Weston. He had discarded his frilled shirt, his fancy sash, and the other trumperies which had generally distinguished him on the track. He was dressed in red worsted tights, a thin white undershirt, and ordinary trunks. He was dressed to compete and not simply to make a show of himself. His face "was shaved smooth, giving him almost a boyish appearance, and the only indications of advancing age were a few gray hairs that showed themselves about his temples."

At precisely 1 a.m. Sir John Astley gave the signal that sent the four pedestrians on their way. Harding and Brown instantly shot into the lead, running as though it were a six-hour race and not six days. Harding finished the first mile in 6:05. He was closely followed by Brown in 6:20. Ennis was running, but at a far more reasonable rate, coming through in 8:05. Weston was where he was expected to be—last in 10:10.

Things quickly settled down with Brown taking the lead in the third hour. By fifty miles, however, the race had taken an unexpected turn. Brown was still in first place in 7:30:14. But, close behind, to the surprise of all, was Weston in 7:47:15. He had shocked the meager crowd with his ability to run with a relaxed and easy flowing stride.

Brown sailed through 100 miles in 17:13:17 with Weston only an hour behind. Promptly at 101 miles Brown retired for a bit of beef-tea and a rest. Weston walked into the lead for a brief time, for when he had finished 102 miles he also stopped to take a rest. Brown was back on the track as soon as Weston stopped and took over the lead once again.

At midnight Brown led with 125 miles to Weston's 123. Brown left ten minutes later for his first extended rest period of the race. Weston ran on until 1 a.m. when he had covered 127-3/8 miles. This was far more than he had ever completed on the first day.

Brown rested only two hours and forty-nine minutes, and again took the lead at 3 a.m. Weston's handlers allowed him to rest only one minute longer than Brown.

By 8 a.m. Brown had made 150 miles, sixty-three minutes ahead of Weston. Brown now began the favorite "stalking" tactic of the experienced peds. John Ennis described this and Weston's counter-tactic in a post-race interview.

> He (Weston) displayed more strategy than he has ever shown before.

> Brown attempted to break the heart of Weston by following close on his heels. Weston saw his game and was equal to the emergency.
>
> It was a great trick of his to reverse in walking, Ennis continued. (The rules allowed for any pedestrian to reverse direction at the conclusion of any lap simply by notifying the lap counter.) Weston practiced this to Brown's disaster.He knew just when he was going to reverse, but Brown did not. He would be walking at a rapid pace with Brown at his heels, when suddenly he would turn about and go the other way. Brown would get some paces over the line before he realized what Weston had done. In this way he lost several yards each time.

Even though Brown was losing those several yards, he was still moving faster than Weston, and by the end of the second day he had increased his lead to seven miles, with a total of 225 miles. Bets were now taken on Brown at 2 to 1.

The second night Brown rested three hours to Weston's two and a half hours. Brown continued to stretch his lead throughout the third day. *Bell's Life* reported that Brown "seemed brimful of confidence" at 3 p.m. on Wednesday. And indeed he should have been. His only real competition was still losing ground. He felt good and had a thirteen-mile lead. He left the track smiling and happy, ready for a well-deserved but brief rest. Weston remained on the track and cut the lead to ten miles.

At 4:30 that afternoon, John Ennis retired from the race. He had never been in contention and was a complete shambles. One week before the race, while he was training along the Thames near Hampton, he saw a tug boat run down and sink a small boat with two men and two women in it. He dove into the river and saved one of the men and also one of the women. But in the process he strained his back. Then, after the rescue, unable to find a carriage to return him to his hotel, he was forced to walk the four and a half miles. He caught a severe cold and badly blistered his soaking wet feet. The cold was barely cleared up by the start of the race, and the blisters never did heal completely. He left the race ill with his feet blistered, infected, and festering. Bad luck had once again struck him down.

Midnight Wednesday saw Brown still holding a comfortable eleven-mile lead over Weston, 318 miles to 307 miles. Brown was six miles ahead of the previous best on record. He had gone to bed at 11:50 p.m. for his longest rest of the competition, and did not return until 3:16 a.m. Weston, sensing that Brown may have been starting to have difficulty, kept going until 1:25 a.m. He was now a mere five miles behind and moving easily.

Weston Closes In

Brown came out of his tent noticeably weaker. Weston charged out of his tent fifteen minutes after a sleep of only two hours. Brown moved stiffly. At 8:30 he took a twenty-three minute rest for a massage. Weston closed to within four miles. Brown came back in obvious pain, his legs no better. Weston was now in control. He gained rapidly, often running up to two miles at a time without a walking break. His adrenalin was rushing through his body. He had waited three and a half days for Brown to crack.

A *New York Times* reporter described the two men at 10 a.m. Thursday. "(Weston) seems hearty and strong and is going finely. Brown is not so strong and his supporters are getting anxious." Brown again left the track at 10:15 a.m. "looking exhausted" with 346 miles 2 laps on his scoreboard.

At 11:01 Weston ran into the lead. "His iron-like legs and indomitable will soon made him the leading figure of the fight" (*Turf, Field, and Farm*). Brown was through. By mid-afternoon he was staggering around the track at two miles per hour.

In the thirteen hours from taking the lead until midnight Thursday, Weston, with a total of 390 miles, gained twenty-seven miles on Brown. Weston had taken only occasional brief rests of a few minutes throughout the afternoon and evening, and slept only three hours Friday morning from 1 a.m. to 4 a.m.

The outcome was now certain. To stimulate interest in the final two days, Sir John Astely wagered Weston $2,500 to $500 that he could not make 550 miles.

Weston was more than ready for such a challenge. He ran effortlessly. At 12:20 p.m. Saturday he ran his 500th mile in 7:39. The fastest mile of the entire six days came at 6 p.m. when he covered his 526th mile in 7:37. He continued "scoring lap after lap with untiring perseverance."

The *New York Times* gave the following description of the last evening.

> A large number of Americans were present and their shouts of encouragement and the many bouquets and baskets of beautiful flowers showered upon their plucky countryman seemed to infuse him with

Weston after Fourth Astley Belt, 1879 ("Weston and His Walks"–Souvenir Program, 1910)

new life, and with a smiling face he reeled off the laps as though he was walking for the fun of it. Whenever the band played he maintained a dog trot that carried him around the track.

He was walking and trotting in splendid form and caused the most undisguised amazement to all who watched him and noted his wonderful staying powers.

The performance is considered the more marvelous that the English public had begun to lose faith in Weston and think that the island could produce a dozen men better than he.

As his score crept past the greatest ever made, the building fairly shook with the tremendous applause of the multitude who watched the sturdy walker and the changing figures on the blackboard. The spectators cheered the American to the echo.

As he passed his tent on the final lap he received British and American flags which he carried around the ring, waving them amid deafening cheering and din of music. The band played first "Yankee Doodle" and ended with "Rule Brittannia."

He covered his last two miles in 11:24 and 11:21, respectively. He stopped his six-day excursion at 10:55 p.m. with a new world record of 550 miles.

Weston was "blithe and chipper to the last, and left Agricultural Hall anything but a used-up man" (*Turf, Field, and Farm*).

Bell's Life commented after the race that Weston was "by no means the weary wobbler he used to be called." He had averaged more than ninety miles per day for the six days and finished as though he had just taken a stroll around the block.

On July 4th, in the theatre of the Alexandra Palace, in London, Weston received the formal congratulations of his friends and admirers. He was presented with a handsome gold watch and chain and a silver cup subscribed for by a number of noblemen and friends. The inscription on the watch read, "Presented to E. P. Weston by some fifty of his admirers as a mark of their appreciation of his great powers of endurance, energy of character, and honesty of purpose, July 5, 1879."

In addition, the park where Weston had trained, Alexandra Park, was christened "Weston Park" in honor of his victory.

A week before the testimonial, Sir John Astley wrote the following letter to *Sporting Life Newspaper* of London.

I venture to think that very many of your readers will agree with me that the feat accomplished by Edward Payson Weston at the Agricultural Hall last week, 550 miles in six days and nights, in the 'go-as-you-please' style is a marvelous performance. Weston tells me he has now covered on foot something like 53,000 miles in America and England and I verily believe he is at this moment in no way worse for his exertions, and he certainly looks better than he did on Monday, the 16th, when about to start.

I have read in many newspapers, from time to time, of the fearful sufferings, of the certain ruin of constitution, of the probable mental aberration, and so forth, caused by overexertion on the track, but the present condition of Weston is the best proof of the utter ignorance displayed by these poor scribes, and confirms me in my opinion that many more men die from not taking exercise enough than from taking too much.

I have known Weston about three years, and have always admired his great powers of endurance and his energy of character, and yet up to this last performance he has never had the good fortune to succeed in the task set before him, ergo, the farther he goes the better he gets. His failure in accomplishing 2,000 miles in 1,000 consecutive hours on the roads of England was to be entirely attributed to the awfully severe weather and the consequent state of the roads, as well as to the enormous crowds that beset him and hindered his progress through the towns on his route. Still, the performance was a most astonishing one, and though Weston did not win, he was far from disgraced.

The expenses attending his walk through England, including the conveyance of his judges and attendants over 2,000 miles for six weeks, were so heavy that his failure cost him over $2,500. This, coupled with serious losses previously, have placed him in pecuniary difficulties from which the poor receipts of the late week's "wobble" (caused by the breaking down of the four other competitors) are not sufficient to extricate him. It is, therefore, proposed by some of his friends and admirers that we should assist him out of his difficulty by organizing a complimentary testimonial on his behalf, and Messrs. Betram and Roberts have generously put their theatre at the Alexandria Palace at our disposal.

I must wind up my long-winded epistle by asking those who agree with me in the above sentiments to take as many tickets as they can afford, particularly impressing on those who have benefitted by Weston's instruction in the art of long-distance progression to lend a helping hand to one who has striven to teach the world what the powers of man are capable of when governed by pluck, perseverance, and abstinence from overindulgence in the so-called pleasures of dissipation. I shall be glad to supply any one who wishes to assist in the above testimonial with tickets if they will apply to me. Yours truly, J. D. Astley.

The day before Astley's letter appeared, the *London News* editorialized about the match.

> There are some slight grounds for hope that the more than usually disgusting spectacle presented by the "Six Days Pedestrian Contest" which ended on Saturday may be the beginning of the end of these senseless exhibitions. If it please anybody to know that rather more than eight miles farther has been walked in the time than has ever been walked before, that knowledge is now open to them.
>
> It is well, however, that they should know something else. The unlucky man, Brown, the winner of the last contest, strained a sinew in his knee or otherwise injured it on Thursday. Notwithstanding this, he continued to hobble painfully along for about 150 miles, the doing of which cost him some three days of constant torture. This was not done in a desperate effort to win, that being impossible days ago, nor merely from a gallant desire to do his best. It was simply done because, owing to the rules of the contest, his share of the gate money could only be obtained by traveling the distance. Brown, of course, has to live by his vocation, and his vocation obliges him to go through several days of absolutely useless torture for the amusement of the spectators.
>
> It is here, however, that the gleam of hope we have alluded to comes in. The spectators, greatly to the credit of those who stayed away, were, comparatively speaking, so few that Brown's gains will amount to nothing. We are sorry for him, but it seems not unreasonable to hope that competitors will scarcely be forthcoming in the future, seeing that there is so much to suffer and so little to get. Appeals to those who encourage these pasttimes have proved futile enough, and indeed, might have been known to be futile beforehand. It is much safer to rely on the common sense and business aptitude of those who have hitherto been encouraged by hope of gain to attempt things which ought not to be attempted.

Regardless of the sentiments expressed in this editorial, Weston had regained the recognition of the athletic world. He had finally won the symbol of the Champion Pedestrian of the World–the Astley Belt. Financially, however, as Astley mentioned in his letter, he made just enough to cover his expenses. He won $2,500 in stake money, $2,500 in the bet with Astley, and a paltry $860 in gate money. This was just three months after Charles Rowell had collected $18,000 in gate money at Madison Square Garden.

In an effort to secure his finances, Weston began a six-week lecture tour throughout the British Isles. He delivered his now famous talk, "What I Know About Walking," and accompanied this with a demonstration of his walking and running styles.

Rowell Challenges Weston

Charles Rowell challenged Weston almost immediately. The two met at the office of *Sporting Life* on the afternoon of August 2 and signed the following rather detailed articles of agreement:

> Memorandum of agreement made and entered into this second day of August, 1879, between Edward Payson Weston, of New York City, USA, party of the first part, and Charles Rowell, of Chesterton, Cambridge, England, party of the second part, witnesseth: Whereas the party of the first part is now the holder of the "Long-Distance Championship of the World Belt," won by him at Agricultural Hall, London, in June, 1879, and the party of the second part has duly challenged him to a pedestrian match therefore pursuant to the conditions upon which the said Belt is held. Now, therefore, this agreement witnesseth, that the parties hereto hereby agree to compete for the said Championship Belt, won by the party of the first part, and the sum of 100 pounds a side. Twenty-five pounds a side is hereby deposited by the parties hereto in the hands of the editor of *Sporting Life* to bind the match, and the remaining sum of seventy-five pounds a side must be deposited in the hands of the editor of *Sporting Life*, or his authorized representative, on or before Monday, the first day of September, in the year before mentioned. The match is to take place in a covered building or ground known as Madison Avenue Gardens, New York, USA, which is mutually agreed upon by both parties, and is to commence at one o' clock p.m. on Monday, September 22, 1879 and terminate at eleven o'clock p.m. on Saturday, September 27, the party covering the greatest distance during that time, by either running or walking, without assistance, to be declared the winner. The match is to be subject to the same conditions as that at which the said Belt was won by the party of the first part, and the Belt is held by the winner on the same terms and conditions on which it is now held. In the event of any other person or persons joining the match, they must each deposit the sum of one hundred pounds with the appointed stakeholder, within four weeks previous to the fixed date for the commencement of the race; and by subject to the conditions and terms of this agreement. The editor of *Sporting Life*, London, England, is hereby authorized to appoint three judges, and the editor of the *Turf, Field, and Farm*, New York, is hereby authorized to engage and appoint the requisite number of lapscorers and timekeepers. A stipulated sum for incidental expenses is to be allowed for each person officially engaged during the contest, beyond which no allowances will be made to them for any purpose whatsoever All matters of dispute or appeals from questions not provided for by these conditons are to be referred to the trustees of the Belt, whose decision shall be final in all cases. The gate receipts (after all expenses have been paid) are to be divided as follows:
>
> If only one man completes 450 miles (or more), then the whole of

the gate receipts (less expenses) to be paid over to him; if two competitors complete 450 miles the winner to receive two-thirds of the receipts, and the second man one-third; if three men complete 450 miles, the first to get one-half, the second 30 percent, and the third 20 percent; if four men complete 450 miles, the winner to receive one-half, the second 25 percent, the third 15 percent, the fourth 10 percent; if five men complete 450 miles, the winner to receive one-half, the second 25 percent, the third 12 percent, the fourth 8 percent, and the fifth 5 percent; if six men complete 450 miles, the winner to receive one-half, the second 25 percent, the third 12 percent, the fourth 8 percent, the fifth 6 percent, the sixth 4 percent; should more than six men complete 450 miles, the winner to receive one-half, and the balance to be distributed among the other competitors in proportion to the miles completed as may be directed by Sir John Astley, Bart M.P., the giver of the Belt. Should there be only two competitors, each man to walk on a separate track, to be laid down according to his own directions, and surveyed by a competent authority in the presence of the judges appointed. The measurement to be made eighteen inches from the border frame on the inside which is three inches higher than the mold. Should there be three (or more) competitors, all to go on one wide track (not less than ten feet wide). Either party failing to comply with any of these articles to forfeit all moneys deposited. (signed)

Charles Rowell
Edward Payson Weston

Witness, W. Potter
Witness, J. Huddart Russell

As Weston prepared to leave England, Mr. Atkinson, the editor of *Sporting Life*, called on him to make the customary $500 deposit on the Astley Belt. Weston, with hardly enough money to get himself, his wife and children, and his valet home, refused. He said that he was a gentleman and they would have to take his word. Atkinson appealed to Astley, and Astley decided that Weston's word was sufficient.

7

Disputes

After being away for more than three years, Weston returned to the United States on August 27, 1879. C. D. Hess and the managers of Madison Square Garden arranged a gala welcoming home for the champion pedestrian and his family. They hired a steamboat to take a large party of Weston's admirers to meet the liner *Nevada* before it would dock in the New York harbor. Six kegs of beer, two baskets of wine, and a large basket of sandwiches were also loaded into the steamboat to keep the guests happy until Weston's arrival.

At one in the afternoon, after a five-hour wait, the *Nevada* was sighted. The steamboat pulled alongside and Weston was saluted with loud cheers and toast after toast as he stood at the railing waving his hat to his friends.

The entire party on the steamboat boarded the *Nevada* and continued the welcoming party until the ship docked.

Weston had received some very bad press during the three years he had been away. Several of the newspapermen who had labeled him as "washed up" and "finished" were now firing questions at him about his most recent victory and the next race that was scheduled to begin in three and a half weeks. Innuendos were made concerning the legitimacy of his performance in England and the chance of invalid record-keeping in the upcoming race.

Weston's countenance changed rapidly from smiling and jovial to scowling and stern. The *New York Times* reporter on board recorded the following outburst.

You want to know whether this walk is going to be square? I have been accused of making unfair walks, but I will give any man $100 for every inch he can prove I claimed without making it. I never made an unfair walk in my life, and would not degrade myself by thinking of such a thing.

Actions speak louder than words, but there's nothing succeeds like success, gentlemen. I have seen the time in this city when I could not borrow $25 to keep the Rink open another day when I was walking. I did not care to bring this belt back to New York. In fact, when I went away I had made up my mind not to walk any more in this city. While in many quarters I always received the kindest treatment here, in others I did not. There was a time when I would have considered it the proudest event in my life to bring this belt back to America, but I have got over that. Still I am glad to bring it back for the sake of my friends here. If I had my way about it, this next walk would not be in New York, but in Australia, but my wife and Sir John Astley overcame my wishes.

One thing you can set down for a certainty. I will not walk in that Garden if smoking is allowed there. It is too hard on the lungs to breathe that foul atmosphere for six days, and I do not intend to do it, and Rowell will not walk if I do not.

Whose make of shoes did I use in the London walk? I have no idea. I bought them and paid for them as anybody would, without inquiring who made them. I did not train at all for the walk, and have never trained an hour in my life. I was in perfect health when I went into that walk, and am now as sound as a dollar. I was shown every attention in England, and could not have been better treated if I had been a prince. Sir John Astley is one of the kindest and noblest men I have ever met.

I must show you my watch. Don't think that this is the Newark watch, for it isn't. Oh no, this is not the Newark watch. I have no Newark property about me. You've heard of the Newark watch, I suppose? After I walked there, the Mayor told me that he and some of the prominent citizens had been appointed a committee to present me with a gold watch as a momento of my long walk. I heard nothing more of it for about a month, and then I met the Mayor one day, and he told me the watch was being prepared, and was almost ready. I told him it was no matter, I was satisfied with what I had done. A few weeks after that one of the "prominent citizens" said to me, "I don't know about the watch; there was a little dispute about the figures, you know." One old Newark citizen said to me, "You ought to come here and live, Weston; this is a splendid place to live." Yes it is. If I owned a house in perdition and another in Newark, I'd rent the Newark house.

> About the next walk? Well, I have nothing to say about that. I shall do my best, whatever that may be. How many miles will I make? I'll try to make a good many. I do not care to say anything about the profits of the London walk, as that would not interest the public.

Weston was asked about the so-called strain of the six-day races.

> Dr. Newman, of New York, preached a sermon about the "brutality" of walking matches. I have walked 53,000 miles in the last fourteen years, and I don't look much like a used-up man, do I? If the ministers would pay more attention to theology, and less to walking, there would be less ministerial scandals.

As the ship pulled into dock several hundred people waited on the pier and several thousand more stood outside the gates, anxiously watching to catch a glimpse of the returning hero. When Weston appeared a loud and continuous cheer went up from the people on the pier and was taken up by the thousands outside the gates. He was surrounded by well-wishers and it was very difficult for Weston and his family to make their way to the waiting carriage.

When Weston stepped ashore the reception that greeted him picked up his spirits immensely. *Turf, Field, and Farm,* the only publication to stand by Weston through all his failures, commented on his rapid change of disposition in their August 29 edition.

> He is the same Weston of old—all gloom one hour and all brightness the next. As he is nervous and excitable, he frequently says things that his friends never think of treasuring up against him. Something occured to chill his spirits just after passing Fire Island. After his reception on the pier he gladly would have recalled the petulant remarks down the bay.

That Friday evening Weston was given a banquet at Madison Square Garden. The opening address, given by a Professor Doremus, discussed walking from a scientific standpoint, and showed how the world was indebted to Weston. He called Weston a "living example of the advantages of temperance." He recounted how Weston had made pedestrianism fashionable and, by so doing had given many people a new lease on life by encouraging them to get out and walk instead of taking streetcars and carriages.

When the professor described Weston as the king of walkers, and warmly welcomed him home, the audience gave him a standing ovation. From *Turf, Field, and Farm:*

> When the champion, in full evening dress, rose to bow his acknowledgments, he looked anything but a pedestrian. His trim figure, neat attire and polished manners, were more in harmony with the drawing room than the cinder path. He thanked the people for the welcome home, explained away the remarks made on the *Nevada*, and called forth a storm of applause by proclaiming himself an American to the core. He eulogized Sir John Astley, and promised to do all in his power to keep the Belt from going back to England.

The next day he traveled to his hometown of Providence, Rhode Island. A large crowd was on hand to greet him and he drove through a "human mass" to the Narragansett Hotel. A reception was held that night at the Park Garden and 8,000 people demonstrated their pride in Weston. Weston left Providence Sunday night for places unknown to the general public until the start of the race September 22.

Charles Rowell had arrived in New York City, accompanied by his trainer, Charles Barnsley, the day before Weston. His arrival had caused none of the commotion that Weston's had. He was greeted at the pier by Hamilton Busby, the editor of *Turf, Field, and Farm,* and Mr. Brockway of the Ashland House Hotel, where he would stay while he was in the city.

When he was interviewed the next day in the lobby of his hotel, he said that at the moment he was tired and not in the best of condition. The voyage over had been very crowded, and he had been unable to do any walking or running. His feet were also giving him trouble of late, and had interfered a great deal with his training since his last race back in March. He explained why he had not started the fourth Astley Belt race. "I had blistered one heel by wearing a pair of old shoes, and a day or two before the opening I put on a new pair. Something in the leather acted like a poison on the blister, and made me so lame that it would have been folly to start against a man like Weston, who was in first-class condition. I shall start this time, though, and I mean to win, feet or no feet."

Rowell considered Weston to be his chief competition in the next contest, and said that he thought this race would be the hardest struggle of his life. While he was very cautious not to commit himself to a certain distance, when he talked about the race his "eyes flashed with quiet determination," and he reiterated his intention to win.

Controversy Surrounds Race

Weston and Rowell had more to worry about, however, than just the prospect of racing against each other. Several months before, Daniel O'Leary had made arrangements to rent Madison Square Garden starting October 6 for a six-day race for the O'Leary Belt Championship of America. O'Leary, concerned that the Astley Belt race would detract from his own competition, solicited the aid of the millionaire Cornelius Vanderbilt.

The Kuntz Brothers had rented the Garden from May 31 to September 30 "as a first-class place of entertainment, amusement and recreation, or religious worship." It had been a bad season, and when Hess, acting for Weston, approached them with the proposition of staging the Astley Belt race, they jumped at the chance to recoup some of their losses. They agreed to pay all the expenses and to take one-fourth of the gross receipts.

Vanderbilt used his influence and began, early in September, to apply pressure to have the Astley Belt race postponed. He threatened to get an injunction to stop the walk. Hess countered with his own threat to get a "writ of prohibition" against any such injunction. Vanderbilt then offered to give the Garden to the pedestrians for nothing but the bar privilege, if they would delay the walk until the beginning of November. He said that that he would withhold his liquor license in case they refused and would make them amenable for every violation of the license law if they attempted to go on. The question of postponing the race was submitted to Sir John Astley. He hired a well-known New York Law firm to study the problem and make its recommendations. The lawyers advised that the walk go on as planned. The O'Leary group then offered a substantial sum to Weston and Rowell to delay the race. They refused.

After two weeks of threats of suits and countersuits, the matter was finally settled. The Kuntz Brothers met with Kelly and Smith, the owners of the Garden, and paid them an undisclosed sum of money to have them obtain the written promise of Vanderbilt not to interfere with the walk. *Turf, Field, and Farm* gave the reason for such a move. "They took this step because they wished to avoid a lawsuit. They had right on their side, but might was on the other side. They preferred to make a pecuniary sacrifice to carry out their contract with Mr. Hess, and Mr. Vanderbilt expressed himself as satisfied."

This was not the only controversy surrounding the race. Ten other American pedestrians, recognizing the opportunity to cash in on the pedestrianism craze, had deposited the $500 entry fee at the office of *Turf, Field, and Farm*. While they were happy at the chance to be part of a certain money-making venture, they were not pleased at all with the proposed management of the race.

There was so much bitterness that the competitors were split into two camps, the Americans and the English. Weston was considered by the other Americans to be in the English camp. The Americans believed that the Trustees (Astley, Atkinson, Hess, Busby) and Weston and Rowell had combined with the "avowed purpose of 'hippodroming' the match." They were upset that Weston and Rowell and their backers had gone ahead and made all of the arrangements and contracts for the match and for the distribution of the gate receipts, without even seeking their advice or approval. They simply did not trust Weston or "his English friends."

A "Pedestrian Congress"

In order to air their grievances they held a "pedestrian congress" at the Glenham House Hotel at Third Avenue and Twenty-Fourth Street on the afternoon of September 7. Invitations were sent to all the competitors and their backers.

Several of the backers and trainers for the Americans showed up at the appointed time. After waiting one and a half hours for a representative of either Weston or Rowell to show up, they began the meeting. The first to speak, as reported in the September 8, 1879 edition of the *New York Times*, was Thomas Scannell, backer of the Connecticut pedestrian Samuel Merritt.

> I am sorry for it, but it is a fact, nevertheless, that this contest is now in a muddle. We don't know for sure even whether it is to come off at all or not, although we have paid our $500 entrance fee and the other expenses of training. The English claim to be the grand patrons of sport. Humbug. They seem absolutely incapable of managing a contest of any kind fairly, and there's no trick in the world they won't play to beat an American.

This Sir John Astley is a smooth one. He's on the "hippodrome," he is. He has got up a sharp set of rules about this belt that allow him to be the final judge in all matters in dispute, and even to make changes in the proceedings after the making of the match. When Rowell took the Belt back and $20,000 besides, it raised a craze among the English pedestrians and showed Astley a new field for making money out of his belt. That's all he got it up for.

I believe that Rowell hasn't got a cent. I believe Astley took all his $20,000 and put it in his own pocket. These English walkers are all too poor to pay their way over here. Astley takes them in hand, offers them wages and expenses for coming over, sends his own referees and agents along to see that they do their work, and that the money is divided fairly, and then just scoops in the cash himself. Why, Rowell is just as poor now as when he first came over. Sir John it was who made the speculation out of the little fellow's legs.

Here's the situation: Weston has the Belt. He is credited with having made 550 miles. I don't believe he did. Brown had made 542 miles, and in the last match, Brown being in it, a score better than his had to be put up to allow Weston to win. Astley wanted him to win so that the Belt would come over here, and he could send over some more hired pedestrians and make another rake. You'll see. I'll bet almost any amount of money that neither Weston nor Rowell will make any 525 miles or better.

After Weston won the Belt, Rowell at once challenged him, and the match was made. The Astley rules allow the holder of the Belt and the challenger to make the match, agree upon the date, arrange the division of money, and choose managers. Weston and Rowell are both proteges of Astley, and he can cook up any nice little job that he likes. How have they done? After fixing everything up to suit himself, he allows as many other contestants to enter the match as pleased to, providing they all pay as entrance fees the sum of five hundred dollars at least four weeks before the day set for the match, which the rules require. The Americans, excluding Weston, paid, making $5,000. After they all paid their money, what did they find? Why, that they were likely to be swindled right and left.

Every contestant covering 450 miles in the match was entitled to a share of the receipts and the return of his fee. At least five Americans can make 450 miles. Guyon, Merritt, Krohne, Ennis, and Pauchot have all surpassed that score. These men, and in fact, all who pay the fee, are interested in the management of the match, and have a right to have a voice in the selection of the treasures and ticket-sellers, in order to protect their interests and secure the true total of the receipts for division. But the English interest is playing a double game, and will not permit it. Astley, Weston, and Rowell have made the arrangement without consulting any of the other walkers.

> We will insist on one thing: to be represented at the box office and at the doors, in order to save ourselves from being defrauded in the matter of tickets sold and receipts. But every proposition we make to the English interest on that score is quietly ignored.

Mr. Charles E. Davis, backer of George Guyon, agreed with Scannell. "The Americans have a right to be represented in the box-office—a moral right, if not a technical one. The English interest could probably claim that technically Weston and Rowell had a perfect right to make that match and the arrangements to suit themselves, and the other contestants were merely "joiners-in" and after the terms were made. But such a position was not an equitable one, and if Weston and Rowell should adhere to it, their conduct would certainly justify the suspicion that they were "hippodroming" the match."

James Cusick, known worldwide as the trainer for the boxer John Heenan, and now the trainer of John Ennis, voiced his opinion.

> I know these Englishmen. I've been among them. They try every time they can to play us. The English have eaten so much bull beef as to have become a race of bullies. That's a fact. I think they want to make all they can by any means out of this contest.
>
> The Americans ought to have a voice in the management of the financial affairs of the match. If they don't get it, they'll be cheated.
>
> The English interest should consent to a meeting of all the representatives of the contestants. At this meeting each contestant should have an equal vote. And then a treasurer should be elected. The meeting should appoint the ticket-takers and sellers. Watchers should be placed in the ticket office and at the entrances to prevent fraud. At the last Astley Belt contest in this city it was notorious that the ticket-takers used to pass large numbers of tickets to confederates outside to be sold on joint accounts. In this thousands of dollars were made, and that is the reason why the receipts in the box office did not tally with the crowds in the building.
>
> Another thing should be prevented. At the last contest the walkers allowed each of themselves to take out of the receipts $1000, allowed certain members of the management to take a similar amount, and then place away some $2000 as a contingency fund to meet unforeseen or unprovided-for expenses. Such business is all "skin" business, and should not be allowed. The contingent fund had never afterward been heard of. If Weston and Rowell refused to consent to such propositions their conduct would be construed as very singular, to say the least.

On Wednesday evening, September 17, the Americans finally got their wish. Everyone concerned with the race met at the office of *Turf, Field, and Farm.* George Atkinson, who had arrived from England just the day before, was Astley's stand-in at the meeting. The Americans presented their case and voiced once more their dissatisfaction at the Hess management of the affair. Hamilton Busby, speaking on behalf of Weston, said there was absolutely no chance that Hess would be removed. Weston was the champion and had the right to select the time, place, and manager of the contest. Hess had made the contract with the Garden and had become responsible to the extent of thousands of dollars. He explained that the "complexion of the match" was clearly defined in the articles of agreement signed in London on August 2 by Weston and Rowell. The other contestants were simply to join in the match and were therefore bound by the conditions previously agreed upon.

The Americans, seeing that it was either agree or not compete, yielded to the management by Hess. Their anger was soothed somewhat when it was decided to organize a Board of Managers, composed of a representative of each pedestrian. Hess was made the president of this board, and given the power to direct all affairs. A resolution was passed authorizing him to appoint a finance committee, a door committee, and a track committee. George Atkinson was appointed head referee and thereby exercised supervisory control over the match, and belonged to the Board of Managers. He was also made the treasurer. The Kuntz Brothers were to turn over 75 percent of the gate receipts every day to the Finance Committee, and this committee would deposit the money in the Second National Bank, subject to the order of the treasurer.

Each contestant would be allowed a representative in the box office to see that the tickets were correctly counted. The scorers and time-keepers were to be appointed by Busby and would be picked from the reputable athletic clubs of New York City and the surrounding vicinity. The price of admission to the Garden was set at one dollar to prevent crowding and to make the gathering select.

Finally, just four days before the start, all the disputed details seemed to be worked out. The American contingent, while not completely happy, resigned itself to the state of affairs and everyone began making final preparations.

8

The Fifth Astley Belt Race

The bickering, however, was not over. John Ennis, the veteran Chicago pedestrian, insisted on another meeting Saturday evening to call the manager of the race, Charles Hess, to account for all the money spent to date and to outline the projected expenses. Hess complained that he had been too busy with the details of the match to prepare a statement of his expenses. After what the *New York Times* reported as "a first class row," Hess was given until Sunday to present such a statement.

The task of transforming the dirt-floored arena into an eight-lap-to-the-mile track had been placed in the hands of George Atkinson. Saturday night at 8 p.m. Atkinson directed a work crew of 100 laborers. They first dug up the ground to a depth of twelve inches, broke the dirt into fine pieces and removed all the pebbles with rakes, then placed a covering of tanbark and loam on the dirt and sprinkled this combination with sawdust. This part of the operation was completed by dawn Sunday. All day long, up to a few minutes before the start, heavy rollers were drawn over the track to make it as firm as possible.

While this was going on carpenters were busy covering over the rest of the floor on either side of the track, and surrounding the track with a strong railing. The *New York Times* described the interior of the Garden in great detail.

> The scorers and reporters are provided with a raised stand with a triple row of desks, one above the other, twenty-seven feet in length.

Opposite these has been erected a board fence six feet high, and on this has been tacked a long and broad muslin sheet, divided into thirteen spaces. Each space is headed with the name of one of the contestants. Below is painted a double circle with the numerals from one to eight inclusive, the number of laps to the mile. A large black indicator turns on a pivot in the center. A peg goes through a hole near the point, and corresponding holes are bored into the dial at each numeral. Between the names and the dials are pegs on which small placards bearing numerals are hung to denote the number of miles accomplished. This novel scoring arrangement is excellent in every respect save one.

None of the spectators, except the few who can crowd immediately in front of it, and the reporters, judges, and scorers, can see anything occurring at the starting point. On the edge of the central floor, between every two alternate pillars supporting the roof, are pitched the tents of the competitors, facing the track. These are surrounded by stout wooden railings to keep off interlopers. All except Weston's are of blue and white striped canvas, with white roofs. Weston's has black and yellow striped sides. They are all wall tents, but are not of equal size. The largest is twelve feet square. All have ventilating holes in the roofs. An enterprising furniture-dealer has fitted each one with a cot and mattress, a table, a washstand, two chairs, a gas stove, and a strip of carpet, in return for permission to hang his advertisement, surmounted by the name of the occupant, on each ridge-pole. Weston has gorgeously furnished two rooms in the corner of the building near his tent, and here he will take luxurious rests, using the tent only for short rubbings-down. He has substituted a lounge for the bed there. In his other quarters he has two beds, one for himself and the other for his trainer; while, in another small room adjacent, are accommodations for a second attendant.

On the central floor near the Fourth Avenue side is a raised platform on which are eight tables for the use of the bookmakers, and fronting the boarded grotto is a tall blackboard, visible from nowhere, on which the record of completed miles is hung. The Garden is lighted at night by electric lamps, which have been specially furnished with extra thick and large globes so as not to injure the pedestrians' eyes. There are numerous petty apple and cake stands, weighing machines, soda-water fountains, and other contrivances for catching stray pennies all around the enclosure, and an extra bar has been fitted up in the north corner. The new decorations consist of advertisements that placard the walls in all directions, and notices to the effect that smoking will not be allowed on the floor.

On Sunday afternoon the pedestrians, who should have been resting, met again at the Garden and received Hess' account. After careful scrutiny it was declared satisfactory by all. Hess' compensation was set at $2,500 without any serious dispute even from the dissident Ennis.

Ennis did, however, have one more complaint. He was not at all happy with the agreement to give the two best tent locations to Weston and Rowell. The pedestrians, tired of all the wrangling, quickly gave in to Ennis and a lottery for the tent locations was hastily arranged with George Atkinson presiding.

Thomas Scannel, Merritt's backer, drew tent number 1 and immediately announced that he intended to turn it over to Weston. He also said that Rowell "wished the tent at the corner of Fourth Avenue and Twenty-sixth Street, so that he might be enabled to run out to the Ashland Hotel whenever he desired," and expressed a hope that the person drawing it would let him have it. This tent fell to Hazael, and he gave it over to Rowell. It was nearly 5 p.m. when the drawing was completed and the pedestrians hurried off to their hotels in order to catch a few hours of sleep before the start.

A United States First

This was to be the first six-day race in the United States with a field of more than four. The arrangement of the tents around the enclosure of the track was nothing short of stupid. From no point in the building could more than a glimpse of the track be seen. The managers recognized this once the tents had been erected, and attempted to have the tents moved to a more convenient location under the seats on the Twenty-seventh Street side. Once more there was a dispute, and again the irascible Irishman, Ennis, was at its center. They absolutely refused to have the tents moved. After a heated debate, Ennis won his third decision in a row. The tents stayed where they were.

At 7 p.m. Sunday there were more than 200 people inside the Garden; scorers, judges, managers, reporters, trainers, bartenders, waiters, regular employees and standkeepers. By 8 p.m. the gas in all the tents was lit and the trainers were busy "arranging bottles and boxes, making up the beds, and laying out the walking costumes of their principals."

The thirteen private boxes in front of the scorers' stand that had been reserved for friends of the competitors were filled long before the doors were officially opened.

The scene outside the Garden was as chaotic as it had been for the third Astley Belt race back in March. Crowds filled the sidewalks in front of the Garden, and made walking impossible on that side of the street. Lines once again extended from the Madison Avenue entrance around into Twenty-sixth Street and Twenty-seventh Street nearly to Fourth Avenue.

The police and management had devised a new plan for handling the crush at the box-office. They hoped to avoid the onslaught and near riot that had occurred in March. Pens had been placed in the center of the vestibules at each entrance, forming a narrow passage next to the ticket windows. A squad of twenty policemen was on hand at each window.

When the doors were finally opened at 10 p.m. everyone remained orderly and quickly filled the best seats in the house—those on the north side, back of the gallery. The bookmakers immediately began doing a thriving business, with Rowell and Hazael as co-favorites at 2 to 1. Weston was given 3 to 1, Guyon 4 to 1, Panchot 5 to 1, Ennis 7 to 1, Hart 10 to 1, and Merritt 10 to 1.

A half hour before the start there were more than 9,000 spectators overflowing the seats and standing room within the track. Charles Hess was beaming with delight, dollar signs in front of his eyes. He told a group of reporters, "Oh, this is the way to do it. We have an orderly, quiet, nice crowd of people and I'd be gratified if the house was only half full, instead of being jammed by a howling mob at fifty cents."

At five minutes to one o'clock the pedestrians were called from the *National Police Gazette* described the start.

> The pedestrians took their places in front of the scorers' stand in four files, each lustily cheered meanwhile by friends. They formed a picturesque group. All the preparations had been made. The scorers and judges were in their seats, and the contestants were called to the front of the scorers' stand. The judges, wearing gay badges, stood in their place, the spectators surged with crushing noise toward the point of interest, and Mr. Hamilton Busby, who had been selected to give the word, stood with watch in hand. The other judges are Mr. Atkinson and Mr. C. H. Pierce, president of the New York Athletic Club. It had been agreed that Mr. Atkinson need not caution the pedestrians against breaches of the rules governing the track by telling them to turn outside their competitor's line of progress, to allow nothing to turn them from the rail when they chose to follow it, or the simpler caution about treading on one another's heels or interfering with each other in any

way. They looked at the judges, the judges looked at each other, and there was a pause.

Guyon, the Adonis of the thirteen, wore blue trunks, a white shirt, and white drawers. He had his hair cut just before he went on the track, and looked trim and in good form. His weight is 152 pounds.

Hart, the colored boy, looked extremely well. His suit was of black and gray, and included a cap. He weighs 140 pounds.

Jackson wore white drawers, blue trunks, and a white shirt. He stood at 125 pounds.

Krohne towered above all the others by nearly half a head, and showed his height far more than when in citizen's dress. He wore white drawers, blue trunks, and white shirt and belt, and around his neck was tied a blue scarf. He weighed 170 pounds. He stepped off with a slight limp, which is permanent lameness.

Federmeyer was amazingly clad in red tights, gray shirt, and a gray hat. His hair had not been cut nor his beard trimmed, and he stood bent forward as if he held an imaginary wheelbarrow and was endeavoring to catch up to it.

Dutcher never looked better. His eyes sparkled and the cheeks were full and rosy. He was attired all in red, except a white hat and white belt. His weight was 145 pounds.

Norman Taylor wore a linen coat and linen trousers, both flapping as he ran. He had told his friends these clothes never failed him, and he had a superstition that any other dress would bring certain failure.

Panchot looked better than he had for weeks previous. He wore blue trunks, balbriggan shirt and drawers, and weighed 138 pounds.

Merritt, the six-footer, half hid his dark, boyish face under a pink cap, and had white shirt and blue trunks.

Rowell wore a jockey cap, and looked exactly as he did in the race by which he won the Belt. Even the striped shirt, which evoked so many jokes about the treadmill, was reproduced. His weight had been reduced to 140 pounds.

Weston showed himself heavier than when he went to England, weighing about 140 pounds He wore the red tights and trunks (that he says he bought for $1.25), a white shirt, and no hat, but carried the inevitable light switch with which he is always pictured. He has with him besides Charley, his valet, his old friend Deputy Sheriff Henry B. Ford of White Plains, who was with him when he won his first 100-mile race. He thinks Ford will bring him luck.

Hazael wore green drawers and a white shirt, and weighed 138 pounds.

"Are you ready?" Mr. Busby asked, a minute before one o'clock.

The men's silence gave assent. The minute seemed like five, but it was over at last.

"Go."

The word was hardly spoken before the thirteen scurried off. The cheering and applause that rose with the music continued until long after the men were sent away, and it was with difficulty the scorers and judges could make themselves heard. The ladies were as much excited as the men, and handkerchiefs were waved frantically in time to the cheering and the clapping of hands. No such scene was ever witnessed in the Garden on any similar occasion.

Hazael sprang into a fast run and took a commanding lead. He covered the first mile in 6:10. Panchot was almost a lap back in 7:00. Rowell, Taylor, and Jackson followed a few seconds later. After the first hour, all of the pedestrians continued to run at an impressive but suicidal pace. Hazael completed eight and seven-eighths miles, Rowell seven and a half miles. Even Weston, who was a notoriously slow starter, made six and a half miles that first hour.

It took several hours before they finally settled down to a more reasonable pace, each one beginning to follow his own predetermined plan of walking and running.

The first real excitement occurred with the race less than three hours old. William Dutcher, "a nice-looking young man with a German cast of countenance and a German build, with a round smooth face and small bright eyes, broad and deep chest and large legs" (as described by a *National Police Gazette* reporter) collapsed on the track, "in a fit." He recovered in a few minutes and was back out on the track, but walking stooped over at a rate of one and a half miles per hour. A short time later he fainted again and "was borne rigid to his tent."

When revived a second time he begged to be allowed to go on. But the doctor for the managers said positively no, and "the young man sobbed like a baby." When he was later asked the cause of his sudden breakdown he said, "Well, I've got some trouble with my heart. I chewed a lot of tobacco while training and that brought on the trouble. Why, my heart beat like a trip hammer. If I had gone on they said it would have killed me."

Soon after 9 a.m. Rowell took the lead for the first time. By 11 a.m. Ennis had also passed the quickly fading Hazael. Rowell dropped into his "incessant dogtrot" which carried him around the tract at the methodical rate of six miles per hour. He passed 100 miles in 16:49, with Guyon now in second place more than two hours behind in 18:58. The others who completed 100 miles the first day followed in this order: Ennis 19:47, Merritt 21:09, Hart 21:14, Panchot 21:39, and Hazael 21:49.

Smoke Clouds the Race

Even though there were signs throughout the Garden forbidding smoking on the ground floor, almost every other man in the crowd held a lit cigarette or cigar. The air was suffocating as described in *Turf, Field, and Farm:*

> Over the heads of the swaying mass, above the din and roar of battle, rolled heavy clouds of tobacco smoke, poisoning the atmosphere and throwing more than one sensitive stomach out of tune.

One of those sensitive stomachs belonged to the defending champion, Edward Payson Weston. About the same time that Dutcher was carried into his tent Weston rushed into his and vomitted for the first time. As the hours passed this became a more frequent event—so much so that after moving along nicely at five to five and one-half miles per hour for the first nine hours, Weston was reduced to two and one-half to three miles per hour. His stops grew longer and closer together.

To compound his woes, the impertinent remarks he had made on his return to the United States the month before came back to haunt him. Weston, instead of being cheered as the returning champion, was taunted by the crowd. At one point during the afternoon he loudly chided the smokers on one turn. The next time around, a man standing by the railing deliberately blew "three puffs of cigar smoke in his face." Weston immediately retired to his tent and sent a formal complaint to the managers. The result was a raid by the police upon the smokers, and for a time the rule was "better observed."

The smoke, however, had taken its deleterious effect. Not only had it robbed Weston of valuable time on the track (time that he knew would be almost impossible to make up on a competitor such as Rowell), but it had shattered his confidence. By Monday evening he was "a beaten man." He could not sleep. His eyes were "wild and staring," and he was unable to take any nourishment. He psychologically conceded the race.

Rowell was the exact opposite of Weston in temperament. *Turf, Field, and Farm* portrayed him:

> . . . Nothing seems to fret or annoy him. He plods along methodi-

cally, eats with regularity, falls to sleep at the mere bidding of Mr. Atkinson and does not waste words in pleading for more time in his tent.

At the end of the first twenty-four hours the experts were calling the outcome a certain victory for Rowell. The standings at this time were: Rowell 127 miles, Guyon 115 miles, Hart 110 miles 1 lap, Merritt 110 miles, Ennis 102 miles 6 laps, Panchot 100 miles, Hazael 100 miles, Jackson 98 miles 7 laps, Weston 95 miles, Krohne 90 miles 2 laps, Federmeyer 85 miles 2 laps, and Taylor 80 miles.

The second day passed uneventfully. The pedestrians had settled down to a more realistic pace. Rowell increased his lead by only three miles by covering eighty-eight miles Tuesday. Guyon, maintaining a steady "heel and toe" walk, held his own with eighty-five miles. Merritt took over the race for third outdoing Hart eighty-seven miles to eighty-three miles. Hart was troubled by stomach cramps early in the day, and the rumor spread quickly that he had been poisoned. Fred Englehardt (Hart's assistant trainer) and Daniel O'Leary (Hart's head trainer and principal backer) stoutly denied the rumor. O'Leary, however, spent the rest of the day walking up and down in front of Hart's tent, closely observing his protege's progress and everything that was handed to him. O'Leary, dressed in a tight-fitting Prince Albert coat buttoned to the throat, and wearing a broad-brimmed soft black hat was dignity personified as he gave Hart the benefit of his pedestrian wisdom.

While Hart was having difficulties, Merritt had slept only two hours in forty-eight but was "the only man who looked as well (Tuesday evening) as when the race began."

Hazael came from seventh place to fifth place with an excellent eighty-six miles to Ennis' seventy-eight miles and a fading Panchot's fifty-five miles. The defending champion, Edward Payson Weston, seemed to have overcome his stomach upset of Monday and covered the sixth most miles with seventy-eight.

It was obvious, however, the Weston was no longer making a real effort to win the race. He carried himself in the most eccentric manner, grimacing and capering all around the track. At one point in the evening, Weston gave George Atkinson quite a surprise by knocking the gentleman's hat clear off his head with his walking stick as he passed by. Later in the evening he walked around feigning an ankle injury, and finally insisted on going to bed over the "protestations of his trainers." Weston's wife claimed that he was "merely nervous," and that his feet and legs were in excellent condition. Of that there could be no doubt. No one prances around with "some antic to perform on almost every turn" unless one is feeling good.

The second day ended with Rowell having 215 miles, a comfortable lead over Guyon with 200 miles, Merritt 197 miles, Hart 193 miles, Hazael 186 miles, Ennis 180½ miles, Weston 173 miles, Jackson 161 miles, Krohne 160 miles, Panchot 155 miles, Federmeyer 150 miles, and Taylor 100 miles.

The early morning hours were far from the loud, exciting hours of the late evening, as the *New York Times* described in its September 24th edition:

> The hours from midnight until daylight are always gloomy, damp, and uncomfortable in Madison-Square Garden. There generally is an overpowering smell of stale tobacco smoke. There are very few spectators, and half of these are asleep, or would like to be. A good proportion of the pedestrians are generally in their tents, and the whole place is sleepy.

The gloomy dampness was intensified Wednesday morning by a steady drizzle and falling temperature. The pedestrians put on heavy coats or wrapped their weary bodies in blankets to shield themselves from the cold.

Neither Rowell's massive lead nor the cold rain, however, dampened the New Yorker's enthusiasm for the spectacle taking place at the Garden. "Down town and up town, in private houses, public resorts, and conveyances, on the streets and in the places of businesses is heard talk of miles and laps, favorites and records. In the cars, on the ferry-boats, on the streets, in the offices, and in the parlors, the walk and the walkers are the uppermost topics of conversation."

Rowell took only four hours of sleep, and seemed greatly refreshed. He still plodded after his usual custom, constantly varying from a walk to his peculiar dogtrot, and covered an amazing ninety-five miles on Wednesday.

Merritt quickly caught the ailing Guyon but could not pull more than a mile ahead all afternoon. But the man of "the long stride and cool self-possession" was in no hurry. He was pacing himself well, and the only indication that he had been racing for

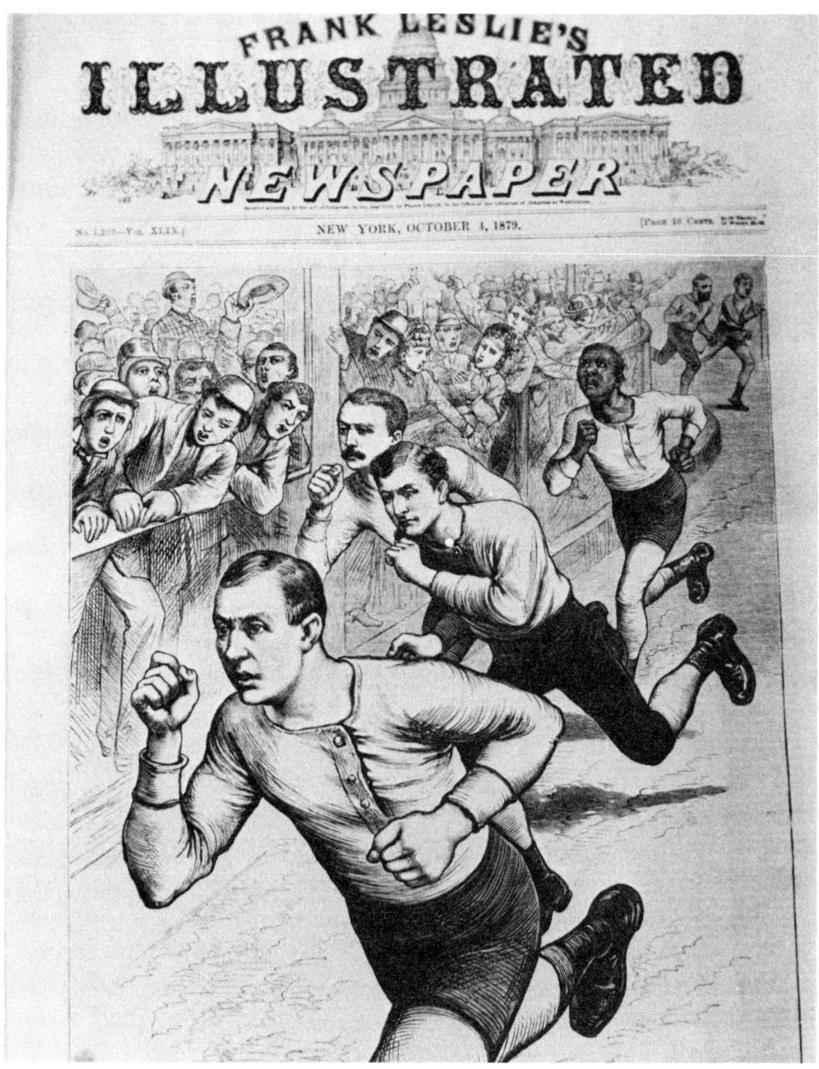

Fifth Astley Belt, 1879 (Frank Leslie's Illustrated Newspaper)

three days showed up in his thinning cheeks. "His thin face was as calm as a summer pool, and his eyes were as clear and steady as his trainer could wish." He completed ninety miles for the day, and was close enough to Rowell to easily take over the lead if the Englishman should falter.

Hart, O'Leary's protege, and the most "stylish" of the pedestrians, became the favorite of the crowd Wednesday. He managed to hold his own during the day and maintained his lead over Weston. Weston seemed to find some of his old zip during the day and ran more than he walked. But, as the Garden began to fill in the evening, so did the smoke. By 11 p.m., with the Garden filled to capacity, the smoke was unbearable for Weston. The skylights were closed and the smoke became so bad in the galleries that it was impossible to see down to the track. Weston left the track upset, discouraged, and sick to his stomach at 11:05 p.m.

While Hart was the favorite during the day, Hazael took over that position during the evening hours. He ran constantly and amazed the crowd. Even Rowell was unable to keep up with him while he was on the track. When he started Wednesday morning he was behind Hart, Ennis, and Guyon. But by mid-afternoon he had run by all three, and finished the day in third place, having covered ninety miles for the day. The betting moved heavily toward him to take over second place before the end of the race.

At the halfway point Rowell had a commanding lead of twenty-three miles. The standings were: Rowell 310 miles, Merritt 287 miles, Hazael 276 miles, Hart 273 miles, Guyon 270 miles, Weston 251 miles, Krohne 233 miles, Jackson 230 miles, Ennis 220 miles, Federmeyer 220 miles, Panchot 205 miles, and Taylor 150 miles.

Rowell took a three-hour rest in the Ashland House Hotel and returned freshly shaved and smiling to begin the second half of what appeared to be a runaway victory. He maintained his even pace throughout Thursday, occasionally taking part in spurts initiated by the other pedestrians, however, never beginning them himself.

Several of the pedestrians requested that there be more music played, so, Thursday the band began to play at 6 a.m. instead of the customary 8 a.m. "The musicians looked as if they had passed the night on benches, after circumnavigating the globe in schooners, and their first toots were not inspiring."

Most of the pedestrians ate their breakfasts right on the track as they were walking. This race saw the introduction of a special eating dish, shaped like a gravy bowl, and about half the size, with a long thin spout. The spout allowed them to drink without spilling the contents.

Hart twisted his ankle in the early morning and was reduced to a painful limp. For most of the day he could travel no faster than three miles per hour. O'Leary was kept very busy massaging the ankle with liniment in an attempt to reduce the swelling. When asked by reporters if Hart was through, O'Leary said, "absolutely not." By Friday, he said, Hart's ankle would be back to normal and he would pick up all the ground he was losing.

The most impressive performance of the fourth day was given by John Ennis. Like Weston, Ennis had been having trouble with his stomach from the beginning of the race. Thursday morning, however, he said that he was "over the bridge" and feeling fine. His wife stayed with him the entire day as he almost matched Rowell's ninety-two miles with a distance of ninety miles.

A Battle for Second

The longer the race progressed the more certain it became that Rowell was going to win back the belt. Even though this outcome was obvious to all there was still a great deal of excitement generated by the battle for second place between Hazael and Merritt.

Hazael continued his excellent running of the day before and slowly cut into Merritt's lead. The young Yankee, surviving on an astonishingly small amount of sleep, could not hold off the charging Hazael, and at 6:50 p.m. surrendered second place to the Englishman. Merritt did not give up. Urged on by the crowd of 15,000 that had made walking anywhere in the Garden but on the

Fifth Astley Belt Begins, 1879

track almost impossible, Merritt kept close to Hazael throughout the night. The longest lead Hazael could secure was one and one half miles. Even Merritt's handlers were amazed at his ability to match Hazael. The *Times* reporter described Merritt at 11 p.m.: "He has a good color, a sweeping step, and a steady motion, and is still doing well, in spite of his youth."

Weston was still having difficulty with the miserable tobacco smoke that hovered over the Garden the entire day. Even with his troubles he managed to do some respectable walking and running during the day and early evening. The band would strike up "Tommy Dodd" and this would send Weston off on a lap or two spurt. The crowd that had initially been very cold toward the champion had warmed up over the past three days and gave him as much encouragement as any of the other pedestrians.

By midnight Thursday his face showed the physical suffering which he was enduring, but he ran nimbly around the track, swinging his riding whip. The crowd cheered him on. At 12:30 a young woman stepped to the railing beside the track and reached out to give Weston a bouquet of flowers. He refused to accept the present and continued down the track. The spectators who witnessed this began to hiss and jeer Weston. Every lap after that as he would pass that spot he would receive a mixture of hisses and cheers. The longer he walked, the fainter became the cheers and the louder the hisses. Once again, Weston's impertinence had upset the New Yorkers.

While the hissing against Weston continued, so did the cheers and encouragement for Merritt. He managed to stay right behind Hazael.

At 12:45 a.m., with Merritt and Hazael walking about four feet apart, a large rock was hurled from the stands in the direction of the two pedestrians. Luckily the rock missed both and the assailant was quickly arrested by the police. He was the well-known Cincinnati gambler, Ephraim Holland. Since neither Hazael nor Merritt were in a position to appear in court to press charges, this was done by Otto Lechla, a spectator at the race. He testified the next day in the Jefferson Market Police Court that he saw Holland make a motion as if to throw something and then he saw the rock hit the track. When cross examined he admitted that he never actually saw Holland throw the rock. The motive given but never substantiated was that Holland had made a bet of $15,000 to $1,500 that Rowell, Merritt, and Guyon would finish in that order and that Hazael's position in the race at that time had upset his calculations.

The defense attorney moved that the complaint be dismissed on the grounds that it was "vague and ambiguous, and that it did not describe the alleged assault with exactness and precision."

The prosecutor asked for and received an adjournment until the next day so that he could find other witnesses who could verify that Holland did, indeed, throw the rock. The next day, however, he was not able to produce any more witnesses, and the charge was dismissed and Holland was set free.

Shortly after the stone-throwing incident Hazael went to bed. Merritt took the opportunity to close the gap on Hazael and took back second place at 1:15 a.m.

At the end of four days Rowell, meanwhile, had a tremendous lead of thirty-four miles. The standings were: Rowell 402 miles, Hazael 368 miles, Merritt 367 miles, Guyon 345 miles, Hart 339 miles, Weston 322 miles, Ennis 310 miles, Krohne 307 miles, Federmeyer 288 miles, and Taylor 180 miles. Panchot and Jackson withdrew.

Rowell rested for only three hours and started the fifth day walking briskly. He gave the scorers a cheerful "good morning" and a smile as he passed their table. His eyes were bright and clear, and he showed no signs of blisters or stiffness. In fact, it was reported that there were "no traces of fatigue" and that he acknowledged the good wishes of the spectators, nodding pleasantly. He quickly ate his breakfast on the track and set out at a pace of four miles per hour.

The morning was damp and cold, as it had been all week. Both Merritt and Hart began the day in an overcoat and a hat. Hazael, wearing his emerald-green waistcloth, struggled out of his tent fifteen minutes before Merritt. He was limping badly on a bandaged and swollen leg. Within an hour, however, the limp disappeared and he began to run at eight minutes per mile. He kept this up for well over an hour and diminished Merritt's lead by two miles. Merritt was unable to match this running and by 7 a.m. Hazael once again took over second place.

However, Hazael himself was not able to sustain such a fierce pace after four days of almost constant motion. His leg began to trouble him again, and he was forced to retire for treatment and rest. Merritt, still in his overcoat and hat, began to alternate two or three laps running with several laps walking. It did not take him long to regain second place, a position he would not give up for the remaining two days.

Rumors of Poisoning

At 7:15 a.m. Rowell had gone to his tent for what usually was a short rest and rubdown. When he had not returned by 8 a.m., questions began to fly around the Garden. At 10 a.m. Rowell had still not returned to the track. Questions stopped and rumors that he had been poisoned began. "Someone had given him a bunch of grapes earlier in the morning and had drugged him in that way." "His legs had given out, and he was unable to stand." "He had gone crazy from too much effort and had to be sedated." These were just a few of the most prevalent rumors. His handlers did nothing to dispell the rumors. All that they would say was, "He is sick, but will be all right soon."

The drugging story caused the managers to hastily arrange a meeting with Rowell's chief attendant George Atkinson. Atkinson stoutly denied that his man had been poisoned. He said that it was ludicrous to believe that Rowell would eat anything not prepared by his own people. Too much was at stake in this race, and every precaution was taken to insure that nothing of that sort occurred. He was"attacked with a rush of blood to the head, and, with proper care, would probably be all right by noon." This explanation satisfied the managers but not the spectators.

Another speculation was that his illness was feigned for the purpose of drawing a larger crowd. It did just that. By mid-afternoon the Garden was three-quarters filled, nearly double the normal attendance for that time of the day.

When Rowell finally left his tent at 12:12 p.m., almost five hours after going in, it was clear that his illness was indeed real. He staggered from his tent pale and worn-looking. He walked slowly, with his head "bobbing up and down on his breast," not even acknowledging the cheers of the crowd as he passed. He covered only one mile and returned to his tent. He was back forty-five minutes later, and this time stayed on for almost an hour before retiring again.

This continued all day. He would walk slowly for an hour or

so, usually carrying a sponge that he frequently used to wipe his face and lips, and then return to his tent once more. He was constantly attacked by fits of vomiting and diarrhea, and walked "with evident pain. . .with his mouth partly opened, his eyes half closed, and his body limp." He was able to move along at only one and one half to two and one half miles per hour while on the track.

Merritt was not to be hurried into catching Rowell. Even

Front page photo of start of Fifth Astley Belt (National Police Gazette)

though he was constantly urged to run hard and immediately close the gap, he kept to his plan of alternating walking and running, never running more than three laps at a time. He knew his strength and used it intelligently and economically. By 4 p.m. this strategy had drawn him within nine miles of Rowell. He had made up twenty-seven miles in only twelve hours of walking and running.

Rowell seemed to pick up a bit later in the evening and managed to stay fairly close to Merritt's pace until they both retired at 11:45 p.m.

In the twenty-four hours of that fifth day Rowell was off the track a total of eleven hours and six minutes compared to Merritt's five hours and thirty one minutes. Rowell covered only 50½ miles, Merritt 74¾ miles.

Weston, fully recovered from the ill effects of the tobacco smoke, completed more miles on Friday than any other pedestrian in the race. He took only a few rests during the day and was covering four to five miles each hour that he was on the track. His walk was sharp and brisk and he did "some fine running." He ambled around the track, making silly grimaces at the scorers and spectators. He would "twist his body into all sorts of apish forms." The press made him out to be a complete fool. The *New York Times* reported, "The opinion was freely expressed that the man (Weston) was insane, and that he would never walk in another race." He was hissed and insulted by the crowd. With all his "antics" and the abuse he withstood, he still demonstrated that there was plenty of life left in his 40-year-old body by covering 82 miles for the fifth day, and coming within 10 miles of Hart.

After five days the race had been turned upside down. It was now a foregone conclusion that Merritt would overtake the ailing Rowell and keep the Championship Belt in the United States. Most even suspected that Rowell would be forced to drop out of the race completely. The standings at the end of the fifth day were: Rowell 452 miles, Merritt 442 miles, Hazael 436 miles, Guyon and Hart 415 miles, Weston 405 miles, Krohne 382 miles, Ennis 377 miles, Federmeyer 348 miles, and Taylor 213 miles.

Rowell's apparent collapse sent tremors through the gambling establishment. They had bet so heavily on Rowell that his failure to win would completely ruin more than half of them. One sportingman was overheard by a *New York Times* reporter to say, "I've

Six top contenders for the Fifth Astley Belt (Frank Leslie's Illustrated Newspaper)

Action during the race for the Fifth Astley Belt (Frank Leslie's Illustrated Newspaper)

heard it broadly hinted that if Rowell couldn't win by fair means, the bookmakers were determined he should by foul. Rather than see him lose, it was said that they would turn out the gas and break up the walk in the evening, when the critical hour arrived."

The speculation of the crowd and the worry of the bookmakers about Rowell's impending doom were, however, premature. When he started the last day's walk around 3 a.m. Saturday morning, his condition appeared much improved. He fell in behind Merritt and "dogged" him hour after hour.

Merritt started that last day full of confidence. "I have got through sleeping and I'm going for the Belt," he said as he jerked the visor of his cap down over his eyes and picked up the pace. But, regardless of his efforts, he was not able to shake off the shadow of the little Englishman. His dark complexion was kept shiny with perspiration which he frequently wiped with a sponge. If he had been able to put in a steady run of ten or fifteen miles he probably could have broken Rowell during the early morning hours. However, he was able to run only a few laps at a time before he was forced by fatigue to slow back down to a walk, never gaining even a full lap on Rowell.

Rowell was again walking "strongly and firmly." He hardly ran at all but kept up a steady four to four and one-half miles an hour while on the track. He stayed on the track the entire day except for two rests that totaled 35½ minutes—a great difference from his more than eleven hours off the track on Friday.

By mid-afternoon, Merritt had still not gained a yard on Rowell and the prevailing opinion had once more turned in Rowell's favor. Even Merritt now saw the inevitable. He slowed up. The spark with which he had started the day had burned out. Rowell actually began to lap the tiring Yankee pedestrian.

Hazael had third place well in hand and it was a good thing indeed. He spent the day walking with a badly swollen tendon in his right leg and carrying a sponge soaked in ammonia that he would frequently put up to his nose in order to keep from passing out.

Hart had a terrific battle early in the day with Guyon, who managed to force his exhausted body and blistered and bloody feet to catch Hart by two o'clock in the afternoon. Hart used some fierce spurts with Weston to hold off Guyon and was able to pull away through the late afternoon and early evening as Guyon was reduced to a two-mile-an-hour shuffle. One of these spurts took Hart to the fastest mile since the first hour of the competition–a 7:23.

Once Guyon faltered, near sunset, Hart took over comfortable possession of fourth place. Hart continued as one of the crowd's favorites in the contest, receiving bouquet after bouquet. While all the pedestrians' tents (except Weston's) were almost hidden by flower gifts, Hart's led the field in this respect.

Weston was not as full of his "antics" on the last day as he had been previously. He did just enough, fifty miles, to secure his share of the gate money and retain sixth place. His bizarre behavior had been an attempt to hide his bitter disappointment with his failure to successfully defend the Championship Belt.

Rowell Takes the Belt

At 8:20 p.m. Rowell and Merritt circled the track with Rowell carrying an American flag and Merritt a large English Union Jack, to the cheers, cat-calls, and waving of canes, hats, and handkerchiefs that "exceeded anything that had been heard or seen during the week." At 8:28 Rowell finished the last lap of his 530th mile and Merritt the last lap of his 515th mile. Together with Hazael, they agreed to stop.

Turf, Field, and Farm described Weston's reaction to the conclusion:

> Stretched upon his bed in his room in the corner of the Garden, the ex-champion heard the roar which greeted the victor, and he buried his head in the pillow and tried to hide his emotion and to still his beating heart. He had dreamed of triumph, but the reality was defeat and disgrace.

Ennis and Krohne had still not covered the required 450 miles at this time. No more than a mile separated the two the entire last day. Ennis stopped first with 450 miles and 1 lap at 9:20 p.m. When Krohne had finished 450 miles and 1 lap at 9:45 p.m. he was urged by his friends to go one more to beat Ennis. The poor German had reached the limit of his physical and emotional powers and could go no farther. He collapsed into his tent. Ennis, hearing the shouts for Krohne, came out of his tent dressed in regular clothes and walked another lap in order to finish one lap ahead of Krohne.

The final results were: Rowell 530 miles, Merritt 515 miles, Hazael 500 miles 1 lap, Hart 482 miles 4 laps, Guyon 471 miles, Weston 455 miles, Ennis 450 miles 2 laps, and Krohne 450 miles 1 lap.

The next day the track was re-measured and found to be 2.47 yards short of the specified one-eighth mile. Rowell's distance was, therefore, officially reduced to 524 miles 77 yards.

The following Monday the fifteen members of the Board of Managers met to audit and pay the outstanding bills and to divide the gate money. After a seven-hour meeting, the managers submitted the following statement, which met with the full approval of all the interested parties. (In all accounts of the report, discrepancies in the figures exist and remain unexplained.)

Gross Receipts	$73,923.00
Kuntz Brothers, 25%	-$18,480.75
Managers' 75%	=$55,442.25
Less expenses	-$15,047.25
Leaving	=$40,395.00

The eight men who covered more than 450 miles had $39,000 divided among them as follows:

Contestant	Percent	Amount
Rowell*	50	$19,500.00
Merritt	18 3/4	$ 7,312.50
Hazael	10 3/4	$ 4,192.50
Hart	7	$ 2,730.00
Guyon	5	$ 1,950.00
Weston	3 1/2	$ 1,365.00
Ennis	2 3/4	$ 1,072.50
Krohne	2 1/4	$ 877.50

*Rowell also received the $6,500 entrance money upon his arrival in London.

It should be remembered that at this time an average man was working sixty to seventy hours a week for a yearly salary of approximately $400 to $500. Charles Rowell had made close to

$50,000 in his two races of 1879. This was almost 100 years of salary in just twelve days.

The entire magnitude of Weston's misfortune was not made public until the October 3 issue of *Turf, Field, and Farm* was published. The day of the division of the stakes, two attachments were made against Weston's share of the gate money. One was brought by George C. Rand and Abraham Avery of New York for $613. The other was brought by David E. Sanders of Boston for between $3,000 and $4,000. In addition Sanders had attached the Astley Belt, which was being held by Tiffany's until the new Champion was decided. When Rowell went to get the Belt on the Monday after the race, the store manager told him about the attachment and refused to relinquish the Belt.

Hamilton Busby, Weston's representative, paid no attention to either of the claims. He said that since Mrs. Weston had put up the $500 entry fee for her husband, the prize money actually belonged to her and not to Weston. He then gave Mrs. Weston the check for $1,365.

The matter did not stop there. Since it was George Atkinson who had signed the check, a motion was made in Common Pleas Court to punish him for contempt of court. Finally, the judge denied the motion, ruling that the money was indeed Mrs. Weston's and not her husband's.

The Astley Belt was also retrieved from Tiffany's after it was explained to the court that the Belt was, like the money, not actually Weston's possession at all.

Turf, Field, and Farm further explained that Sanders had followed Weston to England and for the past year had been hounding him continually over the debt, and that Weston had spent more than $5,000 fighting Sanders in English courts.

As soon as he returned from England his creditors began to harrass him. He had to flee to the country in order to avoid them. Three separate times they had him arrested on the track during the race. All this worry, coupled with the thick smoke, had his nerves "sorely shattered." When he fell behind, he received no encouragement. *Turf, Field, and Farm*, however, supported the fallen hero.

> Had he been some barroom loafer, or some tool of a disreputable gambler, Weston could not have been more abused. Although a beaten

man, he is unquestionably the most marvelous pedestrian that the world has ever seen. At the end of the race his feet and legs were sound. Although he has walked in a professional way more than twice the distance around the globe, and although he has seen forty summers come and go, give him good air and encourage him with applause, and he can surpass his own unequaled performance of 550 miles inside 142 consecutive hours.

9

Odds and Ends

The year 1879 was the high water mark for the pedestrianism craze that Edward Payson Weston had begun five years before. The *New York Times* gave accounts of sixty races and solo performances held that year, varying from twelve hours to 2,500 miles. (This does not include the scores of other competitions that were not considered "important" enough to be covered by the *Times* but were reported by the various sporting journals of the time, such as *Turf, Field, and Farm,* the *New York Sportsman,* the *National Police Gazette, Bell's Life in London and Sporting Chronicle*, and *Spirit of the Times.)* It is estimated that there were well over 100 pedestrian contests in the United States and England in 1879. In contrast, for each year before and after 1879 the *Times* reported fewer than thirty pedestrian events.

The honors, esteem, and monetary rewards amassed by the leading pedestrians encouraged many others less capable to take to the sawdust track and dirt roads. Their exploits were chronicled by the sporting press. The *New York Times* of February 16, 1879, made this observation:

> Each morning's newspapers announce new great undertakings in the peaceful ring, and no well-regulated establishment with anything eatable or drinkable to sell is now complete without its sawdust circle and its pedestrian.

Numerous solo attempts were made to duplicate or better Captain Barclay's 1809 performance of 1,000 miles in 1,000 consecutive hours. William Gale, an Englishman, was supreme in this facet of long-distance rambling. In 1877 he walked 1,500 miles in 1,000 hours, in the style of Captain Barclay. That is, he walked 1½ miles at the beginning of each hour for the entire forty-one days and sixteen hours. in 1879 he did 4,000 quarter miles in 4,000 consecutive ten-minute periods. This allowed him no more than five minutes of continuous rest at any one time for almost twenty-eight days.

Later the same year, Gale attempted to complete five furlongs (1,100 yards) at the beginning of each fifteen minutes for 1,000 hours. With four days remaining, his heel became sore from a nail protruding through the heel of his shoe. After 912 hours he was forced to stop for two hours to put a poultice on his bruised, blistered, and festered heel. He subsequently made up the lost distance and finished the 2,500 miles in the allotted time.

Through November and December of 1880 Gale was at it again. This time he was out to cover 1¼ miles at the commencement of each thirty minutes for 1,000 hours. He averaged nineteen to twenty-two and a half minutes for the five laps around the track at Lillie Bridge. Trouble struck again, however. After 2,232 of the projected 2,500 miles he broke down and could no longer maintain the half-hour schedule. He went on for the entire 1,000 hours but finished ninety-five miles short of his goal.

The Americans were not without their own Captain Barclay. He was Peter Van Ness, who had duplicated Barclay's walk and who in 1879 attempted 2,000 half-miles in 2,000 consecutive half hours. The *National Police Gazette* describes the scene during his effort.

> On the evening of the 3rd, during the attempt of Peter Van Ness, the pedestrian, to walk 2,000 half miles in 2,000 half hours, there was a startling incident, which came near resulting in the killing of many persons. Van Ness had been on the track walking a half mile each half hour during thirty days. He had been suffering terribly during the day, and appeared to be out of his mind. He knocked down his trainer when he would arouse him, and refused to go on the track. Harsh treatment had to be used to compel him to walk. His ankles and legs were badly swollen, and he complained of a burning sensation in the throat and brain.
>
> After finishing his 1,718 half mile he shot his trainer, Joe Burgoine, in the arm, and then fired at everyone he came in contact with. Burgoine fell, and shouted, "I am shot." Manager Levy then rushed in and Van Ness fired at him. The ball went through the band of his silk

hat. Van Ness then rushed into the hall, which was filled with spectators, and emptied his revolver, but the bullets did no damage except smashing glass. The police rushed into the building with cocked revolvers, and Van Ness was overpowered. The crowd of women and men rushed into the street, and intense excitement prevailed. After the shooting, Van Ness fainted and lay in a comatose state, and his trainer, being shot, could not attend to him. Morphine, in hot drops, was administered to the crazy pedestrian, and shortly thereafter he was brought on the track, and resumed his task at nine o'clock. At half past nine, Van Ness had completed 1,721 half miles, and was led around the track. He was suffering terribly.

Van Ness went on to finish his 2,000 half-miles.

Women in Pedestrianism

The women were no longer to be left beside the track waving handkerchiefs and throwing flowers. From *Turf, Field, and Farm* of January 10, 1879:

> Madame Anderson has completed 2,224 quarter miles, leaving 476 quarter miles yet to be made before her task is finished. The attendance for the past week has been very large. After finishing her walk in Brooklyn (Mozart Garden) it is the lady's intention to undertake the same performance in Boston, for which she is to receive the round sum of $15,000.
>
> At 6 p.m. Monday, January 13, 1879, Madame Anderson completed her journey of 2,500 quarter miles in 2,500 consecutive quarter hours. She had walked a quarter mile at the beginning of each quarter hour for twenty-six straight days. She received a purse of $8,000 as her share of the proceeds resulting from her great success.

A week later, again in *Turf, Field, and Farm:*

> Prior to Madame Anderson's walk a prominent sporting gentleman in Brooklyn wagered $500 that she would not be able to keep on the track for the space of three weeks.
>
> It is amusing to see the ruses resorted to in order to keep Madame Anderson awake. When a looker-on falls asleep she is furnished with a tin horn about three feet long and the sleeper is suddenly awoke by a loud blast in his ear. One young fellow we saw served in this manner looked as if he thought Gabriel had blown his horn indeed.

Turf, Field, and Farm—January 31, 1879:

> Since Madame Anderson's success in Brooklyn, every pedestrian

who ever covered twenty-four miles in twenty-four hours imagines himself or herself a wonder and issues challenges accordingly. Mozart Gardens has become the resort of all the pedestrians of Brooklyn and bids fair to continue the scene of many contests.

Turf, Field, and Farm –March 7, 1879:

Miss Elsa Von Blumen is said to have walked last week at Martin's Opera House, Albany, New York, 100 miles in twenty-seven hours. W. T. Cunningham accompanied her, in the task of covering 120 miles in the same time, but he only got up to 100 miles.

At Pedestrian Hall, 489 Sixth Avenue, this city (New York), Miss Cora Cushing and Florence Le Vanion are still plodding on, the blackboard registering nearly two-thirds of their allotted 3,000 quarter-miles in 3,000 consecutive quarter hours.

Dr. Sayre ordered the "Westchester Milkmaid" off the track at Brewster Hall on Thursday evening, she having completed 1,439 quarter miles. Fanny Edwards and Madame Franklin, however, still kept the ball rolling.

Madame Anderson, who originally started the contagion in this country, commenced her feat of walking 2,086 quarter miles in 2,086 consecutive ten minutes at the Exposition Building, Chicago, March 3. She is under the management of A. R. Samuells.

New York Times–March 17, 1879:

Madame Anderson stopped walking a short time after 10 p.m. tonight, when she had completed 2,086 quarter miles in that number of consecutive ten-minute periods.

New York Times–March 17, 1879:

Miss Josie Wilson completed a walk of 2,700 quarter miles in 2,700 quarter hours in Jersey City on Saturday night. She then announced that she would continue until 3,000 quarter miles were finished. The police notified her managers that no tickets could be sold on Sunday. The public were, therefore, treated to a free exhibition yesterday, when the hall was crowded. In the afternoon a party of roughs got into a fight. Miss Wilson fainted, and remained unconscious for over an hour. At a late hour last night she had not resumed her task.

The April 12, 1879, issue of the *National Police Gazette* reported the results of a six-day women's race that was held at Gilmore's Garden beginning March 26th. The first prize of $1,000 was won by Bertha Von Berg with a distance of 372 miles. Only five of the original eighteen starters managed to finish. The *Gazette* called them "a queer lot, tall and short, heavy and slim, young and middle-aged, some pretty and a few almost ugly."

Whatever their looks, most of them didn't belong on the track. The *New York Times* commented on the reason many attempted such a task.

> The poverty that compels some of these women to gain a livelihood in this manner is distressing, and to such straits are some of them reduced that they are actually walking mile after mile, and day after day, without sufficient food.

Sergeant Timms of the Thirteenth Street police station said to a reporter, "One of the pedestrians is dead and another has been taken to the hospital." Captain Williams interrupted the Sergeant. "Sergeant, I order you to give no news to the reporters. All the law requires in this matter, I have done." No further information was obtained by the reporter and nothing more was said in the newspapers or sporting press about the alleged death.

Other six-day women's races were held in New York, Philadelphia, New Orleans, and San Francisco. They did not gain the favor of the general population as the men's races had. In fact, even the *Gazette*, that disseminator of sex, murder, and violence, editorialized against them in its January 3, 1880, edition.

> It is hoped that the recent female walking match (held in New York City and won by Miss Howard with 393 miles) will be the last of these disgusting exhibitions given in this city. Anything more demoralizing and debasing in public amusements can hardly be conceived. The wear and strain upon the constitution of the participants is something which the medical profession alone can realize. That people of evident respectability can so far lower themselves to assist, by paying an entrance fee, in backing up the unprincipled speculators who organize and manage them (note: The *Gazette* had been one of the prime backers of the April 1879 race), is something that is not easily understood. We must congratulate Alderman John J. Morris for introducing at the last meeting, and the other members of the Board of Aldermen for passing, a resolution looking to the supression and prevention of such exhibitions in the future.

Although there is no verification of the death of the female pedestrian, there are records of three actual cases of death during or immediately after a pedestrian effort.

Accounts of Death

On June 14, 1869, James Smith, a carpenter at the Bowery Theatre in New York City, took a challenge to run forty-two laps around the stage of the theatre in seven minutes. On an extremely hot summer afternoon, Smith accomplished the task and won the bet. However, a few minutes later, as he was preparing to go home, he collapsed. He was taken home when he regained consciousness, but died only a half hour later. It appears to have been a case of heatstroke.

The *New York Times* of April 15, 1879, carried this brief announcement:

> Providence, Rhode Island, April 14—In Woonsocket yesterday M. Lavelle, age twenty-two years, started in a walking match. He soon became ill, and died in a few hours.

The most intriguing account of a death was given in the April 17, 1880, edition of the *National Police Gazette.*

> The coroner's verdict in the case of D. H. Hoag, the dead pedestrian, is as follows: "That David Hoag came to his death at the hands of his trainer, Richard H. Nichols, at the M. B. Little Opera House, in Glen Falls, Warren County (New York), at a twenty-seven-hour go-as-you-please match, in which Hoag was a contestant, commencing on the 26th day of February, 1880, and ending on the 27th, at eleven o'clock and two minutes p.m., in which said Nichols drove him (Hoag) until he became so exhausted by overexertion and improper care and ill-treatment on the track and neglect after the race, that he expired at the Lee House, in Port Henry, February 28, 1880." Nichols has been arrested in pursuance of the above verdict.

Attempted attacks upon pedestrians during their races and suspected plots to disrupt and disable were not infrequent. Two such attempts that were successful took place in a seventy-five-hour race in Chicago that Daniel O'Leary sponsored from May 28 to May 31, 1879.

John Dobler of Chicago had been leading the race on the afternoon of the second day. He went into his tent for a short nap that extended into several hours. The *Police Gazette* reported that in "some mysterious way his bed had been saturated with chloroform and four hours were lost before he fully recovered from the stupor that was induced by the drugging." Friends of Dobler accused the "notorious sporting character," Jerry Monroe, for instigating the attack because of bets that he had placed on the Englishman, George Parry.

Parry himself was the victim of an attempted assault on the final night of the race as he was being caught by Dobler. First, Albert Schock, who had quit the race at 100 miles, came back onto the track and walked directly in front of Parry preventing him from passing and slowing him up for several laps. Peter Crossland, Parry's countryman, came to Parry's aid and managed to block off Schock. While Crossland was walking as a shield for Parry, they were attacked by pepper-throwing assailants. Crossland did his job excellently. He took the full shot of pepper and was forced to withdraw from the track. After this Parry was given a personal police guard who walked with him, and he went on to win the race with 268 miles to Dobler's 265 miles.

Accounts of Romance

A pedestrian's exploits on the track were not the only way to get into the press. A detailed article appeared in the *National Police Gazette* concerning Charles Harriman's involvement with Mrs. Katie Stackhouse, the wife of the steward at the St. James Hotel in New York City. Harriman stayed at the St. James while he was preparing for the third Astley Belt race. He became "enamored" of the "beautiful and accomplished" twenty-two-year-old brunette. During the race Mrs. Stackhouse cast "many bewitching glances" upon Harriman as he struggled valiantly. She was a constant visitor to the track and threw him bouquet after bouquet. After the walk, prostrated with exhaustion, Harriman was confined to his bed in the hotel for several days. During his convalescence Mrs. Stackhouse was "indefatigable in her attentions." Mrs. Stackhouse "had become fired by Harriman's heroic efforts, while the pedestrian was rendered doubly susceptible to womanly sympathy by his exhausted condition."

When Harriman recovered he left New York but on his return in May, he met and went out with Mrs. Stackhouse several times. He left once again in June on a tour of the southern states. By July Mrs. Stackhouse could stand his absence no longer. She left home, on the pretense of visiting her family in Philadelphia, and met Harriman in Richmond, Virginia, where he was competing. Her husband discovered the ruse and went after her. However, by the time he arrived in Richmond, Harriman and Mrs. Stackhouse had left.

Finally, after tracking the two to Medford, Massachusetts, Mr. Stackhouse went back to New York City and consulted with his lawyers. He began divorce proceedings and instituted a $10,000 damage suit against Harriman for "alienating the affections of his wife." An order of arrest was granted, the bail fixed at $5,000. Two days later, however, through the efforts of mutual friends an "amicable settlement of the matter was arrived at," and the arrest order was vacated.

Just what the agreement was is unknown. Harriman continued to compete in various pedestrian contests, and nothing more of the matter was mentioned in the press.

The First O'Leary Belt Race

The first O'Leary Belt Race for the Championship of America was held in Madison Square Garden one week after the close of the fifth Astley Belt Race, from October 6 to October 11, 1879. O'Leary's stated purpose in sponsoring this race and the others in the planned series was to develop a pedestrian capable of bringing the Astley Belt back to the United States, and also to give back something to the sport from which he had received so much.

The furor caused by Weston's winning and subsequent losing of the Astley Belt caused a record entry for the race. One hundred and five supposed pedestrians had made initial entrance, without fee, to the race. Fifty-five of these actually paid the $100 entry fee. W. B. Curtis of *The Spirit of the Times* then reduced this to what he considered the top twenty-five. He was pressured by "ex-mayors, bankers, district-attorneys and judges," each pushing for the inclusion of their friend or friends. Finally, Curtis added an additional ten men to the field, bringing the total starting field up to a record thirty-five.

Starting in his first race of more than twenty miles was Patrick Fitzgerald of Long Island. He had run eleven miles in 59:50 and three-fourths seconds on June 16th, just four months before. Fitzgerald had a difficult introduction to the six-day event and was forced to drop out on the second day after covering only eighty-eight miles.

Henry "Blower" Brown, the odds-on favorite, also ran into difficulty and quit even earlier than Fitzgerald, at forty miles.

Second O'Leary Belt Race, 1880, Madison Square Garden (National Police Gazette)

Of the thirty-five starters, more than half had never competed in a six-day race before. One of these novices, Nicholas Murphy, surprised everyone by winning without undue stress with a total of 505 miles. Not one of the other six men who completed 450 miles had ever done that well before.

O'Leary and his co-manager, Fred Englehardt, must have done quite well financially with this venture, because the runners did not share in the gate money but instead received predetermined prizes: first place $5,000; second place $3,000; third place $1,000; and fourth place $500. Others who covered 475 miles received $300, and the rest who covered 450 miles received $100. Subtracting entrance fees, O'Leary and Englehardt probably paid out no more than $7,000 in prize money. The race was almost as well attended as the Astley Belt race that had ended the week before with gross receipts of more than $75,000 and expenses of $15,000.

O'Leary and Englehardt were not the only ones who recognized the possible gold mine in the organizing of six-day races. As the O'Leary Belt race was taking place, two other six-day races were being held. One, in Baltimore, Maryland, at the Academy of

Music was won by John Hughes with 376 miles. He won $300. The other, in San Francisco, was won by McIntyre with a distance of 500 miles.

There were several variations on the six day, 142-hour race. The most popular was the 72-hour version (six days of twelve consecutive hours each day). These were obviously far easier to administer and officiate, but still brought in almost as much money at the gate since the hours not walked were the usual slack spectator periods.

One week after dropping out of the O'Leary Belt race, Patrick Fitzgerald deciding, no doubt, that he should start out slowly and gradually build up to the full six-day event, started and won a six-day, fourteen-hours-a-day, contest. The race took place in Madison Square Garden and Fitzgerald took home $1,200. Another newcomer to the sport, Robert Vint, a Brooklyn shoemaker, took fourth place with 350 miles.

Our amorous ped, Charles Harriman, won a six-day, twelve hours-a-day race promoted by Fred Englehardt on a sixteen-lap-to-a-mile track in Newark, New Jersey, the beginning of November with a distance of 343½ miles.

On the same track three weeks later, Frank Hart won a similar race, beating Fitzgerald (who was back competing after only six weeks) 378 miles to 370 miles. Newark didn't pay as well as New York City. Hart received only $500 and Fitzgerald $300. Still, Fitzgerald had made almost three years' salary in the space of a month and a half.

Three weeks later, Fitzgerald felt he was ready to have another go at a full 144-hour, six-day race. Frank Hart was also one of the sixty-five starters in the race for the D. E. Rose Belt. Rose was another of the promoters who seemed to come out of the woodwork to cash in on the "pedestrian craze."

Fitzgerald was correct; he was ready. He had raced himself into condition. He finished fifth with an excellent first-time performance of 520¾ miles. Hart won the race with a distance of 542 1/8 miles. Eight of the sixty-five starters finished 500 miles and a record sixteen completed 450 miles.

While the Americans were going crazy with six-day races, Charles Rowell was enjoying his new farm in England that he had purchased with a part of his Astley Belt winnings. Because he had already been challenged by Panchot and O'Leary, he had to decide where and when the next Astley Belt race would take place. It was obvious that his fame and reputation would fill any building in this country for the entire six days. But, he didn't need the money and he had spent a large part of 1879 in the United States. He decided that the next race would be in London, at the Agricultural Hall—the site of Weston's fabulous world record 550 miles. As soon as O'Leary and Panchot heard that the race was to be in England they dropped their challenges. Why travel all the way to England, bash out six days, and receive only a fraction of what they could win in the United States?

O'Leary signed articles of agreement to meet Weston in a match race of six days at the Pavilion in San Francisco from March 8 to 13, 1880, for a wager of $5,000 a side. Weston was backed by a Mr. Baldwin, a millionaire horseman, while O'Leary put up his own $5,000.

The race was another disaster for Weston. O'Leary, taking it easy on the last day, won handily, 516¼ miles to 490 miles. Weston "went all to pieces," suffering from vertigo, while O'Leary was "literally striding around the track, from daylight till midnight . . . as if he was some skillfully constructed automaton. . . ." The *Police Gazette* said that O'Leary was now worth $85,000.

Not only did Weston lose once more to his nemesis, O'Leary, but a month before he also had lost his world record. In the third All English Championship for the Astley Belt, "Blower" Brown just surpassed Weston's mark with a 553 mile 165 yard performance. George Hazael was second with 490 miles. Brown said he was "good for twenty-four hours more" when he finished.

Records Set and Broken

Brown's record did not stand for long. Frank Hart, racing frequently and winning each time, set a new world record less than two months later in the second O'Leary Belt race, held in Madison Square Garden April 5 to 10, 1880. After a difficult struggle with John Dobler for the first three days, Hart pulled away to win easily with 565 miles. Enroute he set an American twenty-four hour mark of 131 miles. His prize money brought his winnings up to $27,000. Dobler faded to fourth completing a personal best of 531 miles, behind William Pegram, a black pedestrian from Boston with 543 miles, and H. Howard of Montclair, New Jersey, with 534 miles.

Pegram, Howard, and Dobler now challenged Rowell for the Astley Belt. Hart, like O'Leary, could see no reason to travel to England without the prospects of a healthy reward. Besides, he now had not only enough money to live on the rest of his life, but also a reputation as the best American pedestrian. He had nothing to gain by going to England.

Joining the three Americans in their challenge was "Blower" Brown, who was out to regain the record, and a newcomer, George Littlewood of Attercliffe of Sheffield. Littlewood's debut had taken place September 6 to 11 at Agricultural Hall with a victory of 406¾ miles.

The race started at 1 a.m., November 1, 1880, in front of a meager crowd of 300. The resulting lack of vocal support did not seem to hamper Rowell. He took off fast and after the first twenty-five miles was never passed. He went through 100 miles in a record 13:57:13, and completed a world record 146 miles 250 yards in 22:27:0.

Dobler was not that far behind at the end of the first day, with 138 miles. Littlewood was third, having finished 124 miles before going to bed. Brown was a disappointment when he retired from the race the first afternoon with only seventy-three miles. Pegram and Howard also dropped out before the end of the third day.

The third day also ended any threat to Rowell's supremacy. He slowed considerably over the last three days, making only 226 miles compared with his first three days of 340 miles. Rowell just squeezed by Hart's record with 566 miles 165 yards. Littlewood was impressive the last two days as he overtook Dobler for second place with 470 miles. Dobler could cover only forty miles the last day, and finished with 450 miles.

The failure of the Americans was explained by Edward Plummer, an Englishman who had been living in the United States for several years and who was considered one of the leading authorities in athletic matters. He described the weather conditions inside Agricultural Hall as terrible and "death to any runner who has not prepared for it." He said that the building was "no fit place for such a competition." The pedestrians were exposed to the "raw, chilly fog," with the temperature averaging fifty degrees inside the hall, dropping as low as forty degrees. In addition, he said, "The British public is surfeited with this stuff. The dilatory and slovenly manner in which Agricultural Hall has been kept has done more to killing the goose that laid the golden egg than anything else. Madison Square Garden bears about the same relation to it as a lady's boudoir in Fifth Avenue does to a log hut in the Western wilds."

The *Illustrated London News* commented further.

> The attendance was not very good and we doubt if American pedestrians will care to visit this country again, as the expenses they necessarily incur are too heavy to make the trip a paying one.

This victory left Rowell needing only one more to obtain absolute possession of the coveted Astley Belt. Edward Payson Weston, seeing an opportunity to regain a part of his lost reputation as a leading pedestrian and also a chance to visit again the country where he experienced his most frequent and consistent success, challenged Rowell. Rowell accepted and a race was arranged for June 20 to 25, 1881, at the Marble Rink on Clapham Road in London. Rowell sent Weston $1,000 in expense money for himself and Hamilton Busby, who was to be Weston's handler for the race.

Weston brought out far more spectators than anyone imagined. The Americans came, too. Daniel O'Leary led the pilgrimage, accompanied by Frank Hart, Charles Harriman, and John Ennis. Several other lesser-known American pedestrians traveled to witness what all expected to be the race of the century–Rowell, the world record holder, versus Weston, the former record holder.

Once more fate struck Weston a fierce blow. He was slightly ill the night before the race and could not sleep. He unwisely took an opiate to help him sleep. This just made matters worse and he became more ill. The race was no contest. Rowell covered 140 miles the first day and 100 miles the next. Weston was sick the whole time, but still managed 180 miles the two days. But on the third day he threw in the towel and retired from the race at 12:42 p.m. with 201 miles. Rowell had completed 280 miles and was declared the winner.

The End of the "Golden Age"

This was Rowell's third victory in a row and he became the absolute owner of the Sir John Astley Championship Belt. After seven races the Astley-sponsored series was over, marking the close of pedestrianism's "Golden Age."

During 1881 the world record was advanced three times by three different Americans. In January John Hughes barely broke it with 568 miles. In May, from the 23rd to the 28th, shoemaker Robert Vint covered 578¼ miles in his first victory during an O'Leary Belt race at Madison Square Garden. Hughes finished third with 552¼ miles, and Patrick Fitzgerald set a personal best of 536 3/8 miles for fourth place. George Littlewood traveled to the United States for the first time and finished eleventh with a distance of 480 miles.

Then, from December 26 to 31 at the American Institute Building in New York City, Patrick Fitzgerald came into his own, besting a field of sixteen starters with a record performance of 582 miles 55 yards. George Noremac was second with 564¼ miles and Daniel Herty was third, covering 556 1/8 miles. The attendance had been very sparse the entire week and only 500 spectators gathered to witness the finish of the race. Fitzgerald won $2,000, Noremac $800, and Herty $400. John Ennis, the pedestrian turned promoter, lost $2,000 on the race.

Charles Rowell was in attendance and said that he would begin training the following Monday for his upcoming race with Hughes, an event to take place at the end of February. This was to be his last race in this or any other country.

The British and American publics were not only growing weary of these six-day carnivals, but they were beginning to distrust the results. In the short one paragraph notice the *New York Times* gave of Vint's world-record performance, the reporter said:

> Some extraordinary walking has been done during the week—if the dials are to be believed. Unfortunately for the walkers and the public, however, dials are not always reliable, and the week's records are not considered by well-informed persons to be perfectly correct.

There were also allegations of "hippodroming," or fixing. After one such charge a *Times* reporter commented, "the hope is entertained by even those who have thrived through pedestrian exhibitions that New York shall be cursed with no more of them"—the personal opinion of one newspaper reporter to be sure, but an opinion that had to be discredited if pedestrianism was to survive.

10

Rowell's Magnificent Failure

Charles Rowell had raced to the pinnacle of the pedestrian world. Since his initiation against Weston in 1876 he had decisively won his last four six-day contests. He owned outright the supreme symbol of pedestrian excellence—the Sir John Astley Championship Belt. Along the way he had set two outstanding intermediate marks of 13:57 for 100 miles and 146 miles for twenty-four hours. He had risen from a lowly boat-boy to an honored, respected, and wealthy athlete.

Rowell was ready to retire at the age of twenty-nine but there remained one challenge—the world record. He wanted to set an unbreakable mark. Six hundred miles had been approached but never reached. He would not stop there. He would go on for 700 miles—116 2/3 miles a day.

A race was organized by Peter Duryea for February 27 to March 4, 1882, in Madison Square Garden. It was to be a first-class venture from the start. A $1,000 entry fee was set to discourage all but the most serious competitors. The winner was to receive a large trophy, a diamond-studded whip with the figure of Edward Payson Weston in relief on the handle, 100 percent of the entrance money and 50 percent of the gate after expenses. Duryea paid Cornelius Vanderbilt the sum of $10,000 for the week's rent of the Garden. His out-of-pocket expenses totaled more than $18,000 before the race began. A special nonsmoking section was roped off on the north end of the Garden, and the only spectators that would be admitted were ladies or men accompanying ladies.

The American District Telegraph Company set up two offices, one directly to Wall Street. The Western Union Company also established an office.

Rowell kept his plans, but not his training, secret. He was running and walking forty miles a day at the American Institute Building in Manhattan. He was in the best condition of his life and was ready.

Also training at the American Institute was John Hughes, backed by the *Police Gazette.* Trained by ex-pedestrian and champion bicycle rider William Harding, Hughes was confident of victory even though he was doing only fifteen miles a day.

The world record holder, Patrick Fitzgerald, giving himself little time to recover from his outstanding performance in December, was training twenty-five miles a day at Wood's Gymnasium in Brooklyn.

The other entrants were: Robert Vint; George Noremac from Glasgow, with a previous best of 565 miles; Peter Panchot, the Buffalo mailman trained by "Happy" Jack Smith with a best of 541 miles; William Scott, a California-based pedestrian with a record of 505 miles; and finally George Hazael of England, with a best of 500 miles.

The days before the start were not without controversy. Robert Vint asked to have his entrance money returned because an injury had not cleared up and he felt he had no chance of covering the minimum 525 miles to share in the gate money. He presented a letter from his doctor stating that he was suffering from "rheumatism of a stubborn nature" and that it "would be dangerous for him to go on with his preparations for the walking match at present." The other pedestrians were just as stubborn as his rheumatism and refused his request. Vint would be on the starting line.

Frank Hart had the opposite problem. He asked to be added to the field after the entries had closed. Duryea and Rowell argued for his admission. They thought that even though he had lost some of his following in 1881, Hart would still serve as a popular drawing card. Hughes and Fitzgerald staunchly refused. Hughes had been told that Hart planned to "stalk" him during the race, and this upset the fiery pedestrian. Fitzgerald was against it for another personal reason. Hart owed him $100 and had made no effort to pay him. After some backroom negotiations, Hamilton

Busby gave Fitzgerald $50 and Hart promised to give Fitzgerald the other $50 out of his winnings. Fitzgerald relented. Hughes still held out. Some more private talks followed and finally Hughes also gave his consent.

The gambling fraternity had received information that the police were going to stop them from setting up their tables within the Garden. Thomas Murphy, an Alabama gambler, was successful in obtaining a court injunction preventing the police from interfering with the bookmakers' operations. Sunday night, February 26, they took up their usual positions alongside the scorers, timekeepers, and newspaper men on the Twenty-seventh Street side of the Garden.

Attack on the World Record

Hamilton Busby, wearing a large sunflower-like badge as a symbol of his position as head referee, called the nine pedestrians to the line at midnight. A large, but nowhere near record crowd of 7,000 was on hand. Five minutes later, Busby gave the "go" and Hughes rocketed to the front. He was not intimidated by Rowell's awesome training mileage. He charged through 8 5/8 miles the first hour. The entire field followed almost right behind this suicidal pace. Hart and Fitzgerald covered 8 3/8 miles, with Hazael, Rowell, Vint, and Noremac in a line at 8¼ miles. Only Panchot seemed even a bit reasonable with 7 3/8 miles.

Vint hung on for as long as his sore legs would allow. But by 2:30 a.m., in great pain, he withdrew from the race.

Just after 4 a.m. Hart began to "stalk" Hughes, who had just been passed by both Rowell and Hazael. Disturbed by losing first place and angered by Hart's tactics, Hughes "entertained (the crowd) by a choice flow of billingsgate." Busby once more was called to mediate the dispute. He ordered Hart to cease harassing Hughes or he would be disqualified. Hart left Hughes to himself.

Once Rowell's name was placed on the top position of the huge scoreboard, he never looked back. He broke his own 100-mile world record by more than a full half hour with an incredible 13:26:30. He went to his tent only a few times during the day, and when he did he was inside but a couple of minutes. He followed his theory that it was best to break the field early with a very hard first two days. He left the track, looking "fine," at 10:30 p.m. In the first 22½ hours he had covered a world record and unbelievable 150 1/8 miles. This record would not be broken for forty-nine years. His 100-mile record would take even longer to be bettered—seventy-one years.

Hart was not drawing the enthusiasm Rowell had expected. The *New York Times* commented on this:

> His (Hart's) success as a pedestrian and association with sporting characters seems to have made him mischievous, and he is reckoned among the pedestrians as a "chronic kicker." His once-splendid form has given way to a wasted figure, and he has apparently lost pride in his work.

Lost pride notwithstanding, Hart finished the first day in fourth place with 124 miles. Hazael was second with 135 miles and Hughes was third with 134 miles. Another last-minute starter, John Sullivan, was fifth with 120 miles. Sixth through ninth were Noremac with 115 miles, Fitzgerald with a sane 111 miles, Panchot, sick and on the verge of quitting, with 110 miles, and Scott with 86 miles.

Scott and Panchot retired for good early the second day. Rowell rested only three hours and continued his "incessant dogtrot." He, Hazael, and Hughes spent most of the morning and afternoon running together in a line. Rowell's "light, springy step" was a sharp contrast to Hazael's "heavy, loggy step." Hughes "pranced along like a young colt, jumped, and kicked his heels about," and regained second place. The reason for his newfound energy was "Harding's Lightning Exhilarator," a new drink prepared for him by his head trainer, William E. Harding. Hughes own evaluation of the drink was, "Begorra, I have something now that would make a dead man walk. It lays over all the stuff I've ever tried, and since I began using it I feel like a new man."

In all probability, the "Exhilarator" contained either belladonna or the more potent stimulant, strychnine. The drink would be his undoing in the end. But on the second day he was indeed a new man. By late evening he was lapping even Rowell. He completed 121 miles for the day, eleven more than Rowell, and sat comfortably in second place with 251 miles to Rowell's record 258 3/8 miles.

Third through seventh were: Hazael, 242 miles; Hart, 219 miles; Sullivan, 215 miles; Fitzgerald, 211½ miles; and Noremac, 200 miles. During the day Rowell had collected another world record of 200 miles in 35:09:28.

As Rowell went to bed Tuesday night he said that this race was the hardest battle in which he was ever engaged and it would compel him to do his very best work to win.

It was evident that Rowell was worried. He took a sleep of only one hour and forty minutes, and started the third day at his even five-miles-per-hour pace.

The pre-dawn hours of Wednesday were typical. A few sleepy, dismal-looking spectators were reclining in all attitudes upon the benches and emptiness everywhere else in the Garden, making the men on the track strangely conspicuous as they plodded along on their weary rounds.

Hughes was feeling the effects of too much Exhilarator and began to falter. He turned pale and "coughed like a man seized with consumption. He limped like a bobtail car horse after a hard day's tussle with a truck and a wicked driver."

Hazael moved into second place, and although his knee was beginning to bother him, Rowell was unable to gain on him the entire day.

In the evening Rowell, in an unusual move, left the track for two and a half hours. When he returned at 11:25 his "gait was less nimble," and his "face had a wan and pinched appearance." He was beginning to feel the effort of his fifth world record—300 miles in 58:17:06. In the first seventy-two hours he had taken only thirteen hours and twenty-two minutes rest.

At the end of the third day the results were: Rowell 358 1/8 miles (his sixth world record), Hazael 342 3/8 miles, Hughes 331½ miles, Sullivan 314 3/8 miles, Hart 313 miles, Fitzgerald 313 miles, and Noremac 284 miles.

Rowell was in and out of his tent several times during the morning on Thursday. During one such stop, Dr. Taylor was examining a small abrasion on Rowell's knee, when Rowell called for some beef-tea. In the confusion of cups, vials, bottles, and jugs, his brother-in-law and trainer, Charles Asplan, handed him a cup of warm vinegar that was going to be used to dress the abrasion. Rowell drank it down in one swift gulp, not realizing his mistake until it was too late. At first there appeared to be no difficulty. Rowell left the tent and carried on as he had for the past three and one-quarter days. However, within less than an hour, he was back to his tent, vomiting freely. This began several hours of periodic vomiting. He was unable to put anything, food or drink, on his stomach. He realized that this was a situation that could not be tolerated for long. A few minutes after noon, with his lead reduced to five miles, Rowell went to his tent for an extended rest. The hope was that a few hours on his back would settle his stomach and allow him to continue.

An hour later Hazael took over the lead. The press hovered around Rowell's tent, attempting to pry some information on his condition from his trainers. They sat out in front of the tent, arms folded, "calm and confident." To all inquiries they said, "ho, 'e's all right."

But he wasn't. When he returned to the track at 3:45 p.m. his face was "much wasted and his cheekbones seemed about to burst through his skin." He left the track once more after less than two hours. It was not until 6 p.m. when Fitzgerald passed Rowell that his trainers admitted that he was seriously ill, and told the story of the vinegar.

Hart spent the day walking erect and "with some show of his former greatness." Fitzgerald was running the most evenly paced race of all the competitors. Only Hazael covered more ground on Thursday. Hughes was suffering and could complete only fifty miles for the day. Still, this was two miles farther than the ailing Englishman.

The results at the end of the fourth day were: Hazael 433 5/8 miles, Fitzgerald 413 3/8 miles, Sullivan 409½ miles, Hart 409½ miles, Rowell 406 3/8 miles, Noremac 392½ miles, and Hughes 381 1/8 miles.

At 9:50 a.m. Friday the inevitable occurred. As Peter Duryea and Hamilton Busby emerged from Rowell's tent after a conference with his trainers, they immediately were surrounded by newsmen. They pushed their way through, hurried to the scorers' table, and officially made the announcement that Charles Rowell had retired from the race.

The gamblers were ecstatic. They estimated that more than $100,000 had been lost on Rowell in public and private bets.

Throughout the fifth day Hazael extended his lead over the exhausted field. With a wearied expression. he managed to complete 107 miles on Friday, with the aid of frequent administrations of stimulants, and was almost assured of 600 miles for the entire six days.

Fitzgerald turned in another 100-mile day but, like Hazael, was now depending on the free use of stimulants to keep him going. Hart walked well the whole day.

At the end of the fifth day the results were: Hazael 540 miles, Fitzgerald 513½ miles, Noremac 498 3/8 miles, Hart 490 3/8 miles, Hughes 470 miles, and Sullivan 464 miles.

There had never been more than 5,000 spectators in the Garden at any one time since the first night, and Saturday was no different. In fact, during the day it would have been a very liberal estimate to say that there were 500 people watching the weary and worn pedestrians struggle through the closing hours. Not only were the spectators few in number, but they were also short on encouragement and enthusiasm. Hazael just did not have the charisma of a Charles Rowell.

Six Hundred Miles in Six Days

Four thousand spectators cheered mildly as Hazael and Fitzgerald ran the last fifteen minutes together and Hazael became the first man in history to finish 600 miles in six days. He ran an extra lap and then stopped along with Fitzgerald a little after 9 p.m. Sullivan just managed to complete the required 525 miles. The final standings were: Hazael 600 1/8 miles, Fitzgerald 577 1/8 miles, Noremac 555 miles, Hart 542 miles, Hughes 535 miles 610 yards, and Sullivan 525 miles 170 yards.

The gross receipts for the week amounted to about $45,000. This was $30,000 less than the gate for the fifth Astley Belt Race. Expenses of $18,000 to $20,000 and Duryea's cut of $6,750 left approximately $20,000 to divide along with the $9,000 in stake money. Hazael, therefore, made out well. He took home the third largest purse in the history of pedestrianism–$19,000. The approximate figures for the other peds were: Fitzgerald $5,000, Noremac $2,400, Hart $1,600, Hughes $1,200, and Sullivan $800.

The race that was to be the crowning glory of an illustrious career had turned into a devastating defeat for Charles Rowell. What he may have accomplished had he not taken the vinegar could be speculated upon for hours. He was, without a doubt, quite worn and tired when he left the track Wednesday night. It seems very improbable that he could have continued on to complete 700 miles.

To understand how extraordinary his performance was that first day we must remember that no one in the world bettered his 150 1/8 miles in twenty-four hours until the late Arthur Newton ran 152 miles 540 yards in Hamilton, Canada, in 1931. Rowell's distance still has been beaten by only seven other men besides Newton. No one went farther within the United States for ninety-six years.

Park Barner finally exceeded Rowell's performance in October of 1978 when he completed 152 miles 1599 yards in twenty-four hours. If Rowell had had the luxury of running for a mere twenty-four hours and had, therefore, run the last one and one-half hours of that first day at the same pace he had been running, he would have covered another ten miles for a total of 160 1/8 miles, (This is only 1 mile 345 yards short of the present world record set in 1973 by the Englishman Ron Bentley. Park Barner unofficially broke Bentley's world record June 1 and 2, 1979 at Huntington Beach, California by covering 162 miles, 537 yards.)

Rowell could not retire now. He went home to his farm in England for a brief rest and then more training. He was anxious to compete again as soon as possible. Duryea arranged the next match for October 23 to 28, 1882, in Madison Square Garden. The entry fee was reduced to $500 but the field remained almost identical to the one that started the last race. Scott and Sullivan did not enter. Daniel Herty, with a previous best of 556 miles, was the only pedestrian who had not competed in the March race.

Upgrading the Matches

The Garden went through its usual metamorphosis. The special ladies' section was improved upon. Doorkeepers were stationed "with positive instructions to keep out men unaccompanied by a lady."

For the first time there would be no bookmakers allowed within the Garden. The exact reason for this was never made clear by the press. However, it was applauded by the papers as a positive step in upgrading the pedestrian matches, and considered no loss at all.

Another change would be that the stake money, $4,500 from the nine starting competitors, would not all go to the winner. He would receive only 70 percent, with second place getting 20 percent, and third 10 percent.

Charles Rowell arrived back in New York City September 4, 1882, looking "the picture of health and youthful vigor." He had modified his previous uncautious strategy. He would not attempt to destroy the field on the first day. The race in March had taught him that he must temper his recklessness with patience.

At midnight October 23, 1882, the nine eager pedestrians stood in front of Edward Hanlan, the renowned oarsman, and awaited his signal to begin their formidable journey. Every seat in the gallery was taken. The space behind the seats was packed with standing patrons. Seven thousand voices sent the entrants on their way at precisely 12:05 a.m. as a band played "Yankee Doodle."

The early miles were a duplicate of the March race except that Rowell was content to remain next to last through the first hour with 8 1/8 miles to Hart, Hughes, and Hazael's 8 5/8 miles.

This time, however, it was Hughes who continued the maniacal pace. Hazael, though, did not let him go. He followed only thirteen minutes behind Hughes' time of 13:57 for 100 miles. Rowell, showing unusual restraint, glided by 100 miles in 16:08. Hart was next with a 16:40. Fitzgerald, holding himself in check, was the fifth man through 100 miles in 17:45.

All day long Hughes was running at or near Rowell's record-setting pace. By 11 p.m. he had completed 149 miles and it was assumed that he would break the twenty-four hour record and then go to bed. This assumption was incorrect. At 11:14 he finished his 150th mile and promptly left the track for the night, only one lap short of the world record.

Hart, Hazael, and Rowell were close together in that order with distances of 136 1/8 miles, 135 1/8 miles, and 135 miles, respectively. Fifth through ninth place were: Noremac 126 miles, Panchot 120 1/8 miles, Fitzgerald 118 1/8 miles, Herty 116 miles, and Vint 100 3/8 miles.

The bookmakers, while not permitted within the Garden, carried on a thriving business right outside the doors, giving odds of 7 to 10 on Rowell, 6 to 4 on Hazael, and 4 to 1 on Fitzgerald.

Hughes lost only a little to record pace through the first twelve hours of the second day. He passed 200 miles just thirty-three minutes slower than Rowell had. But then he began to slow down. By the end of Tuesday he had lost eight miles to the record, with a distance of 250 miles. The others finished the day in this order: Hazael 240 1/8 miles, Rowell 238 5/8 miles, Hart 232 ¼ miles, Noremac 224 ¼ miles, Fitzgerald 222 ¼ miles, Herty 217 3/8 miles, Panchot 200 miles, and Vint 190 miles.

The only real excitement on Tuesday took place when a delegation from the Society for the Reformation of Juvenile Delinquents secured a temporary injunction restraining the management from furnishing music during the race under the act prohibiting amusements without payment of a license fee. After much haggling, the managers agreed to take out a license for three months and pay the costs of the injunction ($225) in order to settle the matter.

A look around the dreary, deserted Garden the next afternoon quickly demonstrated the general lack of interest in the present competition. There were no more than 300 indifferent spectators witnessing the drama. Hazael closed in on Hughes the entire day and finally, at 3:40 p.m. caught the stiff-legged pedestrian.

Hughes was not finished however. He tenaciously hung onto the Englishman throughout the evening and at midnight still held a one-mile lead. Interest had picked up a bit during the night and by 9 p.m. there were 5,000 spectators in the Garden. Rowell had moved right along with Hazael and finished the day only a lap out of second place. The longest performance of the day was given by the durable Fitzgerald. He moved into fourth place only ten miles behind Rowell after completing 109 miles for the day.

The standings at the end of the day were: Hughes 342 miles, Hazael 341 1/8 miles, Rowell 341 miles, Fitzgerald 331 5/8 miles, Noremac 330 miles, Hart 325 miles, Herty 309 miles, and Vint 282 miles.

The fourth day was a day filled with drama. Hazael collapsed from exhaustion at 2 a.m. His knee, never completely healed from the last race, swelled badly, and he was forced to take frequent rests during the day. Hughes was also "done in," and took long breaks from his agony on the track. Rowell began developing symptoms similar to those he suffered from in March.

All three leaders moved slower and slower. Only Fitzgerald ran and walked with relative ease. At 3:50 a.m. he passed Hazael. Between six and seven o'clock in the morning he fought Rowell for second place and was successful. At 9:25 a.m. he ran into the lead as he passed the faltering Hughes. In nine hours he had taken only 17 minutes' rest and had made up eleven miles on the leader.

Rowell retired from the race for good at 7:15 p.m. Hazael quit at 10:15 p.m. Hughes stayed in the race, but was now just trying to survive in order to cover the minimum distance of 525 miles needed to share in the gate money.

Rowell was said to be "suffering to such an extent from nervous prostration as to render his further continuance in the race useless." The true cause for his collapse would not be made public for almost a year. When he returned to England, Rowell was examined by Sir William Gull, the private physician to Queen Victoria. He diagnosed Rowell's problem as an enlargement of the spleen brought on by a case of malaria he had contracted while training for the race.

The next two days were anticlimactic. The five remaining pedestrians merely went through the motions. The attendance was miserable. Even on the last night no more than one-quarter of the Garden was filled. The pedestrians were as worn out as the spectators. "The appearance of Fitzgerald, Noremac, and Hughes was wretched in the extreme," was the description given by the *New York Times*. "Fitzgerald, with a bad stoop, limped around the track, as if he were treading upon a bed of live coals."

On the last evening, "an air of gloom, due to the lack of public enthusiasm and empty benches, characterized the closing hours." Hart, seeing the hopelessness of making any money for his exertion, left the track after finishing 500 miles. Fitzgerald, covering a mere 55½ miles the last day, easily took first place with 577 miles. Noremac was second with 567¼ miles, Herty was third with 541 1/8 miles, and Hughes, pale and his swollen legs bandaged, finished fourth with 525 miles.

The gross receipts for the week were only $26,373. This was $20,000 less than the receipts of March and barely a third of the money taken in during the fifth Astley Belt Race. With the rent of $10,000 for the week, the other expenses, and Duryea's 15 percent cut, it is unlikely that Herty or Hughes won enough to pay their $500 entry fee and approximately another $500 in expenses. No formal accounting was given as had been done for the other races. But one can estimate Fitzgerald's winnings to be somewhere around $5,000 to $6,000, Noremac's about $1,500 to $2,000, Herty's about $750 to $1,000 and Hughes' about $500.

11

Rowell Returns

Rowell rested on his farm in England for almost a full year. He spent his time regaining his health and raising stock. Fitzgerald, likewise, rested at his home in Astoria, New York. Neither man competed in 1883. In fact, there were no six-day races of any consequence that year.

Late in the summer of 1883, however, Rowell, completely recovered from his bout with malaria, began to train again and issued a challenge "inviting Alderman Fitzgerald, of Long Island City, to contest a six-day's race." Fitzgerald accepted the challenge and deposited the necessary $100 in the office of *Turf, Field, and Farm*.

Rowell arrived in New York City on October 29, 1883, and immediately began serious training for his return match with Fitzgerald, which was scheduled for Madison Square Garden from April 28 to May 3, 1884. This gave both of the principals and any other interested pedestrians plenty of time to prepare.

Both Rowell and Fitzgerald viewed the upcoming race as far more than just another chance to make several years' salary in six days. Rowell was determined to show the athletic world that his two defeats in 1882 had not ended his career as a pedestrian. Fitzgerald had performed well in both of his races in 1882, but there was speculation in the sporting press that at the age of thirty-eight he was too old to be bashing out these ordeals and would never regain the form that had brought him his world-record performance in December of 1881. This angered the big Irishman and he was out to silence his critics.

Rowell and Fitzgerald began daily training regimens that consisted of between forty and fifty miles a day of walking and running. Fitzgerald trained at Wood's Gymnasium in Brooklyn, and Rowell trained at the American Institute Building in Manhattan.

Before the April 15 deadline for entries was reached, eleven other pedestrians had paid their $100 entry fee and signed the articles of agreement. Besides Rowell and Fitzgerald, the following men were to start the race: Robert Vint, George Noremac, Daniel Herty, Napolean Campana, Samuel Day, Alfred Elson, William Lounsbury, Peter Panchot, Charles Thompson, William Burrell, and Nitaw-eg-Ebow.

By the afternoon of Sunday, April 27, the usual loam, tanbark, and sawdust track had been laid and rolled firm. The new scoring system and large clock, first used in Hazael's world record race, were again in place. The restaurant, bar, and carnival-like attractions were ready to operate.

At 11 p.m. there were more than 8,000 people in the Garden, and the bar and restaurant were packed. The vendors selling photographs of the pedestrians and programs for the race were doing a lively business.

Three minutes before midnight the pedestrians were called to the starting line by Hamilton Busby. Every seat and every inch of standing room inside the track was taken. The judges, Leslie Bruce and L. E. Myers took their places and the band of scorers was deployed. Busby asked the men if they were ready, and after a moment of silence shouted, "Go".

Noremac and Campana shot to the lead as the band struck up "Yankee Doodle," and the 10,000 spectators sent up rousing cheers. Noremac completed the first mile in 6:40, followed closely by the rest of the field. The pace slowed only slightly in the second mile, with Noremac still in the lead in 13:55. At the end of the first hour Noremac, Rowell, Sullivan, Day, Elson, and Thompson had all completed eight miles, with the other seven men all within three laps of this lead group.

Through the early morning hours Rowell and Day alternated the lead. None of the men left the track in the first seven hours. As the first light of dawn forced its way through the dirty windows of Madison Square Garden there were still 5,000 people in various states of sleepiness watching the pedestrians tramp around the sawdust track.

The rest of the first day was uneventful. Day was the first one to finish 100 miles at 3:29 in the afternoon, for a time of 15:29. Rowell passed 100 miles in second place in 15:57.

In the late afternoon as the sun went down it became quite chilly inside the Garden, and the men went to their tents to make a quick change to warmer clothes. Campana, better known as "Old Sport," drew rounds of laughter as he wobbled along wrapped in a waistcoat that was about six sizes too big. He was by far the most awkward man in the building, and he knew it. He grinned with delight when the people laughed at him, and shook his fist at them good naturedly. He plodded along as though he had another fellow's arms and legs by mistake, and his thin face looked drawn and worn.

Rowell took very little rest during the day and evening, and by midnight had a decent but not comfortable lead of nine miles over Fitzgerald. The results at the end of the first twenty-four hours were: Rowell 135 miles, Fitzgerald 126 miles, Day 125 miles, Panchot 123 miles, Noremac 121 miles, Herty 120 miles, Elson 118 miles, and Vint 115 miles. The other six starters completed less than 100 miles, with Lounsbury retiring at forty-six miles.

Rowell had gone to bed at 11:50 p.m., and was off the track until shortly before 3 a.m. He immediately started off on his dogtrot, and was soon joined by the other leaders in the race. Their trainers did not like the idea of Rowell extending his lead over their men. Lap after lap, Rowell, Fitzgerald, Day, Noremac, and Herty ran together in a line, one behind the other. Occasionally one of the men would run past the entire line and take a careful survey of the appearance of the others. Day was the first casualty of Tuesday, suffering from a painfully swollen knee. He would hobble along for two more days before finally dropping out.

As Rowell was steadily increasing his lead and Day was slipping farther and farther behind, Fitzgerald had a firm hold on second place. At the end of the second day the scoreboard read: Rowell 240 miles, Fitzgerald 226 miles, Herty 217 miles, Noremac

216 miles, Panchot 212 miles, Vint 211 miles, and Elson 200 miles.

Nitaw-eg-Ebow was last with only 125 miles. He was a full-blooded Chippewa Indian who the management had brought in as a side attraction. He had no idea of what he was getting himself into when he came to New York. The managers did all they could to keep him out on the track a couple of hours each day because his bright appearance and fancy costumes made him "popular with the women."

Rowell Shadows Fitzgerald

Fitzgerald started the third day at 1:15 a.m. He was followed onto the track very soon by Rowell at 1:30. For the first time in the contest Rowell used his stalking tactic. He ran immediately behind Fitzgerald, never more than four feet away. Unlike O'Leary in the third Astley Belt Race, Fitzgerald didn't seem to be the least bit bothered by Rowell's closeness. "I'll make him follow me closer than that before the week is out," he told his trainers.

Early in the day Thompson and Burrell took their names off the scoreboard. The field was now down to nine men, but it was evident that Day would be conceding at any time. Nitaw-eg-Ebow was still in the race, but he had made only a couple of token appearances on the track since the end of the first day.

Rowell retained a ten-mile lead over Fitzgerald all morning. The weather had changed dramatically from that of Monday. As the afternoon wore on a hot sun beat through the glass roof upon the heads and shoulders of the pedestrians. They became soaked with sweat, and went to their tents to change clothes.

Rowell completed his 300th mile at 1:24 p.m. He had been on the track for nearly twelve hours and except for some slightly sore feet, his trainers told a group of reporters that he was "in good condition," and that they were confident of his ability to maintain his lead. They said that they had no intention of urging Rowell on to the record unless forced to do so.

Fitzgerald finished his 300th mile two hours and fifteen minutes after Rowell. Rowell continued to stalk the tall Irishman. Fitzgerald, showing the first signs of being disturbed by these tactics, offered to run against Rowell in a short race. The *New York Times* reported:

> They spun around the track for a few laps shoulder to shoulder, but the Englishman proved the faster man. Frequent skirmishes of this kind with Herty and Noremac pushed him (Rowell) close to his best record. At 4 p.m. he was only eleven miles behind his March 1882 record for the same number of hours. His average speed (while on the track) since the race began was a trifle over six miles per hour.

At 4:05 p.m. Rowell went in for a brief rest and a change of clothes. Fitzgerald kept on with his steady, swinging gait, and reduced Rowell's lead by two miles within the next twenty minutes. As Fitzgerald continued to run faster and faster, his trainer called out, "Better come in, Pat, and not try to do too much." "Let me alone," was the reply. "I'm all right."

"Talk about endurance," his trainer said to the *Times* reporter, "that man's tougher'n hickory. His early trainin' ain't gone for nothin'."

Rowell came back onto the track at 4:45 p.m. in a new running suit. Fitzgerald was now only eight miles behind. Lap after lap, hour after hour, Rowell ran behind Fitzgerald as though he were his shadow. Rowell knew that his only serious challenger was Fitzgerald, and if he could just stay with him, whatever his pace might be, he could prevent Fitzgerald from gaining any appreciable ground. When Fitzgerald ran hard, Rowell ran hard. When Fitzgerald walked, Rowell walked. When Fitzgerald took a short rest, Rowell took a short rest. In fact, at 10:20 p.m., when Fitzgerald stopped to drink a bottle of Apollinaris water and accept a bouquet from a Long Island policeman, Rowell leaned up against the fence encircling the track and waited for him.

At 11:05, Fitzgerald had been off the track no longer than two minutes at a time since 1:15 a.m. The weary former alderman went to his tent for a well-deserved sleep, having covered 110 miles in twenty-two hours. This was the greatest distance ever traveled by a pedestrian during the third day of a six-day race. Rowell, also, had put in an astounding third day, with 106 miles when he went to bed ten minutes later.

Vint, even though hampered by a sore knee, had run quite hard through the afternoon and evening, and now was only two miles out of third place. He had covered ninety-nine miles for the day.

After three days the scoreboard read: Rowell 346 miles, Fitzgerald 336 miles, Noremac 312 miles, Vint 310 miles, Herty 306 miles, Panchot 302 miles, Elson 286 miles, and Ebow 136 miles.

After a short rest of only one hour and forty-five minutes Fitzgerald left his tent and resumed his tramp. As soon as Rowell's trainers saw this they woke up their charge and said, "up with you, Charlie, Fitzgerald's at work." Rowell, although not at all recovered from his very difficult third day, needed no encouragment. He dressed quickly, swallowed a short drink, and was out on the track in pursuit of the Irishman.

Fitzgerald appeared to be just loping along easily. Rowell, however, was straining for all he was worth. His eyes were sunken and it was evident that he was in trouble. He was forced to take numerous short rests. Fitzgerald kept circling the track at better than six miles per hour. By 4 a.m. Fitzgerald had reduced Rowell's lead to a mere two miles. The race had completely turned around. Fitzgerald, seeing that he had Rowell going, refused to rest.

Fitzgerald Takes the Lead

At 6 a.m., with Fitzgerald only a few laps back, Rowell could go on no more. He stumbled into his tent. His trainers quickly stripped him, gave him a massage, and put him to bed. Fitzgerald rambled on. In just a few minutes he passed Rowell's distance and his name was placed at the head of the list on the giant scoreboard to the cheering of the few remaining spectators and the loud shouts and yells from his own trainers and handlers. Rowell's trainers were noticeably upset watching their man being passed while he slept. By the time Rowell returned, Fitzgerald had a four-mile advantage.

Fitzgerald continued to lap Rowell with ease. After noon it began to grow warm, as it had done the day before. Rowell left the track for about thirteen minutes to change into lighter clothes, and Fitzgerald added another mile to his ever-increasing lead. The *New York Times* described the scene at 1 p.m.

> (Fitzgerald's) perseverance and dogged determination to win were wonderful. He looked thoroughly tired out. His shoulders twitched at every step, and the veins on his brawny arms stood out like whipcords. He reeled off lap after lap with machinelike regularity, never altering his step, and looking straight ahead of him with a dazed stare. A pail of cold water was placed on a chair in front of his tent, and every mile or so he would plunge his face into it. Not even stopping to use the towel, he continued on his course with the water dripping over his bent shoulders.

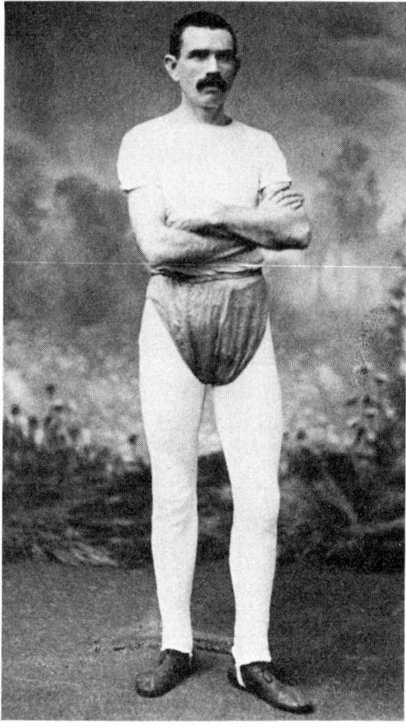

Patrick Fitzgerald, December 1882
(Library of Congress)

Fitzgerald passed 400 miles at 1:52 p.m. Even then he refused to leave the track and started "away at a brisker pace." Rowell was six miles back at this time.

The change in the figures on the hundreds of bulletin boards that were scattered throughout the city intensified the public's interest in the race. The attendance in the afternoon was greater than on any other day and before 9 p.m. more than 9,000 people were crowding each other for seats and standing four and five deep behind the railing surrounding the track. There were more women present on this fourth night than on all the other evenings put together. They waved their handkerchiefs and fans at the foot-sore men and threw nosegays in their path.

Fitzgerald left the track at 11:30 p.m. Incredibly, he had covered more miles during the fourth day than he had on Wednesday—111¾ miles, another record. Rowell went to bed twenty minutes later. He had closed a bit on Fitzgerald's lead in this time but still remained 7¾ miles behind. With two entire days remaining, this was far from a comfortable lead for Fitzgerald, and Rowell certainly knew this. He planned his longest rest of the competition. He would leave the Garden and go to a private residence a few blocks away for a Turkish bath in the hope that it would relieve some of the aching stiffness that pervaded his thighs and calves.

Fitzgerald, veteran that he was, knew that he was far from having the race in the bag. Anything could happen in the remaining hours. He had seen men crumble and retire from the race with less than a day to go. He, himself, had experienced some miserably difficult sixth days. Still, he felt that he could not ease up very much. He had to break Rowell during the fifth day. He would rest only a little longer than the night before, get onto the track before Rowell, and increase his lead as much as possible. If he could get far enough ahead on Friday perhaps he would discourage the Englishman, and be able to have an easy time of it on Saturday.

At midnight on the fourth day the scores were: Fitzgerald 447¾ miles, Rowell 440 miles, Vint 404 miles, Herty 395 miles, Panchot 392 miles, Noremac 392 miles, Elson 372 miles, and Ebow 150 miles.

Fitzgerald, according to his plan, was back on the track at 2:30 a.m., after a rest of only two hours and forty-five minutes. He seemed to be much refreshed by his short nap, and as he passed the scorers' table the first time he asked, "How do I stand?" "You're close to eight miles ahead of Rowell," answered the man in charge. "Good," replied Fitzgerald, "he'll never catch me at this rate."

At 1:20 in the afternoon, Fitzgerald passed 500 miles to the shouts of 2,500 spectators. He had managed to increase his lead to an impressive twenty-three miles. He then took his first long rest of the day. He was off the track for one and one-half hours. When he returned, a *Times* reporter noted, "After a rest of this length his step is more elastic and he walks with greater comfort." The reporter, wishing to know how this was possible, went to Fitzgerald's tent and asked "Happy" Jack Smith, Fitzgerald's head trainer, what they did to him. Here is the reporter's account of the interview.

> He (Smith) led the way into a badly ventilated room about six by twelve feet lighted by an oil lamp. A camp bed covered with thick

blankets stood in the center, with a bathtub directly at the foot. A gallon of beef-tea steamed over a gas stove in one corner, while a dozen bottles of imported ginger ale were packed in a pail of pulverized ice in the other. Bottles, tin teapots, sponges, and a variety of kitchen utensils littered the shelves and tables. Directly over the stove shirts, stockings, and handkerchiefs were drying on a clothesline. "Now," said the trainer, "when he comes in we strip him and tumble him into the bathtub, which is filled with water as hot as he can bear it. He lays flat on his back with his feet up on that shelf. A man gets on each side of him and rubs in a preparation to take the soreness out of his limbs."

"What is that preparation?" asked the reporter. "Oh, come now," said Smith, "it has taken me twenty-five years to find that out. After five minutes steeping we lift our man on the bed and wrap him up in hot clothes. An hour's sleep, a drink of beef-tea or ginger ale, and away he goes again as fresh as a daisy. It's very simple."

The place was as dark and close as a pocket, and it was a relief to get out again into the mixture of tobacco smoke, foul air, and sunshine in the Garden.

Excitement Grows

Interest in the race had grown tremendously in the last two days. By 8 p.m. it was hardly possible to find standing room. The area inside the track became so congested that a patrol of thirty policemen were stationed twenty feet apart the entire way around the track.

Fitzgerald's tremendous running of the past sixty hours had taken its toll. While Rowell was slowly regaining his strength, Fitzgerald was beginning to come unglued. Throughout the evening Rowell was able to close the gap. By 10 p.m. he was only fifteen miles behind. He had reduced the lead six miles in four hours.

Fitzgerald's trainers did all that they could in the way of encouragement and more. They increased the dosage of the stimulants he was receiving. His fellow countrymen screamed and hollered as he shuffled by.

At midnight Rowell was only eleven miles behind. Both protagonists went to bed before 11:30 p.m.

The score after five days stood: Fitzgerald 536½ miles, Rowell 525 miles, Panchot 496 miles, Noremac 494 miles, Herty 483 miles, Vint 480 miles, Elson 455 miles, and Ebow 157 miles.

Fitzgerald was given only a short two-hour rest. Rowell was still off the track, and Fitzgerald's trainers wanted him to gain as much ground as possible before the Englishman returned. When Fitzgerald set out from his tent he was wobbling and groggy. He seemed to perk up a bit under the loud encouragement of the several thousand spectators who could not pull themselves away from the drama of Fitzgerald's struggle to stay ahead.

Less than three hours later, Fitzgerald finished his 550th mile. He was, however, quite exhausted. He groped his way around the track a few more times and then, as he approached Rowell's tent, he stumbled and fell against the railing. Smith and two other trainers ran to his aid. He didn't know where he was. After picking himself off the railing he made a linc for Rowell's tent. One of the handlers took hold of him gently, turned him around, and pointed him down the track toward his own tent. By this time Smith and the others had reached him and assisted him to his tent. At this point he had a twenty mile lead.

Rowell charged out onto the track ten minutes later, after a sleep of almost five hours. He was "as light on his feet as an antelope", and began to cut into Fitzgerald's long lead.

When Smith saw Rowell almost effortlessly scoring lap after lap unchallenged by his man, he gave the order to wake Fitzgerald, and sent him out once more. He had been in the tent only twenty minutes.

The tired Fitzgerald was no match for the well-rested and revitalized Rowell. Fitzgerald, under constant prodding by his handlers, attempted to stay up with Rowell, but it was no use. He continued to lose ground, and was finally forced to his tent at 5:30 a.m.

Drastic measures were now being taken by Fitzgerald's trainers to keep their man on the track and moving forward. A plaster was applied to the back of his neck in the hope that this would draw away some of the heat, and cool him off. The strength of the stimulants was once more increased.

Rowell, constantly squeezing water onto his head from a huge sponge, continued to lap the dazed Fitzgerald. At 7 a.m. he was only ten miles behind. By 10 a.m. he had closed to within eight miles. He had run up twelve miles in the last six hours. It now looked like only a matter of time before the Englishman would dash into the lead. Neither Smith nor Fitzgerald, however, would admit defeat. "I'll die but that I'll keep ahead," Fitzgerald said. He said this with such a determined look that those around him felt that he would, indeed, run himself to death.

Just before noon, as he pulled to within four miles of Fitzgerald, Rowell was carried to his tent, undressed, and given a hot bath.

He fell asleep while his throbbing legs were rubbed down, and he was put to bed. Fifteen minutes later he was awakened, pulled from bed, dressed with great difficulty, and sent back onto the track. He had lost only one mile.

As soon as Rowell appeared, Fitzgerald caught up to him, and fell in behind. Both men settled into their painful walks. Cheers broke out all along the track and followed them as they passed "on their weary way." The cheers would continue unabated for the next nine hours.

Fitzgerald was not done yet. At 12:30 p.m., as he staggered almost blindly around the track, he opened up his bleary eyes at the scoreboard and read his score and that of Rowell. He seemed to appreciate for the first time just how close Rowell was coming. He called out to Smith for a cup of beef-tea. This he received on the next lap and swallowed the whole thing in one gulp. The *Times* described Fitzgerald's reaction to the drink:

> He suddenly put forth an effort and lumbered past Rowell, and his sympathizers sent up an encouraging cheer that made the roof ring, and stimulated by the applause, the long-limbed Irishman made a spurt. Rowell made a spasmodic effort to follow him, but stumbled, staggered helplessly, and almost fell, and then resigned himself to see his big adversary gain on his lead....Although his trainers ordered him to catch up to the leader, the little Englishman did not have the necessary power and only walked slowly down the sawdust.

The spurt left Fitzgerald almost "reeling with fatigue." He pulled up behind Rowell and dropped back into a walk. They continued like this for the next three hours. Both men were fast approaching the limit of their endurance. The emotional strain of forcing a totally exhausted, pain-racked body around and around was especially telling on Fitzgerald.

Rumors had been flying through the Garden all day that Smith had sold out to Rowell's camp, and was doctoring his man's drinks. When one of the spectators hollered this out to Fitzgerald as he went by, he became infuriated. Half dazed, he rushed into his tent and began screaming at Smith. "Someone is trying to fix me. Did Duryea (Rowell's trainer) give you money to lay me out?" Smith was able, within a few minutes, to calm him down and had him lay on the bed. As soon as he did, he fell right asleep. Half an hour later, Smith woke Fitzgerald, told him he had been asleep for four hours and sent him out. Fitzgerald had completely forgotten what he had done.

Twenty minutes later Fitzgerald could hardly move, he was so terribly stiff and sore. The situation was desperate in the Fitzgerald camp. They had tried everything they knew to keep their man slogging ahead. He had now reached the end. He could suffer no more. After much discussion it was decided to attempt something that they had never done before.

Their medical advisor, Dr. Taylor, was called in. Fitzgerald was carried into his tent and placed on a chair. Taylor removed a bronze, rectangular instrument from his bag. This was a scarificator. It had sixteen retractable semi-circular razor-sharp blades. The blades were retracted and the instrument placed on Fitzgerald's left thigh. Taylor then released the trigger and sixteen one-eighth inch deep incisions were instantaneously slashed into the pedestrian's thigh. This was repeated a couple more times and then duplicated on the right thigh.

This bleeding process was intended to relieve the soreness and inflammation in Fitzgerald's legs. While bleeding had been used extensively for just these medical purposes for hundreds of years, in 1884 the medical profession considered it almost "quackery" to use it as a viable therapeutic technique. However, trainers would do anything to their man in order to win the race.

Whatever the cause, Fitzgerald left the tent less exhausted than he went in, and munching on ice, once more took up his now familiar position behind Rowell. While thirty minutes before he was unable to keep pace with Rowell, he now had no trouble "dogging" the Englishman.

Rowell had expected, as did everyone present, that when Fitzgerald returned he would be barely moving, and that his lead would, in short order, be reduced to nothing. What a shock it was to the exhausted Rowell when he found that he could not pull away from the stalking Fitzgerald. He was only three miles behind, but Rowell realized that, with this newfound strength of Fitzgerald's, it was over. The hope that had been sustaining him during his chase of the last thirteen hours was gone. The drive, the enthusiasm that had enabled him to push his body far beyond what most men could endure had disappeared. His eyes showed that he wished now for nothing more than an end to his self-inflicted ordeal. It was 5 p.m.

Fitzgerald Exceeds Record

At 5:25 Fitzgerald passed the world record of 600 miles. A roar of applause broke out and swept through the Garden. He passed this point four and one-half hours ahead of Hazael's time. With Rowell's inability to gain any ground, Fitzgerald had regained his confidence. He perked up, and when he was presented with a gold lined silver cup, he was able to smile broadly and walk a lap holding the cup in the air over his head.

At 6:53 p.m. Rowell completed his 600th mile and became only the third man in history to cover that much ground within 144 hours.

Fitzgerald took a short rest at 8 p.m. When he returned a few minutes later, he was dressed in a bright new suit, one he had not worn at all during the week. The shirt and trunks were red and the breech cloth green. On his head he wore a green jockey cap embroidered with red, white, and blue stars.

After an extended rest, Rowell returned at 8:35. As Fitzgerald passed his tent, he joined in and the two men walked side by side "at the top of their speed." On the next lap Rowell carried an Irish flag and Fitzgerald an American flag. They ran a lap with the flags in their hands, "while men and women stood on their seats and shouted themselves hoarse....The band played and everything that was capable of making a noise contributed to the din."

Three laps later, Fitzgerald completed his 610th mile, and stopped in front of the scorers' stand. He glanced at the score and said, "Let's stop." Hamilton Busby asked Rowell if he agreed. Rowell agreed to stop after he had completed two more laps for a total of 602 miles. He then shook Fitzgerald's hand and the race was over.

Instantly the crowd surged over the railing and poured onto the track surrounding Rowell and Fitzgerald. Cries of "Hurray for Fitzgerald," and "Rowell, Bully boy, Rowell," resounded over and over again. Fitzgerald and Rowell, both on the verge of collapse, were held vertical by the crush of the crowd. It took the police several minutes to push and shove a path for the two men to return to their tents.

The final results were: Fitzgerald 610 miles, Rowell 602 miles, Panchot 566½ miles, Noremac 545 5/8 miles, Herty 539 3/8 miles, Vint 530 miles, Elson 525 3/8 miles, and Ebow 158 miles.

Two days later the six pedestrians who had survived the six days and had covered the required 525 miles met at the Ashland House Hotel with Hamilton Busby for the division of the gate money. Fitzgerald received $8,433.15 as his share of the gate money and $980 of the entrance fees. Rowell was given $3,375.27 in gate money and $280 of the entrance fees. Panchot took $1,856.39 of the gate and the remaining $140 of the entrance money. The others received the following: Noremac $1,181.35, Herty $843.81, Vint $675.06, and Elson $506.28.

A few days later, Fitzgerald was given a Caesar's welcome in Long Island City. He was indeed the conquering hero. He had shown the sporting world that even at thirty-eight he could take on the arduous challenge of a six-day go-as-you-please and not only survive, but regain the status of the best in the world. However, he had paid dearly for this honor. The praise, the excitement, the cheers masked for the moment the tremendous suffering that he had endured. Fitzgerald would never again compete in a long-distance competition. He took his winnings and purchased a hotel and athletic grounds in the Ravenswood section of Long Island City, and lived there peacefully, away from the crowds, noise, and pain of the sawdust track. He died of dropsy in 1900 at the early age of fifty-four.

12

The Record Advances—Interest Declines

The six-day go-as-you-please pedestrian contests had been dying a slow death since the "hippodromes" of the early '80s. A race such as the Fitzgerald-Rowell battle could stimulate interest for only a short time.

There was almost no activity in 1885 or 1886 in the United States. In 1887, Philadelphia was the host of two six-day races. In February, Robert Vint, the shoemaker from Brooklyn, won $4,000 with a first-place distance of 530 miles. Frank Hart was second with 518½ miles. In November, George Littlewood made his second trip to the United States far more successful than his first had been by easily defeating the local favorite, James Albert, 569 miles to 530 miles. Littlewood won $2,200, Albert $1,200. The management made a miniscule $4,000.

Littlewood was now a seasoned veteran. He had achieved personal bests in every six-day race he had entered. He was perfecting the art each time he raced.

Albert, at thirty-three, was also approaching his prime. He had competed in mostly small affairs from his first race in 1879 until the race with Littlewood. He was now ready for a serious all-out effort.

A race was arranged for February 6 through 11, 1888, in Madison Square Garden. Littlewood would not be able to come to the United States before April and so would miss the race. But seventy-two other would-be pedestrians paid the deflated entry fee of $25 to run for glory and fame. Only a handful of the seventy-two starters had ever completed six days before. The old guard of Hart, Herty, Noremac, Vint, and Panchot was there, along with the rising star, Albert. Several other new names appeared, such as George Cartwright of England, with a previous best of 570 miles, and Peter Hegelman and Peter Golden, who were just beginning their pedestrian careers.

In order to reduce the congestion on the eight-lap track, anyone who had not completed 100 miles in the first twenty-four hours would be disqualified and would have to leave the track.

At the end of the first day only twenty-four of the original seventy-two entrants had finished the required 100 miles. There had been no great rush that first day. Hart led Albert by one quarter mile with 130 3/8 miles. Four others had gone over 120 miles. Hart ran into trouble on the second day and there was little excitement from then on. Albert rolled along, day after day, unchallenged. Interest picked up the last two days when it became clear that Albert had a definite shot at Fitzgerald's world record.

New World Record Set

The "natty little Albert" completed his 600th mile at 4:44 p.m. on the last day while the band played "Tramp, Tramp, Tramp, the Boys are Marching." Before his 610th mile he changed his clothes and came out looking "as fresh as a man who had been in a Russian bath and in the hands of a tonsorial artist." He went through the record *on the run*, in contrast to Fitzgerald's blind, exhausting stagger of 1884. The seven other remaining pedestrians left the track to Albert after 9 p.m., and the "redoubtable and graceful Albert ran like a thoroughbred racer until 10 p.m." when the race officially ended with a new world record of 621¾ miles. Second was Daniel Herty with 582 miles 600 yards, third was Guerrero with 564 miles, and fourth was Hart with 546 miles 660 yards. Albert won $4,800 in gate money and $1,000 for breaking the world record.

After the race Albert said that he had had absolutely no problems during the entire six days. He now planned to retire and would resume training only if his record was broken.

George Littlewood made it back to the United States in April for the second Madison Square Garden six-day event of the year, set for May 7 through 13. Littlewood had to fight off two serious challenges during the race. The first came from the Irishman John Hughes of New York. Hughes had grown conservative with age and let Littlewood lead the first day 137 miles to 131 miles. He then moved to the front on Tuesday, while Littlewood suffered a slowdown from an inflamed hip. He pushed too hard, however, and was struck with an attack of rheumatism on the third day. Littlewood regained the lead.

As Hughes was falling back, the Californian Guerrero, was moving up. By the fifth day he had pulled to within two and one-half miles of Littlewood, but was unable to catch the Englishman. Littlewood held on to win with the second best performance ever, 611¼ miles. Guerrero set a personal best of 590 miles. The ever-present Herty was third with 572 5/8 miles.

The extent to which Littlewood had suffered during the race was not made known in the press until the day after the race ended. The *New York Times* of May 14, 1888, described what Littlewood endured for his $3,974.12 in gate money.

> It became known yesterday that it was pluck alone that enabled Littlewood, the Englishman, to win the six-day go-as-you-please contest which ended Saturday night. Littlewood's feet are in a terrible condition. On the second day of the race a huge blister appeared under the ball of his right foot. On the following day another appeared on his left foot. On Wednesday his little toes began to swell, and on Friday they gathered and burst, laying open the flesh so that the bones were visible. His running on Friday and Saturday chafed the broken flesh apart so that it hung in flaps from both of his little toes. In the meantime the skin on the blisters had been worked off, and the man ran for two days on raw flesh. He must have been in excruciating pain during the greater part of the contest. On the third day his hip became swollen and inflamed with rheumatism. At four different times during the race it was thought by his trainers that he would have to abandon the contest, but the plucky fellow determined to go on as long as he could hold the lead.

These two races had been moderate successes for the management of O'Brien and Kelly, and they arranged a third one for November 27 to December 2. Littlewood returned once more. This time he was to be handled by "Happy" Jack Smith, Fitzgerald's old trainer. For four and a half days Littlewood struggled with Daniel Herty, who was competing in his eighth six-day race. Herty, while he had never won a race, never finished worse than third. It was not until 4 a.m. on the fifth day that Littlewood took over undisputed possession of first place. Even then Herty did not crumble.

Record Falls for the Last Time

The Sheffield Blond, as Littlewood had been nicknamed because of his reddish blond hair and moustache, reached Albert's world record distance 621¾ miles at 8 p.m. on Saturday. Albert, who had observed the race every evening of the six days, came out of the stands and accompanied Littlewood on his next lap as the band played "Rule Britannia."

Littlewood walked on for two more miles and then stopped with a new world record performance of 623¾ miles. He could have covered 650 miles easily, but he did not want to make it difficult to break the record the next time he was given the opportunity. He won $4,400 in gate money and a $1,000 bonus for breaking the record.

Daniel Herty remained on the track until the last minute of the 142 hours expired in order to surpass the 602 miles made by Charles Rowell in 1884. He became the fourth best performer with the fifth best performance of all time with 605 miles. He also would be the last man to cover 600 miles or more in a six-day race. Littlewood's record still stands as the greatest distance covered within 144 consecutive hours, go-as-you-please. His record of 531 miles and 135 yards for six days "fair heel and toe" walking also has never been equaled.

There was recurrent speculation that Littlewood and Albert would race at the Garden for $5,000 a side in 1889. The race, however, never took place. In May of 1889, Albert, not able to regain his old form after a layoff of almost a year, managed to scrape by Guerrero 533 miles to 525 miles in a six-day contest conducted in San Francisco. The same week on the East Coast, in the Garden, Daniel Herty finally (after nine tries) won a six-day race by covering 550 miles. But because of very light attendance throughout the contest, he won only $1,000. John Hughes was fifth with 515 miles and took home a paltry $200.

Pedestrianism was just about dead. As one Philadelphia paper said, "After the excitement and interest of bicycle racing, the scene of a motley crowd of quaintly attired athletes slowly

George Littlewood, all-time champion for distance covered in six days (Library of Congress)

ambling around a sawdust path was not an inspiring one." The wheelman soon gained a position of importance that the pedestrians would never regain.

In March of 1891 another six-day race was attempted at the Garden. The small crowds day after day dealt the final blow. Hughes won the race with 558 miles and made $3,750. No one seemed to care. For the next eight years there would be no six-day contest in New York City.

In the fall of 1898, Captain Alexander Samuells, a New York "sporting gentleman," proposed a revival of the "great six-day races of the past." The pedestrians were still around, but on such short notice most could not gather the $100 entry fee. They convinced Samuells to postpone the race until June. Samuells enlisted the aid of J. Henry Webb as his business manager and assistant. Webb traveled to England in March with the intention of securing Littlewood's signature on a contract to compete in the June extravaganza. Webb returned empty-handed. This was to be an omen of things to come.

With the prospect of a full-scale six-day competition later in the year, Lew Morris of New York arranged two races: a twelve-hour and a twenty-four hour go as you please at the Grand Central Palace in New York City.

At five minutes past noon on February 14, 1899, thirty-five pedestrians toed the line before starter Al Smith. Peter Hegelman, competing for the first time in eight years was well prepared. A young Norwegian, Olaf Steen, held the lead for ten hours. But he had run himself out two hours too soon. He tottered, with feet blistered and swollen. Dazed, his head hanging forward and his knees bent under him, his handlers ran alongside "goading him on with threats and shouts." Shortly after 10 p.m. he collapsed. and was carried unconscious to his tent. A short time later he reappeared, supported on either side by a handler. He staggered on in this way until cries of "Shame, take him off" from the meager crowd forced his handlers to do just that. Somehow he managed to hold on to second place and finished only two miles behind Hegelman's seventy miles.

The attendance was extremely light and a Philadelphia newspaper, commenting on the fact that this had been the first "long-distance pedestrian contest" held in New York City in eight years, predicted that it would also be the last one for many years to come. The newspaper miscalculated the tenacity of the pedestrians and their promoters.

Renaissance of Pedestrianism

This was to be but the first race in a four-year renaissance of pedestrianism. Two months later at the same location a twenty-four-hour race was contested. Hegelman was again the victor, with a decent performance of 120 miles. John Glick, a newcomer to the sport from Philadelphia, was second with 113 miles. Eleven of the original thirty three starters were still on the track at the conclusion of the race. Two old-timers, George Cartwright and Gus Guerrero, started the race but did not finish. Alfred Olson at fifty-eight years was the oldest finisher, in tenth place with seventy-two miles.

The long-awaited (by the pedestrians) six-day race began in Madison Square Garden June 12, 1899. It was a complete failure. After two days the gross receipts were a miserable $143. Captain Samuells had already paid out $1,500 in rent for the Garden and was due to pay another $1,000 at the end of the week. It was evident to the competitors, seeing the empty seats throughout the arena, that Samuells would not be able to pay the rent, let alone pay them a percentage of the gate money. They held a quick conference and early on the third day decided to leave the track and go home.

This disappointment did not deter the promotion of a six-day event in Rochester, New York, later that same year. Peter Golden, the Irish champion, set a "world record" of 352½ miles for the vertigo-inducing twenty-lap-to-the-mile track. Martin Fahey, a twenty-year-old youth from Shenandoah, Pennsylvania, was second with 348 2/5 miles. Third and fourth places were captured by two men from the "Golden Age of Pedestrianism," forty-two year-old Frank Hart, who covered 316 2/5 miles, and forty-year-old Daniel Herty, who finished a total of 306.6 miles.

New York City was unresponsive to this new wave of pedestrianism. Other cities took over, however. From 1900 to 1903 the cities of Philadelphia, Pottsville, Pennsylvania, Columbus, Ohio, St. Louis, Shenandoah and Pittsburgh, Pennsylvania, Lynn, Massachusetts, Fall River, Massachusetts, and Detroit, Michigan, were the sites of various pedestrian competitions.

The most enthusiasm was shown by the City of Brotherly Love. A series of five six-day races were held in the Industrial Art Hall at the corner of Broad and Vine Streets, Philadelphia, on its tanbark and sawdust sixteen-lap-to-the-mile track.

Stars of the Renaissance

The "Golden Age" had Weston, O'Leary, and Rowell. The Renaissance had John Glick of Philadelphia, George Tracy, and the foremost pedestrian of the day, Pat Cavanaugh, a Trenton, New Jersey, Irishman. In one twelve-month period, from March of 1901 to March of 1902, Cavanaugh competed in six six-day races, winning three of them. His first victory came at the Old City Hall in Pittsburgh, Pennsylvania, in November of 1901. On a tiny twenty-lap-to-the-mile track he managed an incredible 506¼ miles to win by thirty-one miles. In February of 1902 he teamed up with Peter Hegelman in a six-day two-man relay in Madison Square Garden. They won the race covering 770½ miles—the present world record. One month later back at the Industrial Art Hall in Philadelphia, he won another individual six-day contest with a very fine 532 1/8 miles to Martin Fahey's 514 miles.

Cavanaugh suffered greatly during the race and collapsed a short time after the finish. When initial attempts to revive him failed, he was taken to a hospital where he remained in a coma for several days. He was not expected to live. Nevertheless, he recovered, tough pedestrian that he was, and returned in February of 1903 to win yet another six-day race in Philadelphia for the "Weston Trophy Belt," with 524 miles. His total earnings in seven races, four of which he won, did not amount to more than $4,000. It was still sufficient, however, to allow him to bring his mother, whom he hadn't seen in twenty-five years, to the United States from Ireland.

Hart, Herty, and even Peter Noremac competed in several of these races. The best performance was turned in by Herty in February of 1903, when he finished sixth with 483 miles, for which he won the grand sum of $180.

Death of the Six-Day

The contests had changed dramatically from the days of Weston, O'Leary, and Rowell. The tracks were half the size, and while a race in the Garden was no stroll amid pure Alpine splendor, a six-day race at Industrial Hall was a "pretty stiff thing to go up against," as a reporter for the *Philadelphia Record* put it. He continued, "the hall is so poorly ventilated as to practically amount to no ventilation at all....One whiff satisfies most people that the sanitary arrangements are not what they should be, for the stench at times is positively sickening."

In days gone forever the pedestrians were hailed as national heroes by the sporting press. In 1903 a sports writer for the *Philadelphia Journal* gave this vivid account of his reaction to a six-day race.

> After the first twelve hours the expression go-as-you-please became ridiculous, for no man if he retained his senses pleased to go anywhere. This is where the trainers became valuable in forcing the poor jaded, abused bodies to continue their suicidal work....Imagine the brutality of standing there, eagerly, curiously watching the faces of the contestants, pinched, drawn, and lined with physical and mental agony, and occasionally making cold-blooded comments as to how badly a man's legs were swelled, or as to how much older he looked than a night before....Prizefighting, football, wrestling and the like have been called dangerous sports. But the three played at one time would only represent a game of marbles in comparison with the six-days "go-as-you-please."
>
> It made the writer sick and the memory of it will play havoc with his sleeping hours for many days to come. And he is sure that he is not alone in that feeling.

In February of 1903, Assemblyman Herman G. Hutt from Philadelphia introduced into the State House a bill that would make it a misdemeanor to be in any way connected with an athletic exhibition that would continue for more than twelve hours a day.

It is difficult to attach an exact date to the death of six-day racing. There were a few futile attempts now and then to bring the sport back to life right through the late 1920s. In 1909 there was a two-man six-day relay in Madison Square Garden. The team of Cabot and Orphee won with a non-record 732¾ miles. In 1929 another six-day relay was held at the Ascot Speedway in Los Angeles from July 13 to 18. The field was comprised of the survivors of C. C. Pyles's Second Transcontinental Foot-Race. The winning team of Johnny Salo, winner of the Transcontinental Foot-Race, and Sam Richman covered 749 miles 696 2/3 yards. The runners each received $5, less than a penny a mile.

Six-day racing was dead.

13

Weston and O'Leary Walk On

What of Weston and O'Leary, the two men who began the "Golden Age"?

The six-day race of mid 1880s had become too gladitorial for them. Moreover, they were primarily walkers, not runners, and the pedestrian contests were now dominated by the runner. Weston and O'Leary both knew that they could not, by walking alone, defeat the likes of Rowell, Fitzgerald, and Littlewood. Besides, they did not need the quick-buck promoters and organizers. O'Leary had sufficient money and Weston had both charisma and a sufficient number of contacts to organize and promote their own exhibitions. They did just that for almost forty years.

While Rowell and Fitzgerald were training for their epic battle of 1884, Weston was walking the turnpikes and country roads and circling the rinks of Great Britain. Starting in London on November 21, 1883, he walked 5,000 miles in 100 consecutive working days. That is, he walked fifty miles a day six days a week, resting on Sunday until he completed the 5,000 miles on March 15, 1884. He walked under the auspices of the Church of England Temperance Society, and at the close of each day's walk he delivered a brief lecture entitled "Temperance," in which he extolled the virtues of the active, temperate life.

Weston remained in England until the end of 1885, when he returned to the United States to defend once again the temperate, teetotaling way of life. He was to walk a 2,500-mile race against the one man he desired to defeat above all others, Daniel O'Leary. The race was sponsored by the New York Advocates of Temperance, and would be contested twelve hours per day, six days a week until the first man had covered 2,500 miles. Two thousand dollars would go to the winner in addition to a share of the gate money. The loser would receive $1,000. They would begin December 7, 1885, at the Metropolitan Rink in Newark, New Jersey, and walk at least a week in Newark, New Brunswick, Jersey City, Elizabeth, Brooklyn, New York City, and Syracuse, finishing in Chicago, O'Leary's hometown.

At the end of sixteen days, less than two miles separated the old foes. O'Leary had 754¼ miles to Weston's 752½ miles. They remained very close for more than eight weeks when finally the constant strain of seventy-two hours of walking each and every week began to take its toll on O'Leary. From the third week on he had been forced to use various stimulants to keep him going. He also drank alcoholic beverages freely during the competition. On Tuesday of the last week of the race, after completing 2,292 miles, he collapsed "from too free use of stimulants" the *New York Times* reported, and was unable to return to the track. Weston continued on alone and finished the 2,500 miles on Saturday, February 6, 1885, to the unbounded delight of the New York Advocates of Temperance. Weston finished in so little distress that he was able to wash, change, and catch a train to New York City within an hour of leaving the track. It had taken eleven years, but Weston finally had beaten Daniel O'Leary.

The two men would never compete against each other again, even though they both would continue to walk professionally for the next thirty-six years.

O'Leary's Greatest Feat

After his defeat by Weston, O'Leary traveled the world, giving exhibitions of his walking prowess. He was able to support himself and his family (a wife and three children) quite comfortably in this way. In 1902, at the age of fifty-six, he walked from Boston to Albany, New York—187 miles in forty-five hours. In 1904 he walked from New York City to Toronto, a distance of 535 miles in exactly nine days. At the age of sixty-one, in 1907, in what he regarded as his greatest feat, he walked a mile at the

Edward Weston

beginning of each hour for 1,000 consecutive hours at the Norwood Inn in Cincinnati, Ohio.

On his 35th birthday he had begun the custom of walking 100 miles within twenty-four hours. He was able to keep this up through his 75th birthday, in 1921, when he completed the 100 miles in 23:54.

He outlived his wife and only son and during his later years spent his summers in Chicago and his winters in Southern California. There he would pick up money at baseball games by heeling and toeing it around the bases six times in five minutes. After one such exhibition he said, "I used to do twelve in ten minutes and I'll have you know I'm walking six times around because the price of everything has gone up and I'm selling my product in small packages. I could do twelve now if I wanted to."

His old age was comfortable and relaxed. He ate breakfast at 5 a.m., lunch at 10 a.m., supper at 5:30 p.m., and never retired later than 9 p.m. His diet was simple, with apples and grapes his luxury. He said that he never took medicine.

He walked constantly until 1932, when he was compelled to retire because of a tumor on his hip. When questioned regarding his exceptional powers of endurance he said, "I never stay in one place long enough to get stale. Life is always fresh for me. That is my secret."

He died in Los Angeles just short of his 87th birthday on May 29, 1933, of hardening of the arteries.

Weston Continues Walking

Weston, like O'Leary, continued to give exhibitions after their race in 1886. But his were far more flamboyant than those of O'Leary. At the request of a number of prominent gentlemen "to demonstrate that his great walking feats had not injured his health, and that, though age considered, he was still vigorous," he set out on the night of December 18, 1893, to walk from the Battery in New York City to the state capitol in Albany, a distance of 160 miles, within seventy-two hours. Although the entire route was covered by ice and snow, his fifty-four-year-old legs carried him to his destination in 59:59, more than eleven hours ahead of schedule.

Three years later, at the Lexington Avenue Skating Rink in New York City on the day after Christmas, he covered 103¼ miles within twenty-four hours.

In 1906, still in the public mind, he accepted an invitation from thirty prominent medical men of New York and Philadelphia to duplicate his feat of 1870–a walk from Philadelphia's City Hall to the Fifth Avenue Hotel on Madison Square in New York. He left Philadelphia on May 23 and with only a thirty-minute sleep at New Brunswick, walked into Madison Square twenty-three hours and fifty-four minutes after starting. He was sixty-seven years old.

The next year, determined to test himself against another of his earlier records, he set out to duplicate the performance that brought him into public prominence in 1867–Portland, Maine, to Chicago. He astounded everyone by walking the 1,345 miles in twenty-four days and nineteen hours. This was twenty-nine hours faster than he had done forty years before at the age of twenty-eight.

Harper's Weekly has this to say about the old pedestrian as he strode into the Windy City.

> But for the whiteness of his hair and dragoon mustache his bright blue eyes and ruddy cheeks would make him appear as young as ever.... He goes at a light, steady pace of five miles per hour, rolling his

> shoulders a little and swinging his arms, never lifting his feet high from the ground and sometimes making a little hitch in his stride.

In 1908 he walked from San Francisco to Los Angeles, 512 miles, in twelve days.

If Weston's confidence needed lifting, the last two walks certainly did it. He now planned one last colossal venture. He was certain that he could walk across the United States in less than 100 days. He would not take the straightest and shortest route, but a devious one of 4,000 miles from New York City to Chicago, St. Louis, Kansas City, Denver, Ogden, and San Francisco.

He left New York City on his 71st birthday, March 15, 1909. All went well for the first seventy days. Then the weather turned bad. The last part of the trip turned into a nightmare, with storms lashing down on the old man, soaking him to the skin day after day. At times he was forced to walk up to his knees in slush and mud. During a spring snowstorm in the Rockies he crawled on his hands and knees along railroad tracks for almost twenty-four hours because he could not stand up against the force of the wind. He covered only four miles for his effort.

He finally pulled himself into San Francisco four days and seven hours behind schedule and 105 miles short of his projected 4,000 miles.

His friends urged him to retire. They were afraid that he was overtaxing himself. He refused. Still convinced that he could cross the United States in 100 days, he planned another excursion. This time he would start on the West Coast, in Santa Monica, to take advantage of the easterly flow of the wind. He would travel across the desert, make a detour to the Grand Canyon, and then follow the right-of-way of the Atchison, Topeka, and Santa Fe railroad into Chicago. From there he would take the main roads east into New York City.

Why would a man approaching seventy-two years old wish to take on such an arduous task? The souvenir program for the transcontinental walk was put together by Walter H. Molar and answered this question.

> ...to prove simply that the feat is not one of superhuman or even unusual effort, but simply an educational and healthy exercise which any man of normal health and temperate habits can successfully follow....He simply feels that if people at large would walk more they

> would be the better for it, and if he can bring this truth home to the great American people by any effort of feet or tongue he will feel he has not made his great trial in vain.

A close friend who believed that Weston's athletic achievements were "a sterling example to the young and an encouragement to all to lead the careful and simple life" advanced him a sufficient sum of money to defray expenses, and Weston left Santa Monica on the morning of February 1, 1910. Three thousand six hundred and eleven miles and seventy-six days twenty-two hours and fifty minutes (Sundays excluded) of walking brought him on May 2 to the steps of the New York City Hall. He strode triumphantly through a cheering, screaming crowd of 20,000 that completely drowned out the sound of a brass band and was officially welcomed to the city by Mayor Gaynor.

> I am mighty proud of you, Weston. The whole world ought to be proud of you....This is marvelous. There never was anything like that in the history of the world. You are one of the benefactors of the human race. You have made people go out in the open and taught them how to live. If they would follow your teachings they would live 100 years instead of fifty.

Weston's exploits once again stirred the heart of the nation. But his two trips across the country were extremely expensive. Each one cost him about $6,000, and once again he found himself in debt. Weston's own comment on his continuous financial plight was expressed in an interview in the *Saturday Evening Post* some years later. "While I have never dissipated, I fell into the age-old habit of sportsmen of spending all I earned." His almost constant state of insolvency had, in fact, led to permanent estrangement from his wife and family.

No novice at public speaking, Weston went onto the the church lecture circuit. Through 1911 and 1912 Weston delivered his humorous talk "The Vicissitudes of a Walker" in more than 170 churches. He hired a young Irish girl, Anna O'Hagan, from Philadelphia to act as his secretary. She would remain with Weston for the rest of his life.

His presentation met with acclaim from all who heard it. A visiting Englishman said, "He poured out experiences and convictions richly spiced with humor, not unworthy at times of Mark Twain."

From the *Evening Gazette*, Haverhill, Massachusetts, December 15, 1911:

> He (Weston) talked straight from the shoulder, told his hearers how to walk. How to care for their feet. How to cure rheumatism. How to prevent colds. How to keep healthy. He gave walking as a prescription for nearly everything, laughed at the medical profession in general, and told so many interesting stories and amusing anecdotes that the audience was loath to let him go.

From the *Troy Times*, December 22, 1911:

> His talk of an hour was as entertaining a combination of wit and humor and homely sense, reminiscence and advice as one would wish to listen to. Many in the audience who came to see rather than hear Mr. Weston, because of his international fame, were really surprised to find that he was a charming speaker, with native eloquence and wit.

After two years of lecturing, Weston still owed more than $4,000. In May of 1913 he was invited to walk from New York City to Minneapolis to lay the cornerstone of a new $400,000 building for the Minneapolis Athletic Club.

Weston jumped at the chance to win some money and in the process make good on a boast he had made thirty-seven years earlier. One night during the height of his career, while in England dining with Sir John Astley and a group of sportsmen, he wagered that in his 75th year he would attempt to show that a seventy-five year-old man who had taken care of himself could perform a feat that would be considered beyond the strength of an average man of fifty. He proposed to walk the 1,450 miles from New York to Minneapolis in sixty days (excluding Sundays). Weston left New York on June 2, 1913, and covered 100 miles more than he expected in sixty-one days, receiving a royal welcome in Minneapolis on August 2. He was escorted by the governor of Minnesota and his staff, the National Guard, 2,000 members of the Athletic Club (mounted and on foot), representatives of other clubs and civic organizations, and 500 decorated automobiles. It was a fitting end to an incredible athletic career.

Weston's last years were not years of comfort and relaxation as were O'Leary's. Through the '20s Weston slipped out of public view and into increasing poverty. The East Coast life of the "roaring '20s" had no time for a shuffling old man who said you should walk and not ride. On June 8, 1926, Weston was found wandering aimlessly on First Avenue in New York City. He had left the Philadelphia home of Anna O'Hagan the day before but could not remember how he had traveled to New York. He was taken to Bellevue Hospital and was said to be suffering from partial amnesia and "senile psychosis."

A small notice was run in the *New York Times* concerning this episode, and a month later Weston was visited by a reporter from the *Saturday Evening Post*. A long article appeared in the July 31 edition of the *Post* that described Weston's colorful pedestrian career of half a century. Weston may have been old and entering the early stages of senility but he could still espouse the merits of walking.

> Sometimes in watching the mad pace of modern life I (Weston) wonder if they (younger men) are not more in need of hikes than their grandfathers....The great thing about walking, after all, is that it is Nature's remedy. It isn't exercise in the ordinary meaning of the word. If you do it regularly and easily it is more like a perfect massage.

On learning to walk he said:

> A lot depends on the frame of mind....Unfortunately we can't automatically turn off one set of thoughts and turn on another; if we could there'd be less misery in the world. What we can do is to let Nature turn'em off, and many good doctors have discovered this method. If the patient can be induced not only to shuffle along—to go slowly and easily—but to keep on going for enough distance, and to keep repeating the stunt day after day, he will find himself enjoying his walks. Instead of trying to rush through to the finish he will want to prolong them, and right there, when his mind is at ease, the walking will begin to benefit his body. When a man is highstrung and nervous he is in effect yanking one set of muscles against another, and the result is simply to wear himself out....The only thing you will need to remember is not to overdo it.

But on August 15, fear of old age and poverty gripped Weston and he fled in panic to the scene of many triumphs, New York City. Anna O'Hagan reported him missing and he was found four days later sitting in a daze on the steps of a house in Brooklyn. He said that he had spent a night or two in a hotel room but with his money exhausted, he was thrown out of the hotel. He then strayed through the streets during two days of heavy thunderstorms finding shelter in doorways and halls. A compassionate policeman took Weston home until Anna O'Hagan could come for him. O'Hagan left her job in a store in Philadelphia and came to New York with her adopted son, Ray Donaldson, to take care of the ailing Weston.

An article in the New York *Telegram* early in March of 1927 made known Weston's plight.

> Just a few feeble, tottering steps across a dingy tenement room. Famous feet, that once bore Edward Payson Weston, grand old man of the open road, across continents are pacing the worn carpet in a cell-like place he now calls home. He who never knew what it was to tire, who received kings and hoboes alike under the only roof he called his own, the sky, now lies exhausted on a bed for long hours at a time, gazing wearily at the ceiling.

The article brought Weston his first good fortune in many years. Anne Nichols, author and producer of the hit play "Abie's Irish Rose," gave $30,000 for the care of Weston. The interest from the

Weston, age 70, walking across country in 1909 ("Weston and His Walks—Souvenir Program, 1910)

endowment amounted to $150 per month on which Weston could live.

On March 15 the Press Club held a special birthday luncheon for the eighty-eight-year-old ex-pedestrian. There was a big cake with eighty-eight candles and a roomful of admiring spectators. After the luncheon Weston was taken to a reception given in his honor by Mayor Jimmy Walker.

But tragedy struck again just five days later. While walking to church with Ray Donaldson, Weston was hit and hurled several feet by a taxicab. He received a severe head injury, and spent almost three weeks in St. Vincent's Hospital.

Weston walked little from the day of the accident. While his body was deteriorating he was still able to quip with a reporter for the *New York Eagle* a short time after his 89th birthday.

> The trouble with people nowadays is automobiles. That's why there are so many in the hospitals. It's all wrong, it is not common sense to eat a big meal and then sink back in a car and ride. What they ought to do is walk, but they haven't the brains to know it. Now don't forget to walk every chance you get and keep out of taxi cabs and automobiles. If you do you'll live to be eighty-nine, the same as I do.

O'Leary died less than one and a half years after he could no longer walk consistently. Weston survived a bit more than two years. He died from "the infirmaties of old age" on May 13, 1929, at the age of ninety. The *New York Times* in its obituary gave Weston a fitting eulogy.

> He has gone at last on what one has called the "perfect walk," the walk for which solitude is essential. But in his pilgrimage across the earth he had led a multitude who will keep on walking till they, too, come to the end of the road which is the longer for going on foot.

Sources for Part One

Newspapers

Chicago Tribune
Los Angeles Times
Newark Daily Advertiser
Newark Evening Courier
Newark Morning Register
New York Eagle
New York Telegram
New York Times
New York Tribune
The Times (London)

Periodicals

Bell's Life in London and Sporting Chronicle
Frank Leslie's Illustrated Newspaper
Harper's Weekly
Illustrated London Times
Nation
National Police Gazette
New York Sportsman
Saturday Evening Post
Turf, Field and Farm

Books

Astley, Sir John Dugdale. *Fifty Years of my Life in the World of Sport at Home and Abroad.* London: 1894.

Harding, William E. *The Pedestrian Manual.* New York: 1880.

Lupton, James E. *The Pedestrian Record.* London: 1890.

Moler, Walter H. *Weston and His Walks - The Wonderful Record of Edward Payson Weston.* New York: 1910.

Plummer, Edward. *The American Championship Record and a History of Mixing Races.* New York: 1881.

Tansey, John E. *Life of Daniel O'Leary.* Chicago: 1878.

Thom, Walter. *Pedestrianism.* Aberdeen: 1813.

Weston, Edward Payson. *The Great Trial of Endurance at Barnum's Roman Hippodrome.* New York: 1874.

Part Two

The Art of the Ultramarathoner

by Tom Osler

1

Dispelling Myths

We are growing accustomed to marathon race fields numbering in the thousands. Such is the popularity of the sport that even recent converts to jogging are contemplating the marathon as perhaps their very first (and last?) race. By comparison, ultramarathoning remains a lonely sport. In October 1977, I ran the New York City Marathon in the company of 5,000 runners. Two weeks later, the same city played host to the most prestigious ultra of the year, the National AAU Fifty Mile Championship. A mere thirty-eight runners started the race! Perhaps because so few participate in this sport, it is very misunderstood. I will try to dispel some of the popular myths surrounding ultramarathoning.

Myth: Ultramarathoning is the lunatic fringe of running. No sane person would want to go beyond the marathon.

I argue that the opposite is true. Racing at distances from 100 meters up to the marathon is popular primarily because of the revival of the modern Olympic games in the late nineteenth century. In addition, people who live in the age of auto travel easily forget that humans are designed to cover great distances on foot. Our forefathers knew that through walking, and walking mixed with occasional slow trotting, even an untrained man could cover several miles on foot, while a trained "pedestrian" could negotiate hundreds of miles in a few days. The armies of previous centuries travelled immense distances by walking. The great explorer, Richard Burton, searching for the source of the Nile, walked hundreds of miles through teeming, disease-riddled jungle. Burton was not a trained athlete; he simply accustomed himself to the journey at hand when the need arose.

History records the deeds of men especially gifted at such footwork. Herodotus tells us that the herald Pheidippides ran 125 miles over rugged mountain trails from Athens to Sparta in a futile effort to procure military aid for the famous battle of Marathon in 490 B.C. Jonas Cattel (1758-1854) was a well-known "strongman" in southern New Jersey during the revolutionary period. At the age of fifty-five Cattel won a wager by running the eighty miles from Woodbury to Cape May, New Jersey, in one day. Other examples of the enormous capacity of the human motion on foot could be given.

At this point, it is well to make one important distinction. Going an immense distance is one thing, but racing it is another. The legs can cover hundreds of miles through easy walking, and their owner can arrive at his destination in cheerful good health. Racing distances much beyond even a few miles is, in contrast, most unnatural and can be very destructive to one's health. For this reason, ultramarathon racing must be approached with a far more casual attitude than is appropriate in shorter events. Not doing so can lead to serious breakdown.

Myth: Walking is of no use in racing or in the training of runners.

Walking is perhaps the finest single health-generating exercise known to man. It is superior to running because it does not place as great a load on the tendons of the feet and leg, thereby reducing the probability of injury.

As I studied the faded pages of the scrapbook whose story Ed Dodd related in his Introduction, I was astonished to find the names of men like Peter Hegelman and James Cavenaugh, now totally forgotten, but great athletes in their day. I thought the marathon was forbiddingly long, but these men were competing in races lasting six days! Not only were the races hundreds of miles long, but the competition was frequent. Often only a few weeks separated these contests and essentially the same names kept appearing at the starting line! How could these men endure such exhaustion? It took me far too long to catch on to their technique. After fifteen years of intermittent study and research, I finally saw that the secret lay in *mixing walking with running.*

Walking is not in vogue today. It just doesn't seem strenuous enough to be truly athletic. However, the sooner the would-be ultramarathoner conquers this prejudice the better. Walking is an extremely efficient means of travel. The trained runner who runs a few slow miles, then walks for five minutes, runs a few miles, then walks for five minutes, and so on, will find that he can run twice as far as he can with steady slow running.

The reason for this is simple. Walking utilizes different muscles than running. Thus the running muscles have a chance for recovery and rest while the athlete continues moving forward, covering distance.

It was in December 1976, that I first tried this technique. Each Christmas the freshman class at Glassboro State College, where I teach, sponsors a fund-raising drive for needy families in the county, for which faculty members are asked to perform fund-raising stunts. I decided on a twenty-four hour run around our outdoor quarter-mile track. This would not only assist the project, but it would also provide a stem test of the method I felt I had uncovered. I decided on a ratio of seven laps running to one lap of walking. Thus I would walk one quarter mile at the conclusion of each two-mile segment.

I had never managed more than sixty miles in training prior to this effort, and I was delighted to find that I could maintain this walking-running mixture right through one hundred miles in 18:20:0. A rest for dinner, followed by an additional fourteen miles of walking brought my total to 114 miles. The post-race recovery produced no leg stiffness, a happy outcome that Ted Corbitt attributes to the frequent walks. I now knew how the great pedestrians of the past century had achieved seemingly impossible mileage.

Myth: Only those gifted with superhuman strength should attempt ultramarathons.

While it is true that only the best-conditioned runners can run continuously for fifty miles, an average marathoner could cover fifty miles in seven to ten hours using the proper mix of running and walking. To go this distance requires learning when to walk, when to run, and how to handle fluids; it does not require additional training mileage for the person who already can run the marathon.

In June 1977, several of us staged an exhibition run of sixty-two miles from Independence Hall in Philadelphia to Convention Hall in Atlantic City. Norm Draper, a 3:15 marathoner, decided to try the distance even though he had never gone beyond the marathon before. I told him simply to walk and run as I did, and to drink as frequently as I, and he would probably make it. We started at 4 a.m. on a humid but clear summer morning. When we stopped at two miles for the first five-minute walking break, Norm immediately protested. After all, he was just getting warmed up! I repeated that he must get into the proper run-walk rhythm from the start, and not wait until fatigue began to set in. Norm reluctantly agreed. After twenty-five miles, he no longer complained about walking. At the finish (in ten hours, thirty minutes), he was beat, but still in command of himself all the way. Thus, ultras are not only for those with unusual genetic gifts.

Myth: Post-race recovery will be even worse, and longer, following ultramarathons than the week of leg soreness that follows a marathon.

If you are strong enough to run the entire distance of a fifty-mile race, then recovery will indeed be longer and more frustrating than that following the marathon. However, if you mix walking and running rather than running continuously, the recovery likely will be easier than that following marathons.

When in top condition, I can run fifty miles in about 5:50. For me this is a difficult run requiring a steady speed of seven minutes per mile. Without doubt, the recovery from these efforts is harder than that of any of the other 800 races I have tried. My thighs and calves can be very sore for more than a week, and an unpleasant weariness can shadow me even longer.

In contrast, none of my three twenty-four hour races produced any post-race leg stiffness. I am not strong enough to run continuously for an entire day. I use a mixture of walking and running. Even my recent 200-mile trial in seventy hours produced no leg stiffness.

Myth: Training for ultramarathons will require even more time than training for the marathon.

Surprisingly, this is not the case. A recent survey of America's best ultramarathoners revealed that they did even less training than the best marathoners. Many never trained at distances greater than twenty miles. Park Barner, of Harrisburg, Pennsylvania is the American record holder at twenty-four hours and he averages about eighty miles of running per week.

Myth: Experience at racing the marathon is a necessary prelude to racing ultramarathons.

It is true that a survey of the contestants in any ultramarathon will reveal that most have had extensive experience in marathons. But there are a few who are successful and have had no marathon experience. This is particularly true in the longer events, such as the twelve-hour run, the one-hundred mile run, and the twenty-four hour run. In these events performers with a background in hiking and comparatively little running can do surprisingly well.

While it is true that training for and racing the marathon is probably the best physical preparation for the ultras, it is not the best mental preparation. Indeed, if the intensity with which these shorter races are approached becomes habit-forming in the marathoner, it can cause him to "burn out" too soon in the ultras. In contrast, those who are familiar with all-day hikes have a better appreciation of how the body functions over periods of time measured in half and in full days.

A striking example of the latter is my colleague Professor Benjamin Trimble. Ben is a computer specialist who has an interest in bird watching. Ben jogs three miles each day, but he and his wife watch birds on frequent hikes that last nearly all day. When I told him of my first attempts at twenty-four hours, he was eager to accompany me on the track. I suggested that he alternately walk and run laps. To my amazement he managed forty miles in eight hours. Later he tried a twelve-hour track race, but managed only fifty miles because of badly blistered feet. Keep in mind that Ben runs only three miles each day, and has never entered anything resembling an ordinary race!

Myth: Champion marathoners would be champion ultramarathoners if they would only try the longer races.

Some might, but most would not. Remember that there is a great range of distances to consider when you think of the ultras, fifty miles, 100 kilometers, 100 miles, twenty-four, forty-eight, or seventy-two hours, six days and more! Could Olympic Marathon Champion Frank Shorter better Ted Corbitt's American record for 100 miles? One hundred miles is just under four times longer than the marathon distance. To run Shorter at this distance would be comparable to the Olympic 400 meter champion racing for the one mile record.

Because of the wide range of distances for the ultramarathoner to try, no one dominates them all. Park Barner was voted Ultramarathoner of the Year by the staff of *Runner's World* in 1978, yet he was frequently beaten at fifty miles. Park gets rolling at about 100 miles, and his twenty-four hour record has not been matched by any other American. But if six days were tried again, would Park be victorious? Here again, some unknown athlete might emerge champion.

Myth: Ultramarathoners are by nature masochistic, with unusual capacity for suffering.

Men and women, with proper training and pacing, can cover distances from fifty to several hundred miles without overtaxing their energy reserves or willpower. While some athletes do approach this sport with an "all-or-nothing", "blood-and-guts", "never-say-die" attitude, this eventually will be their undoing. Ultramarathoning is simply too difficult to be approached with such intensity. After driving oneself to exhaustion in a few misguided efforts at racing, the gutsy competitor will likely be the victim of an injury from which he will never spring back. The experienced ultra-distance specialist knows that there will be some mild discomfort in the final miles of a race, but these are easy to bear in the atmosphere of competitive excitement. It is the wise competitor who quits with the onset of serious discomfort or pain. It is best to be patient and wait for a day when one is better prepared.

Myth: Ultramarathon races are incredibly boring and are a seemingly endless succession of dreary miles.

On the contrary, the longest races can be the most interesting. The marathon runner has few parameters to play with. Besides some rather mild accelerations or decelerations in the pace, little else takes place. On the other hand, the ultramarathoner has much more to be concerned about. When and what should be eaten and drunk? Should you stop for five minutes and rest? Should you sleep for an hour? Should you take a warm shower? Should you change shoes or clothes? How will you run in the dark?

The longest races require carefully thought-out plans and alternatives. It is not always the strongest athlete who wins, but sometimes the shrewdest.

2

Running with Class

In the fall of 1963 I ran my first sub-three hour marathon, a 2:41:59 performance in Atlantic City. I have forgotten nearly every detail of that race, but the scene immediately upon crossing the finish line remains vivid in my memory.

I was elated with my time, but my legs were very stiff and weary. I grabbed my sweatsuit and walked over to the curb to sit down. My father, who was always enthusiastic about athletics but not a runner himself, walked over to me and asked, "Why are you sitting there on the curb?" I replied, "Dad, I'm exhausted, I just ran a marathon!" While this seemed a reasonable excuse to me, it did not conform to my father's image of what a trained athlete should do. He continued, "The winner kept right on running to the field house. I thought you said you were in good shape!" I shook my head. "Dad, you just don't understand this sport." As he turned and walked away he muttered, "You've got no class."

Sixteen years have passed since that incident, and I now know that my father was right. In recent years we have been able to watch the finish of the Olympic Marathon live on TV. There was no fatigue evident when Abebe Bikila finished in Rome and Tokyo and immediately proceeded to do calisthenics. I recall Frank Shorter's victory at Munich and the one-two finish of Cierpinski and Shorter at Montreal. Did these men collapse upon crossing the finish? On the contrary, they continued running and waving to the crowd.

The well-trained athlete, who knows himself and his sport,

maintains a dignified and professional appearance even in the most difficult moments. Limping, staggering and collapsing, are not the gestures of the heroic, but a clear sign that the runner has misused the body's energy reserves.

In short, running with class means knowing your own strengths and limitations, and understanding how they can best be utilized, not abused, in long distance racing competition. The athlete should finish looking like a "pro", with things well under control. Introducing the idea of *running with class* might seem like a glorified personal opinion about the correct appearance of a runner. However, this concept reaches beyond my own personal judgments. The fact is that most marathon runners require no additional physiological training in order to compete in the ultras, however, they *are* in great need of *psychological* preparation. As the individual expression of a necessary approach to the sport an entire chapter to this concept of the runner with "class" is justified. It is through this portrayal that the reader will best learn how to orient his or her mind and body for the best results in very long races.

An Ultramarathoner's Creed

Running distances of fifty to one hundred miles and beyond can have severe negative effects on an athlete's health. But ultramarathoning can also be most rewarding and healthful, if it is undertaken with the proper psychological, almost spiritual, restraint. I want to keep moving my feet in this joyous sport until I am called to leave this world. I do not wish to run one or two good races, only to spend the rest of my life nursing an injury that arose because I was too foolish to realize my limitations. For this reason I have composed the following creed as a pact with my body. It is based upon the faith that if I take good care of my body, it will reward me with robust health and respectable athletic performances. I believe it to be a practical foundation for running ultras with class.

1. My body is the source of my running joy. I will respect its needs and not subject it to the foolish abuse.
2. Pain, discomfort, and fatigue are my body's signals that it is being overtaxed. When these arise, I will take appropriate

action by slowing down, resting, or quitting as the degree of the symptoms indicates.

3. Running is to be enjoyed. I will endeavor to maintain a playful attitude toward competitive races, and not take victory or defeat seriously.
4. I am a trained athlete. I realize that my appearance in competition provides an example to others of what the healthy body can achieve. For the good of sport as well as my own health, I will at all times endeavor to walk and run in good form. I will quit rather than give the public a degrading display of overfatigue.
5. Running myself to the point where I stagger or am totally drained is not heroic, but a poor show of misused engery. I will retire from the race long before I reach such a state.

This creed is designed not only to protect the competing athlete from his or her overzealous enthusiasm, but the good name of the sport as well. The intense drive over the final miles of a ten-mile road race has no equivalent in a 100-mile run. The abandon with which the ten-miler may expend his energy without fear of collapse or serious injury cannot be permitted in the ultras. The athlete must restrain himself, or his career as an ultramarathoner will be remarkably frustrating and short.

The Challenge of the New Frontier

You may wonder how you can ever cover such great distances on foot without great discomfort. Short races are tiring, the marathon is exhausting; must not the ultras be frightfully fatiguing? From direct personal experience I can answer "NO." True, a fifty-mile race run with the abandon suitable for a marathon can produce record times as well as fatigue of positively awesome proportions. But fifty miles of gentle running mixed with frequent walks can be accomplished by many average marathoners with only slight traces of weariness.

Today, ultramarathoners are rediscovering the techniques that made the great records of the old-time pedestrians possible. Four years ago twenty-four hour races were unheard of in the United States, but they are now growing in popularity. Even longer events are beginning to appear on running schedules.

The record for racing the marathon is now 2:08:33. Never

before in history has the art of running this and shorter distances reached such a high state of development. In contrast, the art of covering great distances reached its peak in 1888, when George Littlewood set the all-time record of 623.75 miles in six days. The great challenge for today's ultramarathoners lies in rediscovering this forgotten art. I do not believe that any living runner could match steps with the great Charles Rowell at races of 24 hours or longer.

If the reader likes racing with crowds, then perhaps he or she should stay with the marathon. A sub-2:30 marathon requires conditioning of the highest levels, yet thousands of runners can achieve this time. One hundred miles in twenty-four hours is also very difficult, but certainly not as hard as the sub-2:30 marathon. Yet few have ever managed 100 miles within the span of one day. The ultramarathoner of today is a modern-day pioneer of sorts. He is one of those exceptional souls who would leave the thousands who crowd the starting line of the marathon, and face instead the challenge of distance of nearly inconceivable length. Fifty miles, one hundred miles, two hundred miles and more—these seem at first to be impossible on foot! But they are indeed within the grasp of most athletes whose hearts are stirred by the challenge. Not only can such distances be achieved, but they can be achieved *without great fatigue*.

To show the world what the human frame was designed to do, and do well, is the great challenge facing the runner who would call himself an ultramarathoner. Miles measured in the hundreds, covered with only slight fatigue are, in short, performances with class!

The Great Edward Payson Weston

I have discussed, in abstract terms, the mental outlook I believe to be most advantageous for the athlete who would test his or her strength against great distances. I have chosen to call this view of the sport running with class. However, I am not by any means its originator. In formulating this outlook, I had in mind the great walker Edward Payson Weston, whose performances have been tremendously inspirational to me. Much was said of Weston's career in the other half of this book; still, reviewing certain of his exploits and their significance can be very instructive for today's ultramarathoners.

Weston was born in Providence, Rhode Island in 1839. He claimed to be frail as a youth and took long walks for the purpose of restoring his health. If this story is true, it is one of the great success stories of all time, for he lived to the age of ninety when he was run down by a New York City taxi.

As a young man he worked as a reporter for the *New York Herald*. Since there were no telephones, the reporter who could get back to his desk most rapidly was the one who most often earned the "scoop." Naturally Weston found his walking prowess of great service here.

In 1861 he walked the 443 miles from Boston to Washington to attend the first inauguration of President Lincoln. Typically, he arrived a few hours late. Nevertheless President Lincoln saw fit to greet the remarkable pedestrian personally.

After using his walking powers to advantage during the Civil War when he served as a spy for the Union forces, Weston undertook his first professional walk in 1867. In this cross-country effort he walked the 1,326 miles from Portland, Maine to Chicago in twenty-six days. In doing so, the journals of the day reported that he won a wager of ten thousand dollars. Weston's name became a household word.

It is important to note that Weston was never a stranger to failure. He tried forty-seven times before successfully covering 100 miles in twenty-four hours. This he achieved in 1870 during a solo indoor walk.

For the first half of the twentieth century, the four minute mile was the great challenge of track athletes. The name of Roger Bannister will be remembered forever as the first man to break the famed barrier. In the nineteenth century, (as seen in Part I) the equivalent barrier for pedestrians was the walk of 500 miles within six days. Many great pedestrians in both Britain and the United States had tried this monumental walk, and all failed until Weston tried in 1874. He had failed on three earlier occasions that year at Madison Square Garden, but in December he moved the scene of his solo trial to Newark, New Jersey. Here the sporting world went mad as Weston became the first man in history to negotiate 500 miles in less than six days. He was declared the "pedestrian champion of the world."

Shortly after Weston's 500 mile success, another giant arose to challenge him, the great walker Daniel O'Leary. O'Leary was an Irish immigrant who made Chicago his home. As a direct result of the Weston-O'Leary duels in America and England, the Astley Belt for the Pedestrian Championship of the World was established. The championship was always staged as a six-day contest.

One of the most noteworthy of these championship struggles came in the fourth contest for the Astley Belt in 1879 in London. Due to numerous recent failures, Weston's popularity with the public was low, and the odds against him were set at ten to one. He was now forty years old, and for the first time he abandoned walking as his exclusive means of progression and practiced running as well. Not only did his mixture of walking and running result in a startling new world's record of 550 miles, but the ease with which Weston negotiated the final miles was never before or since matched. He ran his 501st mile in 7:39 and his 526th mile in 7:37. On the last lap he was given British and American flags. The band played "Yankee Doodle" and "Rule Brittania." The old man was once again world's champion and record holder.

Weston continued public exhibitions of his foot powers in both indoor and cross country events to the extent that his racing mileage totaled an incredible 75,000 miles. This distance would circle the earth three times!

Famous as he was, his most talked about pedestrian achievement was to await his seventieth year. In 1909 he announced that he would walk from New York City to San Francisco over a zig-zag route of 4,000 miles. This he would attempt to complete within 100 days. Typical of Weston, he again failed. It took him 105 days and the route proved to be only 3,900 miles. Nevertheless America was taken by storm by the old man's courage. The *New York Times* carried daily accounts of his progress. Many adults who were privileged to see him pass remarked that they remembered seeing him on his great walks when they were children. When he entered a town huge crowds came to greet him. Frequently he spoke in town halls on the "Vicissitudes of a Walker," a speech delivered in a form which some reporters compared to the style of Mark Twain.

Weston died on May 13, 1929 as a result of being run over by a New York City taxi at the age of ninety. His career as a professional pedestrian spanned a full fifty-two years in what has to be one of the most brutal sports ever devised. How did he survive? Weston had class. He knew his powers very well. He knew when he was ready for an all-out effort, as in his 550 mile six-day record in 1879, but more importantly, he knew when to ease up, as evidenced by his numerous failures. Other men showed more guts and courage, but they did not last. Blower Brown broke Weston's six day record, but he died at the age of forty-one. Patrick Fitzgerald managed 610 miles in six days, but he died at fifty-three. Charles Rowell won fifty-thousand dollars in 1879, but he died at fifty-five. (Fitzgerald died from a kidney related disease, but the cause of Brown's and Rowell's deaths cannot be determined from the newspaper accounts. While it cannot be proved that any of these men had their natural lives cut short from the extreme exertion of professional pedestrianism, it does remain a possibility that should give all present day competitors pause.) Weston lost many races, but before his days were to end, no pedestrian could match the esteem in which the public held his accomplishments. Few athletes in history have ever demonstrated that they knew their own capacities so well, and exercised such self-control even in the heat of professional competition.

Today's ultramarathoner can aspire no higher than to imitate the self-awareness and control of E. P. Weston. He had class!

3

Training for All Distances

Training for ultramarathons does not differ from training for the marathon or shorter road races. Runners who have completed the marathon several times have attained the physical condition necessary to cover fifty or more miles. However, while they possess the sheer power required most would fail if they tried. First, they would lack knowledge of how to mix walking and running. Second, they would not know how to take fluids so as to remain hydrated. And third, their psychological orientation likely will be too intense and they will squander valuable energy in the early miles. In this chapter we will review briefly the most popular forms of marathon training, as well as consider warming up, stretching, training in heat and cold, diet, and injury and illness. We will take a closer look at those areas of training of special interest to the ultramarathoner in the next chapter. These include walking, the selection of fluids to be used while running, psychological preparation, as well as a glance at the training techniques of the great pedestrians of the past.

Mileage and Speed

The first question today's runner asks when he considers training is, "How many miles should I run each week?" As mentioned earlier, ultramarathoners generally run no farther in a week than well-trained marathoners or 10,000 meter specialists. The ultramarathoner of today is in the enviable position of being able to compete at a great variety of distances. Most are no strangers to five and ten mile road races, as well as the marathon, fifty miles, 100 kilos, 100 miles, and beyond. Those who consider themselves ultramarathon specialists will use the very shortest races as tune-ups for speed.

Just how many miles should you run each week? This varies with the individual runner's basic strength and opportunity to train. Few will run less than sixty miles per week, and few will go more than 120; most will average seventy to eighty miles over seven days. A typical schedule will look something like this:

Day	Mileage for 60 mile week	Mileage for 80 mile week	Mileage for 120 mile week
Monday	5 miles	7 miles	10 miles
Tuesday	10 miles	13 miles	20 miles
Wednesday	5 miles	7 miles	10 miles
Thursday	10 miles (including 3 mile time trial)	13 miles (including 3 mile time trial)	20 miles (including 3 mile time trial)
Friday	5 miles	5 miles	10 miles
Saturday	10 miles	15 miles	20 miles
Sunday	15 miles	20 miles	30 miles

The essential feature of these schedules is the following:

1. There is an observable easy, hard, easy, hard pattern. Monday's run is short, followed by Tuesday's, which is long, and so on. *Rest is as important as stress when training*, and the shorter days provide insurance against overtraining.

2. There is a long run every week, or every two weeks. These serve to re-acquaint the athlete with the difficulties involved in prolonged footwork.

3. There is a short time trial or race each week to help the runner develop the important ability to relax at a fast pace.

The speed attained in these workouts varies with the individual's strength, level of fitness, and goals. In general, the pace should be easy and relaxed, with no difficulty maintaining a conversation. The runner should be moderately tired at the conclusion of the workout and should have sufficient reserves *to repeat the workout immediately if necessary.* Overtraining to the point of exhaustion will eventually cause illness or injury.

What pace is typical in these workouts? A 2:18 marathoner can probably relax at six minutes to the mile, a 2:30 marathoner at seven minutes per mile, a 2:45 marathoner at seven and a half minute speed, and a 3:00 marathoner at about eight minute speed. These times are only guides, and a particular athlete might find that his or her pace varies considerably from those mentioned. I can run a marathon in 2:50 at any time, yet I frequently run at nine minutes to the mile, especially in the early morning hours.

Sharpening Training

The training pattern described above is frequently referred to as *base training.* Base training differs from the present consideration, *sharpening training,* in that there is little emphasis on the development of speed that is so useful in short races. Even though the ultramarathoner will rarely have reason to run faster than six minutes per mile in races of fifty miles or more, sharpening techniques can assist substantially in running performances. In addition to teaching the runner to relax at a fast pace, proper sharpening training calls forth those precious endocrine supplies, such as adrenaline, that give the athlete an extra edge.

In sharpening training repetitions of a short distance, perhaps one-half mile, are run frequently at a fast pace with a short rest between them. During these fast bursts, the runner concentrates on relaxation at the quicker speed.

Experience shows that peaks in performance level, resulting from this type of training can rarely last for more than six weeks, due to additional strain placed on the body by a heavier running load. Such sharpening work should begin about six weeks prior to the runner's first important race, and terminated six weeks after that race. Failure to terminate this form of training can result in the body being driven headlong into a deep racing slump with possible injury or illness developing.

I assume here that the reader is familiar with sharpening techniques as described in detail and used so successfully by the great New Zealand coach Arthur Lydiard. There is no space here for a detailed account of these methods which are of primary importance to those interested in shorter distances. Sharpening will assist the ultramarathoner, but many specialists in this area ignore it. For further details the reader should consult the many articles and books by Lydiard as well as the author's *The Conditioning of Distance Runners,* 1967; and *Serious Runner's Handbook,* 1978, (World Publications).

Warming Up, Cooling Down, and Stretching

Since the training pace of the ultramarathoner is rarely swift, warming up is not of great concern. I usually find that it is a bit harder to get started in the early morning hours than it is in the afternoon, because the motion of daily activity acts as a partial warm up.

I usually begin my workouts with a fifty yard walk, followed by a trot at the slowest speed for another fifty yards. I repeat this sequence of alternately running and walking fifty yards for a distance of one-half to one mile. By this time I am ready to run at a steady speed of seven to eight minutes per mile. If I plan to do a time trial, I will run one or two easy miles followed by five sprints of fifty to one hundred yards at nearly full speed as a preliminary warm up.

For most workouts, the only cool-down that seems necessary can be obtained by simply slowing up in the last two miles. On very long runs, I like to end by walking segments of the last two miles.

In recent years artificial stretching exercises have become very popular in running circles. Many runners are being urged by their coaches to spend considerable time bending to touch the toes, both before and after running. I must confess that I never do these stretching exercises, and am not alone in in this matter. Park Barner, America's greatest ultramarathoner, termed stretching exercises a "waste of time" in a recent magazine article. Frank Bozanich, the American record holder at 100 kilometers, told me that he never does these exercises either.

The running public has been misled into believing that stretching exercises will prevent injury to runners. This is true only if the runner's injury is due to an awkward fall in which the limbs are stretched beyond their normal range of motion. Such falls are common in sports like football and baseball, and thus stretching exercises are of great value in those sports. But virtually no running injuries are due to clumsy falls; overuse and fatigue are the primary culprits in running injuries.

Rather than preventing injury, many athletes have found that stretching can induce injury. Runners are often tired from all this unnatural footwork. If tired muscles and tendons are stretched daily, they sometimes become inflamed. Stretching *will* make you more flexible; if this is your goal, then stretch. But don't be fooled into believing that stretching will prevent running injury. Only careful attention to the degree of fatigue generated in each workout to avoid overstress, will prevent injury.

Diet

Runners, like any other people, vary considerably in the importance that they attach to diet. The two extremes are represented by the great runners Park Barner and Don Choi. Both these men broke the American record for the twenty-four hour run in 1978. Choi stayed overnight with a friend who reported that he arrived with a box full of vitamin and mineral supplements. Barner, on the other hand, gives little thought to diet and eats whatever is conveniently at hand. In spite of all the bad press received by the American diet, there remains no proof that it fails to be adequate for even the most strenuous athletic performance.

In the absence of conclusive proof on the subject, I will simply describe what has worked for me. I like to get plenty of fresh fruit and vegetables, and to eat them with as little preparation as is necessary. I am not a vegetarian, but I eat little meat. I try to avoid cakes, pies, ice cream and other food loaded with sugar; I always have difficulty keeping my weight low. I don't use vitamin or mineral supplements because I have little faith in manmade nutritional products.

A word should be said about salt. Some runners believe that extra salt is always necessary, particularly when training in hot weather. Others advocate a low-salt diet at all times and urge that the salt shaker be removed entirely from the table. Who is right? They both are!

The average American is addicted to salt. His diet has contained excessive salt since childhood, and now he is a "salt-junkie." Like any addiction, when the source is removed, there are withdrawl symptoms. Thus, many runners, who develop a salt deficit due to excess sweating, will experience muscle cramps and nausea. They are urged to take salt supplements, which will relieve these withdrawal symptoms.

On the other hand, those who have become accustomed to a low salt diet do not have difficulty with salt depletion. They have broken the habit and need never concern themselves with use of table salt. A low-salt diet is preferable for endurance athletes because it places less strain on the circulatory system. (Recall that doctors always place patients with circulatory problems on a low salt regimen.) If the reader chooses to discard the salt shaker, he or she should start in the cold winter months so that the adjustment will be easier. When the hot summer months arrive, the runner's sweat will be less salty and the tolerance for punishing heat will be higher.

Weight

Every additional pound of fat carried on the runner's frame results in reduced athletic performance. As a rough rule, runners find that they lose about two seconds per mile for each pound above optimum weight. Thus a runner overweight by only one pound will lose ten seconds in a five mile race and twenty seconds in a ten miler. A runner who is only five pounds overweight will lose ten seconds in a one mile race, fifty seconds at five miles and one minute forty seconds at ten miles. Excess weight is a serious concern to all competitive runners.

For some reason, runners who are drawn to the ultramarathons appear to have more weight problems than people who compete at shorter distances. I don't know why "big" runners abound in this sport. The fact that it is necessary to eat and drink considerable quantities during the longest races might be a factor. Thus a runner with an efficient digestive system—the proverbial iron stomach—has an advantage over those who are less hearty eaters. Whatever the reason, excess weight is a serious handicap to the ultramarathoner as well as the marathoner.

How does the runner shed excess poundage? More mileage is often inefficient, since it takes about thirty-five miles of running to burn off one pound of fat. The difficulty I have with this method stems from the fact that extra running increases my appetite. Thus, without exercising great self-control, the good done by extra mileage will be lost due to extra eating. Unfortunately, only a restriction in my food intake really helps me lose weight. The best reducing diet for runners consists in eating a wide variety of wholesome foods, but in very small quantities.

One dimensional diets, such as the all-protein diet, or the grapefruit diet, are to be avoided because they can quickly lead to nutritional deficiency. At all times, the dieting runner should drink large quantities of water or diluted fruit juices. Dehydration can cause very serious health problems while dieting.

Heat and Cold

With appropriate clothing, the runner can train in nearly any extreme of weather. I don't like winter's cold, but there is no danger associated with running in freezing temperatures. Cold rain is another matter. I have never found a sweat suit that would protect me sufficiently from cold rain, and in such weather I usually skip training to avoid getting sick or injured.

Hot weather is dangerous; most deaths while running occur in the heat. Here in New Jersey the summers bring high temperatures and humidity, a combination which is especially lethal. The dangers of running under the direct rays of the sun when the temperature is high are very real. Marathoners often remark that the sun is their worst enemy.

In conditions of extreme heat I recommend that training take place in the early morning or late afternoon when the sun is low. Some runners insist on training at midday in order to get "accustomed" to the heat. But in the hottest weather, running at noon isn't training, it's more like taking a beating. You can't get accustomed to being hit with a stick; you just get reduced to a pulp. Likewise, the weakening effects of training under a direct noontime sun are simply more pronounced than the beneficial effects.

A light hat to protect the head from the sun, a visor, and sunscreen lotion to protect the skin are all of value to the sun-drenched runner. Above all, the runner must take care not to dehydrate: drink frequently during the workout. If necessary, sew a small pocket into your shorts so that you can carry change to purchase soda at vending machines. Dehydration can not only make you sick, it can kill.

Injury and Illness

Injuries of the foot, leg and hip are all too common amongst runners. When training and racing properly, most athletes should remain free from injury and illness. That this is not the case with many runners reveals that stress—brought on by too much running—is very widespread. We like to think that we can train 100 miles per week, but if our body will only endure seventy comfortably, then injury will eventually occur. I have been running for twenty-five years, but it took the first ten to learn my limitations. During that time I had every injury a runner can get. Arches, achilles tendons, shin splints, knees, hips all failed at one time or another. After learning to respect my body, and avoid abuse, I have sustained only three injuries during the past fifteen years and have had to stop running for only four weeks in that long period.

How is injury prevented? By staying FRESH. Don't strain while training, and be protective of your well-being. If you're tired from a hard run or race, take things easy for a few days or weeks; a short rest won't significantly reduce your conditioning, but if it prevents an injury, you have gained considerably. When in doubt, err on the side of training too easily, rather than too hard. In this way you will actually do more running because you won't lose time nursing injuries.

Another frequent cause of injury is worn shoes. As a shoe wears, its shape changes, and your running stride is forced to change with it—an unnatural alteration that can culminate in an injury. A simple procedure for keeping shoes in good repair is to glue a small portion of rubber, perhaps from an old tire tube, over those parts of the sole of the shoe that wear quickly. With most runners this means gluing rubber to the outside area of the heels. As this rubber wears, simply glue additional rubber over it. Not only is the chance of injury reduced, but the life of the shoe can be doubled in the bargain.

At times the runner's overall resistance will drop and a cold or fever will result. If the illness is very mild, a short slow run can actually help. In other cases, rest is preferable to medication. Once the symptoms of the illness vanish, the runner should be careful not to hurry back into full training too quickly—a rule that applies to the recovery from any injury or illness. The comeback should be gradual and spread out over a period of at least one week. If a runner was averaging fourteen miles per day in training prior to the illness, his return might start with two miles the first day, with two miles added each succeeding day until the fourteen mile distance is reached.

Further Reading

Only an outline of the most fundamental aspects of marathon training has been given in this chapter. For further study I recommend the following: *The Self-Made Olympian* by Ron Daws, *Women's Running* by Joan Ullyot, and *Running the Lydiard Way* by Lydiard and Gilmour. All are published by World. Joan Ullyot's book is of value to both men and women, in spite of its title. For other works by this author that might be of help, refer to the section on sharpening training.

4

For Ultramarathoners Only

We now come to a consideration of ideas of special interest to modern day pedestrians.

The Training of the Great Pedestrians of the Past

I have the good fortune to have a copy of a remarkable book by Walter Thom published in 1813, entitled "Pedestrianism or an Account of the Performances of Celebrated Pedestrians During the Last and Present Century; with a Full Narrative of Captain Barclay's Public and Private matches; and An Essay on Training." In this book we get a rare look at the unusual customs, habits, and prejudices of British athletes and trainers of the early nineteenth century. Captain Robert Barclay-Allardice, better known as Captain Barclay, was a well known "strong man" and endurance athlete of his day. He was responsible for "the most famous feat in the history of pedestrianism"; he was the first man to do "1,000 miles in 1,000 hours." This event, which appears so strange to us, had been tried by many pedestrians without success. It requires that one mile be walked during each and every hour for 1,000 consecutive hours. For a period of forty-two days, the athlete must walk one mile during each hour of the day. He could not walk five miles in one hour and then rest for several hours. By requiring motion during each and every hour, over forty-two days, the athlete could never get continuous sleep. Barclay won 100,000 pounds by performing this feat at Newmarket in 1809. He was 39 years old and lost 32 pounds during the trial.

Here is a summary of Thom's detailed account of Barclay's training methods:

> The pedestrian who may be supposed in tolerable condition, enters upon his training with a regular course of physic, which consists of three doses. Glauber Salts are generally preferred; and from one ounce and a half to two ounces, are taken each time, with an interval of four days between each dose. After having gone through the course of physic, he commences his regular exercise, which is gradually increased as he proceeds in the training. When the object in view is the accomplishment of a pedestrian match, his regular exercise may be from twenty to twenty-four miles a day. He must rise at five in the morning, run half a mile at the top of his speed up-hill, and then walk six miles at a moderate pace, coming in about seven to breakfast, which should consist of beef-steaks or mutton-chops under-done, with stale bread and old beer. After breakfast, he must again walk six miles at a moderate pace, and at twelve lie down in bed without his clothes for half an hour. On getting up, he must walk four miles, and return by four to dinner, which should also be beef-steaks or mutton-chops, with bread and beer as at breakfast. Immediately after dinner, he must resume his exercise by running half a mile at the top of his speed, and walking six miles at a moderate pace. He takes no more exercise for that day, but retires to bed about eight, and next morning proceeds in the same manner.
>
> After having gone on in this regular course for three or four weeks, the pedestrian must take a four-mile *sweat*, which is produced by running four miles, in flannel, at the top of his speed. Immediately on returning, a hot liquor is prescribed, in order to promote the perspiration, of which he must drink one English pint. It is termed the *sweating liquor*, and is composed of the following ingredients, viz. one ounce of caraway-seed; half an ounce of coriander-seed; one ounce of root liquorice; and half an ounce of sugar-candy; mixed with two bottles of cider, and boiled down to one half. He is then put to bed in his flannels, and being covered with six or eight pairs of blankets, and a feather-bed, must remain in this state from twenty-five to thirty minutes, when he is taken out and rubbed perfectly dry. Being then well wrapt in his great coat, he walks out gently for two miles, and returns to breakfast, which, on such occasions, should consist of a roasted fowl. He afterwards proceeds with his usual exercise. These sweats are continued *weekly*, till within a few days of the performance of the match, or, in other words, he must undergo three or four of these operations. If the stomach of the pedestrian be foul, an emetic or two must be given, about a week before the conclusion of the training, and he is now supposed to be in the highest condition.
>
> Besides his usual or regular exercise, a person under training, ought to employ himself in the intervals in every kind of exertion, which tends to activity, such as cricket, bowls, throwing quoits, etc. that, during the whole day, both body and mind may be constantly occupied.

The reader need not fear. We will not recommend "purging by drastic medicines" nor a diet of "beef and strong ale." We included Thom's description of training to show how things have changed and how really tough the old timers were!

Long Training Runs

Long training runs of thirty or fifty miles and beyond are not necessary in order to develop the endurance required for ultramarathons. However, preparation of the body is only half the athlete's work. His mind must be trained also. There is no better way to gain the confidence needed for the ultras than to have undertaken workouts in which the runner is afoot for six, eight or twelve hours. In addition, the runner must learn how to combine walking with running and discover which drinks suit him best on the run.

For these reasons I strongly recommend that runners "go the distance" in training before they try it in racing. In doing so, the runner will learn that by rationing energy properly, almost any distance can be achieved. The old timers often remarked that distance does not kill, but speed does.

These long training efforts should be *easy* trials. The athlete should never experience real discomfort; if real fatigue surfaces, the long run must be terminated so that the runner's reserves are not depleted. After all, the race can't be left on the training road.

The specifics of walking, drinking and "psyching" will now be considered. A description of how these elements are combined in a successful training run will be given in the next chapter.

Walking

The art of mixing walking with running is one of the ultramarathoner's most important skills. A runner who can race the marathon in 3:15 would have great difficulty running more than thirty-five miles at a continuous jog, regardless of how slow the pace was. However, the same runner could run for fifteen minutes, then walk for five; run fifteen, walk five, etc., and complete sixty miles in good form. The athlete who can run the marathon in 2:35 can probably run fifty miles at a steady, seven minute per mile pace. But even runners of this class can profit from walking. They find that a blend of walking and running allows them to cover great distances in training without generating fatigue. Finally, even the greatest runners in the world cannot run continuously for periods approaching forty-eight hours. Races lasting two days and more are beginning to appear on road racing schedules, and they present yet another running challenge. Here even the most gifted athletes must employ walking for optimum results.

What do I mean by walking? I don't mean race walking of the heel and toe variety; I mean ordinary brisk walking. Most marathoners will find that they can walk for extended periods at a speed of about 3.5 miles per hour. With practice, walking speeds close to 4.5 miles per hour are possible without employing race walking technique. The great Edward Payson Weston, America's greatest walker ever, did not use race walking form. He often poked fun at race walkers and said in an article in the *Saturday Evening Post*, "Heel and toe walking isn't really walking at all, but is straight-legged running. And there is nothing natural about it."

Neil and Pat Weygandt, Ed Dodd, Tom Osler, Bob Zazzali, and Norm Draper finishing a sixty-miler on the famous Atlantic City, New Jersey boardwalk (Tom Powell photo)

Dr. George Sheehan has suggested that the most efficient walking for runners might be that of a race walker who cheats. He suggests that utilizing the race walker's style, but in addition, bending the knee slightly on impact (a violation of race walking rules termed *creeping*), is the most economical walking style. I am a trained runner, not a walker, and I don't have final answers to these questions. The reader should experiment to uncover the walking form which works best.

The exact division of an ultramarathon into pre-set walking and running segments will depend upon the circumstances of the race. In a track effort, it is best to measure these segments in laps. When I first covered one hundred miles I used a quarter mile cinder track and ran seven laps, then walked one; ran seven, walked one, etc. When on the road, it is more convenient to gauge these segments by time rather than by distance. When a group of us ran from Philadelphia to Atlantic City in the summer of 1977 (sixty-two miles in 10.5 hours) we ran slowly for fifteen minutes, then walked for five; ran fifteen, walked five, etc.

Few runners have tried walking in races. Walking is viewed by runners as something you do when you can no longer run. Sometimes, the poorly paced marathoner will "hit the wall" in the last few miles of the race. Such a runner may find that stopping to walk causes the legs to knot up, preventing further running. They have lost the rhythm of continuous running, and once this rhythm is lost, it is not easily regained. For this reason, the marathoner will be skeptical about the usefulness of walking.

The marathoner knows only this one rhythm of continuous running; there are other rhythms of which he has no knowledge. The body becomes used to the rhythmic pattern that is established while the runner is fresh. For this reason it is essential to begin the walking segments of an ultra in the very *beginning* of the run while the runner is still feeling very good. Let us assume that a mixture of ten minutes running to five minutes walking is selected before the run starts. After the first ten minutes of running the runner MUST STOP AND WALK FOR FIVE MINUTES, EVEN THOUGH THIS FEELS MOST UNNATURAL. It is very hard to stop because the runner is fresh and just beginning to get warmed up. Nevertheless he must establish the rhythm at the start. After an hour, stopping will no longer seem unusual and the rhythm of running and walking will have been established.

After several hours of "mixing" in this fashion, fatigue of a mild nature will slowly settle in. At this point runners find that when they begin a running segment, the body feels reluctant to resume. This sensation leaves after about thirty seconds. As the runner approaches the end of his running segment he will again find his body growing reluctant to run. This is a sign that the runner's inner clock has grasped the appropriate rhythm and is preparing the body for the walking phase.

How fast can you cover fifty miles while walking and running? Let us suppose you are on a quarter mile track and choose to run seven laps and walk one. Also, assume that you walk comfortably at four minutes per lap (3.75 mph). If you run at a speed of 7:30 per mile for the seven lap segment you will cover fifty miles in seven hours and eight minutes, a very good time. If you run at a speed of eight minutes to the mile then the fifty miles will be complete in seven hours and thirty minutes. If you run at nine minutes to the mile, you will do the fifty miles in eight hours and thirteen minutes.

Suppose now that you need more walking. You select a ratio of three laps running to one lap walking. Again, you walk at four

Stopping for refreshments on the same run (Tom Powell photo)

minutes per lap, but you jog the three laps at a comfortable nine minutes to the mile. You will complete fifty miles in eight hours fifty-eight minutes. One hundred miles would pass in seventeen hours and fifty-six minutes, a time bettered by only a few Americans.

Should the runner take long, continuous walks as part of training? I doubt that these would be necessary for races shorter than twenty-four hours. I recently underwent a three day trial in which I covered 200 miles. So much walking was necessary here that I now feel that I need long walks as specific training for events lasting two days or more.

Finally, I should mention that walking is useful not only as a means of greatly extending the distance that a runner can go on foot; it is also a marvelous restorative exercise by itself. After a hard day of training, a brisk walk of thirty minutes to an hour in the evening will accelerate the recovery process by stimulating the circulation. Walking places only one third the pressure on tendons of the foot compared with running. Edward Payson Weston described walking as a gentle massage, and claimed that many ailments could be cured through its employment.

Drinks for the Long Run

While learning to mix walking with running during the long workouts, the athlete must also discover which drinks can be ingested on the run. Even on the hottest days, I rarely drank much fluid in marathon races. I usually elected to pour available water over my head and neck in an effort to keep cool. Because the ultramarathoner is working at a much easier pace than the marathoner, he is able to drink fluids more easily. In particular, the walking phases of the effort provide an ideal time to drink. In addition, the ultramarathoner is much more likely to dehydrate than the marathoner due to the long period of time over which he will work. Even on the coolest days, considerable quantities of fluid must be taken. At all costs, serious dehydration must be prevented.

The most important component of the runner's drink is the plain water that it contains. If he takes nothing else, he will have at least avoided dehydration. How can you tell if you are drinking enough? You cannot wait until you feel thirsty. On hot days, twelve ounces every quarter hour should be enough. On very cold days, sixteen ounces per hour might be enough. If you feel the need to urinate frequently, then you can be sure that you are drinking a bit too much. I feel that it is better to drink a little too much than to risk dehydration.

Many runners put sugar, sometimes in large quantities, in their drinks; other runners find it difficult to handle heavily sugared fluids. The runner can experiment with these in training. I first learned the significance of sugared drinks in 1967 when I was preparing for my first fifty mile race. It was summer, and I was taking a long run each week, adding three miles each week to the previous distance. All went well until I reached thirty-five miles. For two weeks in a row I found that I felt great at thirty-two miles, but at thirty-five, I felt like a car with a suddenly empty gas tank. I recalled the words of my old mentor, Jack Barry, himself a champion marathoner in the mid-1950s. Barry ate dates during his longest training runs and races. He claimed that the sugar in dates went directly into the runners fuel tank. At the five mile mark of my next long run, I decided to mix a little sugar in the iced tea that I had been using as a fluid replacement. When I mixed in two teaspoons I was surprised to find that I did not taste the sugar. I tried a few more teaspoons and still could not taste it. I immediately suspected that my body was urging me to use more and more. I dumped a large quantity in...*now* I could taste it, and deliciously inviting it seemed! When I began running again I was amazed to find that I felt stronger immediately. I had discovered an important trick! The next week I ran forty-eight miles and the following week fifty-five. I did no more long training, for I now knew that I could go the distance.

The quantity of sugar that should be included in the drink is a matter of personal preference. I have placed as much as a two pound box of sugar in a gallon of iced tea and consumed the entire gallon during a fifty mile track race on a hot and humid summer evening. Not every runner can tolerate that much sugar. I always have a gallon of plain water available and should the sugar begin to bother my stomach, I take plain water until I feel relieved.

I have used the following drinks with success: apple juice, grape juice, orange juice, various sodas, powdered milk and plain water. All the above can contain extra sugar at a concentration that the runner prefers. My favorite drink is tea with sugar. I use iced tea in the summer, and hot tea in the winter.

If the long training run takes place on a track, or relatively small loop, then the runner can have a variety of drinks available with which to experiment. If the workout will take place on the road, then he must carry sufficient change with him so that he can buy available drinks at vending machines and grocery stores.

Mental Preparation

Learning to mix walking with running, and the preparation of appropriate drinks, are technical problems that are relatively easy to master. Altering the psychological outlook of the marathoner to ultramarathoning is a more difficult task. The marathon is a race of great intensity when compared with races of fifty or one hundred miles. A much more casual approach is required for ultras. The marathoner is on the move every instant, unwilling to relinquish a precious second. The athlete in a two-day trial, by contrast, takes brief naps, pauses to rest, has nearly complete meals, and so on. The longest events are more like taking a trip than running a race.

Competitors in marathons and shorter races think of their event in terms of miles or kilometers. They can comprehend the entire race in terms of distance, since they have probably run that far many times in training. On the other hand, races of fifty or one hundred miles are too long to comprehend in terms of length in miles. It is easier for the runner to view these in terms of the hours to be spent afoot rather than in terms of miles to be covered. For example, a seven hour fifty-miler stands at the starting line of a race that begins at 9 a.m. Although he finds fifty miles difficult to comprehend, he can easily imagine the time from 9 a.m. to the finish of his seven hour run at 4 p.m. He must stay in easy motion, walking and running gently. In order not to go out too fast, he thinks of the 4 p.m. finish. Can he remain in motion that long? If not, he must either reduce the pace or do more easy walking. The ultramarathoner constantly reminds himself of the finish time and the number of hours during which he must remain in motion. With his mind's eye thus fixed on the finish, he can monitor the intensity of his efforts. Ultramarathoners often remark that the distance covered in training is not important, but the number of hours spent on foot is.

A race of fifty miles, 100 miles or more would be remarkably frightening—and physically destructive—if it were approached with the intensity that I use in the marathon. In fact I approach these events in a playful, joyous manner. They are to be days of great fun—a celebration of life and an exuberant display of my body's energy. I promise myself that I will not tolerate pain or heavy fatigue. Should these unexpectedly occur, then I, like the great Edward Payson Weston before me, will walk off the track. Quitting in such cases is no loss of honor, but a sign of common sense and mature self-control.

Of all athletes, the ultramarathoner is among the most fortunate. His events bring him out into the fresh air for hours or even days. His body flows with easy rhythms. He becomes one with nature, and his spirit rejoices for every cell in his body is being flushed with energy.

5

Diary of a Long Distance Run

I discussed the technical aspects of long training runs in the previous chapter. Details on how to mix walking with running, the selection of drinks, and psychological preparation were all considered. In this chapter I will describe one such workout, drawn from the pages of my own training diary.

The Day Before

It is Saturday, September 2, 1978. Several times each year I arrange one of my favorite workouts, a fifty-mile run from my home to the seashore at Atlantic City. My wife and two sons will be driving to the beach tomorrow, and I can meet them there at the conclusion of my run. A check of the weather forecast reveals that Sunday will be clear and hot; a perfect day for swimming, but a trying day for a pedestrian.

It is best to do very little running the day before such trials, and I elect to sit around the house and read, staying off my feet as much as possible. This run will take from eight to nine hours. I don't want to leave too early in the morning, for it will be dark until 5:30 a.m. Not only is it difficult for motorists to see a runner at night, but there are probably drunks on the road returning home from a Saturday night binge. I decide to compromise and start at 5 a.m. I inform Kathy, my wife, that I will meet her at the beach at 2 p.m. I ask her to keep an eye out for me as she drives there; in case I meet with unexpected difficulty, she can give me an early lift.

I go to bed at 9 p.m. and set the alarm for 4:30 a.m. My running shorts and sleeveless running shirt are set out for my quick morning get-away. My softest training shoes, as well as a cap with a large sun visor, are placed beside them. In addition, a small change purse is prepared. It contains about three dollars for the purchase of drinks at vending machines. An additional forty dollars in bills is included to buy yet more drinks and supplies as well as a taxi ride home if the need arises.

The Big Day

As usual, I awaken before the alarm rings. It is 4:15 a.m. I check my weight—two pounds over my usual morning reading. This is a good sign, for it means that I am hydrated. I will need this extra body fluid during this hot, day-long run. It is very bad to arise on the day of a long run to find your weight a few pounds below normal.

A bowel movement and shave help get my system going. Soon the kettle is boiling for a cup of tea with plenty of honey. As I sit and drink, I try to calm myself. I *always* get too excited before these runs, which are among my most enjoyable undertakings. I decide to take an additional drink, for there is no place to purchase drinks on this course before the eight mile mark. I select a large glass of apple juice.

I pin the change purse to the inside of my running shorts and stuff an old handerchief there as well. I leave a note for Kathy telling her that I left on time and will see her at the beach between 1 and 2 p.m.

The Start

I walk out the back door at 5 a.m. Except for a street light, it is dark. On most mornings at this time the sound of traffic from a highway 200 yards away would be heard, but it is Sunday, and a strange quiet fills the air. It is damp, nearly 100 percent humidity, but the temperature is only seventy degrees. The weatherman predicted clear skies, but as I look up no stars can be seen.

It is important to get in the proper mood. I walk easily for fifty yards, then begin moving in a gentle trot. Normally I have difficulty running this early in the morning, but the excitement of a special workout has my juices flowing and my running steps seem remarkably easy. I stop and walk a few yards during the first half-mile to make sure that I warmup slowly.

I have now left our housing development, which offered the protection of street lights, and turn onto a narrow, dark country road which I must travel for 4.5 miles. I am uneasy about this stretch because of the danger of not being seen by the occasional motorist. As always I stay on the left side of the road facing traffic. For ten minutes, I am left to my own thoughts as no cars appear. I try to keep my stride as short as possible, for I can barely see where my feet hit the road.

I hear a car coming from behind. As it approaches I stop and walk off the road until it passes. I am paranoid about being hit.

Before the run, I had planned to walk every fifteen to twenty minutes, for about five minutes. As the time for the first walk approaches, I decide to forego it, due to my uneasiness about this dark stretch of the road. I want to get off it as quickly as possible. It is undeniably important to start walking at the very start of a long workout, to establish the proper run-walk rhythm. But I am just too uncomfortable, and decide to wait until I reach the five mile mark at Cross-Keys.

Cross-Keys (5 Miles)

Five country roads meet at this little backwoods center. Usually there is heavy traffic here, but at this hour there are no moving vehicles. I hear the sound of voices–loud semi-hysterical female voices. As I approach the intersection, I see a car parked near the trees and several teenagers standing around, apparently drunk. They don't notice as I trot by and turn onto the three mile stretch of road that leads to Williamstown. Normally there would be some daylight by this time, but the heavy cloud cover postpones the dawn. Suddenly it begins to rain, hard-driving downpour that immediately chills me to the bone. Worst of all, my shoes are drenched, and my feet begin to slide in them. After about five minutes the shower stops and the sky begins to open; at last there is light on the road.

In spite of my heavy, flopping shoes, this is the first time that I feel really cheerful. I simply can't relax when I'm on the road in darkness. Six miles have passed and I still have not walked. Normally, I would have walked twice by now. I would stop immediately for a walking break, but I am cold from the rain. I relax and keep moving towards the eight mile mark.

Williamstown (8 Miles)

I have now been running without a walking break or a drink for one hour and fifteen minutes. I certainly would not recommend that a long workout begin this way, but I have had little choice. I enter the small center known as Williamstown. Thus far, there have been no gas stations or stores at which to buy drinks. Now I have a choice of both. I select a twenty-four hour, chain grocery store, since it might offer fruit juice, while the gas stations have only soda machines. As I walk in, I am instantly made aware of my appearance. The glance from the clerk is intimidating; I am wet with rain and sweat, and my calves are covered with grime from the road. I quickly select a sixteen ounce container of orange aid. As I remove the change purse from my shorts the clerk looks at me with further wonder. "Where are you going?" he asks timidly. I always enjoy startling people, so I pipe up, "Atlantic City." He looks at me in total disbelief. "I'll be there by 2 p.m.," I reply as I walk out the door. He grins. "Good Luck!"

At last I begin walking a few steps and drinking. How refreshing this feels. I wonder if I will pay a heavy price later for not stopping sooner to walk. Suddenly I feel slightly weary. Is my mind playing tricks, or am I deteriorating already? I'm taking no chances, and sit down on a nearby concrete step..

It feels good to be off my feet—too good. Oh well, I can always call Kathy and get a ride home. How often I have thought of doing this in previous workouts, but in eleven years of marriage, I have only called her once to rescue me. It is now 6:30 a.m., and I enjoy the view of this quaint town as I sip the remainder of my drink.

As I rise to continue, my concern is not with my recovery, but with how best to discard my empty paper container. I'm not a "do-gooder," but I just can't leave this on the road. Years of running have given the road an animate quality. Littering would be an act of disrespect towards the road on which my feet must travel. I have been trained in modern science all my life, but when I'm in physical labor, I think as my Stone Age forefathers did and see spirits of non-living things. I crumple the container in my hand and wait until I find a trash container in which to discard it. I have carried bottles many miles on previous runs for the same reason.

I've resumed running again and feel refreshed. Once more I face barren country road, but now I have daylight. Seven miles will pass before I reach Winslow and the next opportunity to buy drinks. The sun is rising and would be directly in my eyes were it not for my visor. I need to urinate, and relieve myself in the cover of the trees. This is a good sign, for it means I am not dehydrated. I stop and walk every fifteen minutes. It's beginning to get warmer, but I do well in heat and am not too concerned.

Winslow (15 miles)

I trot into the tiny rural cluster of old homes called Winslow at 7:45 a.m. One hour and fifteen minutes have passed since my only opportunity to drink, and I now eagerly anticipate arriving at a soda machine which I have used on past occasions.

My rising joy as I near the long-sought oasis is abruptly stilled as my eyes focus on a hand-printed sign that says "out of order." Five more miles separate me from Hammonton. I really need a drink.

I begin to walk, I say to myself, "relax, relax." I begin to look at each little country home that I pass, hoping to see someone whom I can ask for a glass of water. I'm in luck! There is an old woman sitting in a rocker on her porch. I walk up, and again am immediately intimidated by the reaction to my appearance. "Good morning," I say, "could I trouble you for a glass of water?" The woman says nothing, but rises and enters the house. She returns a minute later with large glass of water. "That's pure spring water, not pipe water," she says proudly. I drink it down quickly. " Could I trouble you for another one?" She smiles and seems delighted to be of help.

I must have consumed a quart of water on that stop, and my stomach feels really full. I walk for a few extra minutes to let it settle down. When I start running again, I feel the water sloshing about in my stomach, but I am relieved. I know this will pass, and I've been rescued from dehydration.

Hammonton (20 Miles)

Old Hammonton is a picturesque, medium-sized town in the heart of South Jersey. It is in a conservative area originally settled by Italian immigrant farmers who have prospered remarkably.

(The number of millionaires per capita in Hammonton is one of the highest in America.) It is 8:40 a.m. and there are several people in the streets. They barely notice as I trot down Main Street, as usual, looking for a grocery store.

When I leave Hammonton, there is a ten-mile stretch of highway with little chance for refreshment. I buy two sodas and sit down to drink them. After the first is consumed, I don't feel that I can handle the second. I begin walking, hoping that the first drink will settle in and make room for the other before I start running. It doesn't, and the precious second drink must be discarded.

As I leave Hammonton, I am leaving the quiet country roads behind. I will now travel over Route 30, the White Horse Pike. This major artery from Philadelphia to Atlantic City was one of the first paved roads in the nation.

Thirty miles to go! The thought is intimidating, because the next ten mile stretch on the White Horse Pike is psychologically the most difficult of the entire run. The road is as straight as an arrow. There is heavy traffic, but the shoulder is adequate. There are no towns; only an occasional roadside produce stand. More importantly there are no shade trees—I will be exposed to the sun for two hours straight!

At such times, I assess my condition carefully. My legs feel good, with no signs of stiffness. I try to accelerate my gentle trot to a speed of about six minutes to the mile, to see how it feels. Unfortunately, this acceleration reveals that I am more fatigued than I thought. Damn it! Why didn't I walk during that first hour?

As I approach White Horse Pike, with its continuous noisy flow of cars, I spot an open gas station. I pause here and relieve my bowels. In addition, I soak my hat and shirt with water. Leaving the rest room, I look like I've just emerged from a swimming pool. Water is dripping all over from my hat, trunks and legs. This will give me some protection against the increasing heat.

A Long Ten Miles

I'm now on the White Horse Pike, with traffic whizzing by. I hate traffic, and take every opportunity to run on the grass rather than the shoulder of the road. I concentrate on keeping my stride smooth and easy. I hear the words of a popular tune, "take it easy, take it easy, don't let the sound of your own wheels drive you crazy," again and again in my mind.

There are few landmarks on this truly boring stretch of road, and the two hours required to traverse it go by ever so slowly.

After five additional walks and one stop to drink, I at last enter Egg Harbor City.

Egg Harbor City (30 Miles)

The large green road signs remind me that I have twenty miles left to run. It is 10:30 a.m. and really hot. An inviting cluster of trees, surrounded by rich cut grass appears during my next walk; I sit down under their shade. Sitting there sipping iced tea, I wonder what the motorists zooming past must think. I really don't care though; it feels good to be off my feet. After five minutes I rise to continue walking, only to discover a serious problem. The nail on the large toe of my right foot is beginning to feel strange. It doesn't quite hurt, but the fact that I am conscious of it at all indicates the onset of damage. This has happened several times previously, and is due to my left foot being slightly larger than my right. As a result, the nail gets pressured by the end of my shoe. If I don't relieve the pressure now, I will probably lose the nail.

Concern over my nail has caused me to forget the gradual fatigue that is slowly surrounding me. I begin to look for a piece of sharp glass with which to make a hole in the front of the shoe. These days you don't have to look far to find broken glass on the road. In fact, I soon have several sizes and shapes to choose from. I stop, remove my shoe, and quickly make a one inch slit through the soft nylon upper of the shoe, right at the spot where my toe is being irritated. This isn't the first time I've repaired my shoes on the run with broken glass. I smile inwardly. How many runners could fix their shoes on the open road? Ah, there is a certain pride. . . .

Pomona (35 Miles)

Only fifteen to go; I feel relaxed and confident, and begin to enjoy the prospect of a successful run. It is 11:20 a.m. and I am trotting through the parking lot of a small shopping center in Pomona. A car driven by a teenager starts up as I pass through, and I step in front of him unknowingly. He guns his motor and I immediately flinch with fear. Instantly I am angry and stop. I look at him defiantly, as he stands some ten feet in front of his car. He smiles and slowly heads toward me. Immediately I check myself, remembering past encounters like this when I was fatigued from running. I can get very aggressive at such times, much like a soldier suffering from battle fatigue. I have learned that it is best not to confront people at such times, but to leave as gracefully as possible. I turn and continue running.

My body is now flooded with adrenalin. I am so angry! I notice that I am no longer weary and am probably moving at a pace close to 6:30 per mile, rather than my usual nine minutes. It seems funny, but I should go back and thank that kid! He energized me, and now I feel like I just started. I deliberately check my speed—there is a long way to go.

Moving along comfortably, I am suddenly conscious of being watched. I turn to the right and see a car slowed to my speed on the other side of the road. I look carefully to see if it is anyone I recognize, or possibly that crazy kid from the parking lot. But it is neither. The car is beginning to tie up traffic, so it accelerates and leaves. Who was that?

A half-mile further down the road I see the same car again. A slender young man steps out in shorts and waits for me to approach. "Are you Tom Osler?" Now I haven't run well in short races since the late 1960s, and I'm always surprised when someone that I don't know recognizes me. The previous year five friends and I made a well-publicized fun run from Philadelphia to Atlantic City. The distance is 60 miles, and while ultramarathoners know that it can be easy to go that far, the uninitiated find it impressive.

We run together for an hour while his girl friend drives the car ahead to meet him. At first I have great difficulty slowing him to my pace, but after the first walk, I have him under control. He gives me a detailed history of his running career, from high school to his present college status. I find listening to him very enjoyable, for he takes my mind off the miles at hand. He seems surprised that I stop to walk so often, and remarks that he has never purchased drinks on the run. He is especially uneasy when I walk up to a garden hose and douse my head, neck and back with water.

Absecon (40 Miles)

It is now ten minutes past noon, and my groin is beginning to chafe. I stop at a drug store and purchase a small jar of vaseline. At the next gas station I stop and put plenty of this jelly on the affected area. Immediate relief!

My college friend and I continue to get acquainted. The White Horse Pike now becomes Absecon Boulevard. This is a six mile stretch of divided highway built over marshlands that separate the island of Atlantic City from the mainland of New Jersey. On either side of the road is an endless expanse of water in which tall reeds grow. In the distance the skyline of Atlantic City is visible, with the famed Convention Hall clearly in view. A pleasant breeze blows across the marshes. With my destination in sight, and the realization that I am still moving easily, I wear a broad smile. Soon my friend's car appears and we shake hands and part.

I'm glad that I will run the last miles alone. I really enjoy the last hour of these workouts. All psychological doubts and fears are gone. I can savor the sound of my easy footsteps as a reward for years of preparation.

Atlantic City Boundary (46 Miles)

A long steep bridge marks the edge of Atlantic City. This bridge has special significance for me. In 1967, in training for my first fifty-mile race, I made my goal to run from my former home to this bridge. This fifty-mile jaunt was only possible after I learned to prepare sugared drinks. Every time I see this bridge I think of that first workout of over fifty miles, taken many years ago. How absolutely delighted I was with that achievement!

I go over the bridge and four more miles to the beach. Many of the streets in Atlantic City are desolate with entire blocks leveled in quiet anticipation of the city's revival thanks to legalized gambling.

Desolate or not, I am joyous as I stride down the sidewalks with the boardwalk just up ahead.

The Beach (50 Miles)

I stop one block from the boardwalk, and walk the last 100 yards. It is 2 p.m.—I'm on schedule. My wife, my father and two sons, Eric and Billy, are playing in the sand. "Look mommy, there's daddy!" I pull off my shoes and walk over to them through the hot sand. Kathy is pleased to see me looking fresh.

I quickly remove my shirt and take a short swim. If I don't jump in the water at once, my body temperature will drop and I will never get in later. How refreshing it feels!

After lunch on the beach and a nap in the shade of the boardwalk, Kathy and I take a walk of two miles on the boards. A walk at this time helps relieve fatigue in the legs.

The Next Days

On Monday, I awake and feel no leg stiffness whatsoever. This indicates that the run was done "well within myself." While I feel good, I elect not to overwork and run only three miles, to make sure that I am recovered. Normal training can resume on Tuesday if no further evidence of fatigue appears.

6

Racing for Half the Day

Having examined methods of training for traveling very long distances on foot, we now consider the needs of the athlete who could test his or her ability against other runners and the clock. In this chapter we explore races of fifty miles, 100 kilometers (62.2 miles) and twelve hours. Of these, the fifty-mile race is the most common in the United States. Fifty kilometers (thirty-one miles) is also considered an ultramarathon, but in my eyes it's really a long marathon. The fifty-miler is the shortest ultramarathon worthy of the name.

Two Types of Races

Should the athlete run the entire distance, or should he mix running and walking? This is a basic consideration, and must be settled before further race plans are made. For novice runners, regardless of their demonstrated marathon capability, running and walking is best. In fifty-milers, it may be difficult to cover the distance in under six hours thirty minutes while mixing, but the quest for fast times should be deferred until experience is gained.

Why should a 2:30 marathoner walk and run in his first fifty-miler? He surely will not produce a time worthy of his marathoning potential in this way. But remember that these races are very difficult. Reckless ultramarathoning can produce lasting injury. An inexperienced fast marathoner, who sees fifty miles as a long marathon, might produce a record time in his first race, but he could also do his legs lasting harm. Patience is a required virtue in this sport if months or even years of agonizing recovery from leg trouble is to be avoided.

Who should elect to run continuously, rather than mix? Marathon runners who cannot break 2:50 should not consider running fifty miles continuously, but should mix walking with running. Experienced ultramarathoners who can race the marathon in 2:45 can probably run fifty miles in 6:10 without harm. Marathoners of the 2:35 class can likely cover fifty miles in 5:50; marathoners of the 2:25 class have demonstrated that they can run fifty miles under 5:30. To achieve the fifty mile times that I roughly projected from known marathon performance, it is assumed that the runner can master the necessary special techniques of the ultramarathoner. These include the ability to relax while others run out of sight, and the ability to handle large volumes of fluid.

Before leaving the subject of continuous running in ultramarathons, we should note that the world's record for 100 miles is 11:30:51, held by Don Ritchie of Scotland. Needless to say, Ritchie's pace of under seven minutes to the mile did not allow him to walk. But the average ultramarathoner had best not be fooled by such performances; they are as far from his or her reach as a sub-3:50 mile is from the average miler.

Time Limits

Many ultramarathon sponsors place time limits on their event. These time limits are important, and must not be ignored by the competitor. For example, a fifty-mile race might have an eight hour time limit. Any runner who finishes after eight hours is disqualified. There are many reasons why sponsors impose such time limits. In road races they allow for traffic control by the police. They allow the officials, who are probably volunteering their time, to know exactly when they can return home.

If you cannot meet the advertised time limit, then out of courtesy and awareness of the enormous job of the race officials, you should not enter. If you do enter and subsequently find that your progress will not allow you to finish in time, then you must graciously retire. For no reason should you remain on the course after the time limit expires without having consulted the race director first for permission. There is always great concern for a missing runner.

Never bicker with a race director over these matters. Even if you have someone following you in a car, and are willing to take responsibility for yourself, you should quit when ordered to do so by the director. Why? You may not be aware of arrangements made before the race. For example, the director might have promised the police that all athletes would be off the course by a certain hour. You and your handler can become a traffic nuisance after that time.

Always defer, with grace, to the wishes of the race director. If you have other thoughts, you are showing poor sportsmanship and no class.

Handlers

While international rules forbid the use of handlers in marathon races, handlers are permitted in the ultramarathons. In fact, some race promoters insist that each entrant provide a handler so that his needs will be adequately met. By pouring your drinks, handing you towels, providing directions, etc., the handler will save a runner precious time that can mean a place or two in the race. Even on a track, the simple act of being handed a drink, rather than reaching for one on a table, will save time.

Your handler should be very familiar with the way you race and your probable needs. Long before the race starts you should sit down together and discuss every detail of your preparations. You should provide him with all necessary drinks and containers. Alternate shoes and clothing for potential changes in the weather should be available. A complete first aid kit with band aids, tape, petroleum jelly, and foot pads is a necessity. It is also advisable to discuss your prerace strategy; your handler can assist in letting you know if your pace is consistent with these plans.

Most important, you must be able to quit the race at any time should fatigue of a serious nature develop. Of course, there is no problem in quitting on a track or small road loop. On courses that take you many miles away from the finish line, your handler should be available every few miles if a rescue becomes necessary.

In road races, handlers should not stay with their runners on bicycles or in cars, for this can create a traffic hazard. The handler should drive ahead of the runner by a few miles, pull off the road, then stand and wait for you.

Finally, unwritten rules of sportsmanship dictate that any runner should be helped when help is requested. While your handler is "your man," he should give assistance to others when called upon, provided that it will not detract from his primary concern which is to assist you.

Psychological Preparation

Whether you are a novice and hope to run and walk fifty miles in twelve hours, or a world class runner shooting for under five hours, you should be willing to retire from the race should fatigue become excessive. This is not marathon racing where a "blood and guts" attitude will probably do no lasting harm. The potential for damaging the runner's health is far greater in ultramarathons, and neither the runner nor the sport is served by unwise acts of so-called courage. The athlete who would drive himself to the point where he gives a degrading display by tottering about the track looking half dead should recognize that he is a nuisance to others. In particular, he becomes a problem for officials who must worry about his well-being. Mature athletes should not subject spectators and handlers to such needless worry in order to satisfy a perverse view of sport. If running yourself to death is your thing, thén do it in training where no one else need watch.

In planning for these races, as with shorter races, I find it convenient to divide the race into thirds. Thus a six-hour fifty-mile race is conceived in distinct phases each lasting two hours. My psychological attitude towards and within each of the three phases is different.

During the first phase I imagine that I am not running at all. Ideally I would feel as relaxed as if I were sitting at home in a chair. If even the slightest fatigue is felt, the pace must be reduced, more walking employed, or rest periods begun.

In the second phase I expect to be fully aware that I am running, but I should still be moving in comfort. Some small effort might be employed here to maintain the pace, but it must be slight. In this phase remain non-competitive. Should a runner challenge and try to pass me, I do not pursue him but will reduce my speed momentarily to let him pass.

The race really starts in the final third. Some discomfort can be expected here as I start working towards the finish. For the first time I allow myself to be competitive and will "race" if challenged. While I have planned the entire race to be run comfortably, it is likely that the final hour of running will be somewhat unpleasant as fatigue sets in.

While the effort put forth in each of the three phases feels different, the pace within each phase will hopefully remain. Here, as in shorter races, a steady pace is preferred.

A 50-MILE TRACK RACE

I will now describe two fifty-mile races based on entries in my training diary. The first is a track race, the second a road race.

August 6, 1977

It is early morning. This evening at 6 p.m. I will be running the Fort Meade 50-Miler. This is the third consecutive year that I will have started this event, which is run on a 440-yard, all-weather track for 200 laps. The first year I set the meet record at 5:49:14. The second year I quit at ten miles because of a leg injury inflicted by a piece of broken glass.

For breakfast I have a bowl of spaghetti. This is certainly not my usual breakfast, but I won't be able to eat much later because of the late start of the race.

I nap for an hour at noon, then leave at 2 p.m. by car for Maryland with my running partner Bob Zazzali. I hate driving, and Bob graciously agrees to drive the entire distance while I try to nap in the back seat. We arrive at Fort Meade at 4:15 p.m.

The track has a carnival atmosphere. A 24-hour relay race started at noon and there are hundreds of runners on the field. Tents, cots, and lounge chairs dot the area inside and outside the track. As soon as I see all these athletes I start to get nervous and excited. This is bad because the race doesn't start for almost two hours.

It is *very* hot: ninety degrees, sunny and humid. I find a tree away from the view of the track and lay down on a blanket in the shade. I stay there alone, trying to relax and forget the race.

Several friends from South Jersey arrive. Some will race and others will serve as handlers for the entire group. At 5:10 p.m. I assist them in setting up the "rain machine," a large galvanized tub which we keep filled with ice water and sponges. It is placed on the infield just off the curb of the first turn. This will be our

Park Barner, current world record holder in the twenty-four hour ultramarathon, cools off during the Fort Meade fifty-miler, 1975 (Ed Dodd photo)

"handling station." The sponges will be used to douse our heads and backs with ice water. This is a remarkably effective way to stay cool and will allow a runner to race under the most torrid conditions on a track. Multi-gallon containers of various drinks are also available. I have one gallon of iced tea containing my standard two pounds of sugar. In addition I have a gallon of ice water, which I use if the sugared tea starts to bother me. The handlers will also be busy counting laps and recording lap times. Several lounge chairs have been brought for their comfort.

I dress at 5:30. Plenty of vaseline is applied between my thighs to prevent chafing. I wear nylon shorts and a cotton sleeveless shirt, and will use a visor until the sun sets.

I am told that Nick Marshall is here. He won this race in a fast time last year, as well as the Lake Waramug 50-Miler in May. Park Barner is also here. Park is always a threat, but he often runs slowly in hot weather. I suspect that Marshall is the man to watch. I am in good condition and plan no walking. I should be able to maintain a seven minute mile speed for the entire race; at that rate, I should finish by midnight.

At 5:50 p.m. I leave the field house and walk to the track. I have deliberately remained clear of my competitors. Meeting them will make my heart beat faster, and I want to stay as calm as possible.

The Start

We are called to the starting line. I see Barner and Marshall for the first time, but we don't even have a chance to say hello. There are twenty-eight starters, all in three rows on the outside of the track to avoid interfering with the relay.

The starter's pistol is fired, and I trot easily towards the inside lane. There is no hurry. This is phase one, and must be run with genuine ease. Someone is running like crazy in front, and I'm roughly in tenth place. I can't see Barner, but Marshall is about thirty yards in front of me.

The sun is incredibly hot, even though it's early evening. I pass the first mile in 6:30, and my head is beginning to feel uncomfortably warm. I ask for my first sponge. It is dripping with ice water and I place it over my head and squeeze. The water pours over my scalp and down my neck. Truly instantaneous relief. I slowly accelerate, I carry the sponge for one lap, and then throw it back into the tub.

Shortly after the first mile I pass Marshall. I'm not trying to pass him; my legs are running without any real direction from me.

Osler runs easily during phase one of a fifty-miler (Ed Dodd photo)

During this first segment of the race, I like to think I am distinct from my legs. They run, and I sit on them and take a ride. In this way I don't force the pace.

I go to the sponge every mile for the first ten miles, which pass in 1:05:45. The pace is too fast, but I am not concerned because I do not command my legs; they move freely, of their own accord. I am now soaked with water, including my shoes, but it is this water that saves me from the tremendous heat. I drink twelve ounces of sugared iced tea every half-hour.

I don't really know what place I'm running in, since there are so many runners circling the track. I can distinguish relay entrants from fifty-milers because the former carry a baton. I have been lapped several times by some fool who is running at a world record pace. I keep my eyes on Marshall and forget everyone else.

Shortly after ten miles, Marshall passes me. I am trying to remain non-competitive, but the sight of him spurs me on and I pass him in turn without trying.

I pass fifteen miles in 1:38:54. Suddenly Marshall makes a dramatic move, shooting past me looking very strong. I am running at 6:45 pace, and am no longer in the mood to give chase. If Marshall can sustain this pace, well, good for him; I certainly can't. I relax and notice that my pace seems slower. Have I been running too fast? Phase one will be over shortly and I will "take control" of my renegade legs.

Phase Two

At 8 p.m.I have run eighteen miles and the long second phase has begun. I take stock of myself. My legs no longer have that tremendous zip that I enjoyed at the start, and my pace has slowed to 7:15 per mile. Nevertheless, I feel no real fatigue and look forward to passing the marathon in good time.

Marshall laps me. It's somewhat depressing, for he looks very fresh and is not drenched with water as I am. How can he run that dry in this heat? I let him go without a fight; too many miles remain. Marshall passes the marathon distance in 2:53:00 and I in 2:56:30.

But at thirty miles my lap counter, Mike Brasko, rushes down to the side of the track. "Marshall is off the track and you're now less than one lap behind him!" Perhaps Nick is cracking and I'm back in the race! The excitement generated by this good news brings my next mile to 6:54, even though my last few miles were all over seven minutes.

My enthusiasm is short lived. A few minutes later Marshall passes me again. "Blisters," he says, "I had to change shoes." Not only does Nick look great but, more significantly, his voice reveals no sign of fatigue. I settle back to an easy 7:30 pace, hoping to reach the finish line without too much difficulty.

I am not uncomfortable, but my legs know that they are working. Soon I shall reach thirty-five miles and the third and last phase of the race will begin. Marathoners often say that their race begins at twenty miles, but fifty-milers say their race starts at thirty-five.

Phase Three

I pass thirty-five miles in ten seconds under four hours. I feel slightly weary, but should be able to move well for two more hours.

Suddenly Marshall leaves the track again. This time he takes off his shoes and just sits in a lounge chair on the inside of the track! To my amazement, and delight, he is out of the race. Blisters, not fatigue, finished him. The race is now mine. What a glorious feeling! All I need to do is run around the track for less than two hours, without concern for the opposition, and I will win. This time, the unexpected excitement does not cause any acceleration in my pace.

My complacency is short lived, for a few laps later I am passed by a slender young man looking very smooth and strong. He is not carrying a baton...must be in the fifty! My God, who is this? I rush up to catch him and ask, "Are you lapping me? What place are you in?" His reply is short: "I don't know." I get very angry. When runners are fatigued, it takes little to cause their tempers to flare.

I call my lap counter, Mike, to the side of the track. "Find out who that guy's lap counters are and see if I'm behind him. He looks too good!"

A few minutes later Mike returns with bad news. The phenom is Jim Czachor, running in his first fifty, and he is one lap ahead of me. Damn it! Not only will I not win, but I'll be beaten by an unknown!

Now Czachor is lapping me, and I am growing fatigued. I take the sponge every lap, but Czachor laps me for the third time, still looking great. "Keep rolling and the track record is easily yours" I shout to the impressive conqueror. He wins in 5:44:30, a superb time given the hot weather. I finish almost one mile behind him in 5:51:13.

It is best to keep moving after such extended efforts, so I go to the outside lane of the track and begin a brisk thirty minute walk. In the past I have learned that this exercise will reduce tomorrow's leg stiffness. After circling the track several times, Mike Brasko walks over and points to Czachor sitting in the stands, because he can't stand up. Well at least he had to *work* to beat me. One month later Jim Czachor proved that his victory at Fort Meade was no fluke. He won the National AAU 50-Mile Championship in California in his second race at the distance.

Bob Zazzali and I leave Fort Meade at 2:30 a.m., and arrive home at 5 a.m. I sleep until 7 but no further.

Post Race Recovery

Before this race I had felt I might be getting a cold. After the race I did develop a cough which lasted for three months. Hard ultramarathon races, in which the runner does no walking, are very hard on the athlete's overall health.

I had some leg soreness in my thighs for three days, and was able to resume normal training in one week following the race.

A 50-MILE ROAD RACE

Shortly after the Fort Meade 50-Mile Track Race described above, I accepted an invitation to speak and run at the annual "Michigan Fifty" at Copper Harbor, Michigan.

Kathy and I were the guests of Professor and Mrs. Otto Ruehr of Michigan Technological University. Otto agreed to serve as my handler, and we discussed race plans and filled the back of his station wagon with drinks and other provisions.

I gave my lecture on Saturday, and was troubled by coughing as I spoke. This cough had hounded me since Fort Meade and I seriously wondered if I should be racing here at all. But since I don't get invited to race that often, I reasoned that I could simply ease up on the pace and take a good workout.

Race Day September 18, 1977

The course for this Michigan Fifty is one large loop within Copper Harbor, a small mining town on the shores of Lake Superior. The first half of the course rolls gently along a narrow traffic-free road that gives a continuous view of the lake. The remainder of the loop moves inland and is very hilly. The pre-race entry form described the course as "rolling," but you can never trust these descriptions. What is "rolling" to a mountain man is like crossing Everest to athletes from the plains. Although there are few hills where I live, I don't worry about racing over them. Experience shows that a good runner on the flats should run well over hills. In the words of the great Australian coach Percy Cerruty, "A good runner can run anywhere."

I arrive at the starting line twenty minutes before race time and use brisk walking to warm up. The fields in ultras are usually very small; nineteen men are at the start today. Most were from Michigan, with other entrants from Chicago, Georgia and New Jersey. It was cloudy and fifty-five degrees–ideal racing weather.

Just before the race started, Bob Olson, the race promoter and an entrant himself, unveiled a large wooden sign that read "Tom Osler Mile," to be placed at the forty-nine mile mark! I am always responsive to flattery, but this is beyond all imagining. My heart rate accelerates even more.

The gun is fired and we are off. I quickly take the lead, which my better sense tells me is bad. Out of nineteen runners there should be someone willing to go faster than I. I have not planned to walk in this race, and while I didn't recognize any of my fellow starters, I had been hopeful that an easy run in six hours and fifteen minutes would win the race. That time requires an average of 7:30 per mile, a pace I feel I should be able to sustain despite my cough.

The sun rises late in Copper Harbor, and it is a bit dark as I stride by the one-mile mark. An official drives by and says "You'll slow down a lot later." Does he know something I don't? I try to relax, for I am in phase one of this race, in which my body should be taxed only minimally. I try to enjoy the beautiful views of Lake Superior.

At the five-mile post I get my first clocking–I am running

slightly faster than seven minutes per mile. Good. I can slow up a bit later.

At eight miles reality begins to unfold. Ken Rogotzke and Larry Swanson draw even with me. Ken looks great and begins to open ground; Larry starts a running conversation. I don't like to talk during races, because talking expends valuable oxygen and slows the pace. When I tell Larry that I'd rather not talk, he seems insulted and accelerates his pace. In a few miles both of them are out of sight.

Otto Rueher, my handler, stops every two miles and meets me with my favorite drink of sugared tea. He keeps telling me that I look strong, but I'm worried. I have no zip. Every time I run up even the slightest incline I feel the strain of the climb. For a runner in phase one of an ultra, I'm being taxed far too heavily.

My wife is riding with Otto, who is now tour guide as well as handler. Even though it's chilly out, I begin to use cold sponges to wipe my head. A few more runners pass me. I can't find a pace that is sufficiently easy, but I don't want to walk. I've never walked in a fifty before, and I should be able to survive running.

At twenty-five miles we turn left and leave the pleasant lake shore. Now there is a steady two mile climb, and I'm beginning to fall apart. My thighs are really laboring, and my pace feels like a crawl. I pass the marathon in 3:11. Bob Olson, the race director, overtakes me; I'm surprised that he is running so well. I know from personal experience that directing a race is very demanding. I have never raced well in a competition that I had directed. I assure Bob that though I'm in difficulty, I can probably finish. He begins to open ground, moving easily.

After twenty-seven miles the course becomes even more hilly: long rolling hills all the way to the finish. The twenty-eighth mile was a gentle downgrade, but on the twenty-ninth we start back up again. I am too weary. I break into my first walk.

Surprisingly, the walk feels good. My handler seems surprised to see me walking, but I tell him that there is no need to be concerned. He probably was hoping that I could run a swift final twenty miles, but I will feel happy to finish in reasonable shape. I walk briskly uphill for 150 yards. When I start running again I feel better immediately. This is a good sign; if I were really fatigued my return to running would be lethargic. I am now convinced that I can walk and run to the finish without overextending myself.

There are markers painted on the road every five miles. I am now walking every two miles and the markers seem to pass very slowly. However, walking always helps to revive me. I walk up all the big hills.

With four miles to go I catch Larry Swanson, who is walking. "Don't quit," I tell him. "You can walk to the finish in less than an hour." Larry is speechless. I always seem to say the wrong thing to him. Two miles further down the road I hear someone rapidly catching me. Larry overtakes me and beats me by 400 yards at the finish.

For the last thirty miles I have been dreaming about the finish line. My body is weary; I should not have started this race. I'm going to take a long rest after this—a very long rest. My cough was an indication that my resistance was too low for serious racing, but I was not wise enough to read my body's signs.

As I approach the finish line, I start laughing. I am so tired and happy to get off that road. I finish fifth in 6:29:25. I'm surprised that I could finish so fast with so much walking. I learn that Ken Rogotzke won in 5:48:35, while forty-six year old Bob Olson was second in 6:01:01. These are fast times for this difficult course.

I grab my sweat clothes and walk the half-mile back to the motel room with Kathy. She tells me that I still look good, but I know better. "I'm not going to race again for some time, I need a long rest."

Following this my legs were stiff for nine days. A few weeks later my left heel began to hurt and prevented me from racing until February of the next year.

7

Racing All Day

In this chapter we examine races of 100 miles and twenty-four hours. In the past, runners were warned to avoid these distances, or advised to try them at the conclusion of a career as a grand finale to serious competition. Few ever raced these lengths more than once. Even the great Ted Corbitt established the present American record of 13:33:06 for 100 miles in 1969, in his first and only attempt at the distance. At that time there were so few 100 mile races that Corbitt went to England to set the record. He also established an American record of 134.7 miles for twenty four hours, again in England and again in his only try at the event. In those days runners saw these as grotesquely long marathons, to be run every step of the way. Walking was not yet considered a serious skill within the sport, even though both these records could be matched by an athlete who knew the art of mixing. Since running the entire distance would sometimes "destroy" the runner, it was thought best—perhaps correctly—to retire after one such race.

Today we know that twenty-four hour runs, as well as 100 milers, are well within the capacity of trained athletes who mix walking and running. By doing this, such distances can be enjoyed and not feared. I have run three twenty-four hour runs in the past three years, as well as two 100-milers. In all these races I combined walking and running and had very positive experiences. My best twenty-four hour distance is 114 miles, and my fastest 100 miles was run in 16:11:15. While these are far short of records, they provided me with an opportunity to explore new dimensions of my athletic potential. They were not devastating; in fact, my recovery from these ultras was more rapid than recovery after many difficult marathons.

Continuous Running or Mixing

While many well-trained runners can race fifty-milers using only steady running, only the world's finest athletes should attempt to cover 100 miles without some walking. It would be far easier to negotiate 100 miles in fourteen hours by mixing than it would by trotting at a steady 8:24 mile pace. One hundred miles in fourteen hours in an excellent time, and would win most races of this length. In a 1978 100-mile road race that was run in New York City, my good friend Nick Marshall tried steady running and turned in a brilliant 14:37:05 performance, the sixth best American ever at this distance. Unfortunately Nick's legs have not yet returned to normal, even though a full year has elapsed. Nick is one of the finest athletes ever to attempt these distances, and I have respect for him as a competitor. No doubt he will soon recover and we will once again match strides on the track and road, but I would not want to endure the frustration that I know he feels when he cannot race.

On the other hand, Park Barner established the American twenty-four hour run record in 1978 without walking a single step. Park stopped only twice, once to change shoes and once for a bowel movement. There is no doubt that he has exceptional genetic gifts for this activity; the average ultramarathoner would take great risks if he used steady running only in races of this length.

Road and Track

Nearly all twenty-four hour runs take place on quarter-mile tracks. Races of 100 miles are also frequently run on a track, and when a road is used the course usually consists of a small loop that is repeated many times. Tracks and small loops are desirable because they require far less help from officials. These days, runners are never in short supply, but it is often difficult to find volunteers to help direct the race.

Many would-be ultramarathoners are intimidated by the track. They fear that circling a small oval all day will be unbelievably monotonous and detrimental to their performance. Surprisingly, most athletes who have run in long track races discover that boredom is rarely a concern. Ultramarathons are not even like 10,000 meter races. Here you do much more than simply circle the track. You walk, drink, eat, do exercises, reverse direction, sit, stop and talk to reporters and even nap on occasion. There is far too much happening in an ultra to ever cause boredom.

Most runners who have tried twenty-four hours on the track, and have been schooled in mixing, find upon finishing that they are eager to do it again. Rather than experiencing boredom, they discover that the track becomes a good friend. Where else can you find refreshment every quarter mile? There is no concern for losing your way, and officials can help a man if he gets into difficulty.

Because long distance track races have not been common during the past fifty years, one important feature has been ignored by race directors–reversing direction. In bygone pedestrian races, athletes were often free to reverse the direction in which they had circled the track. This is healthy for the legs and feet. While I am not recommending that runners reverse at will, they can reverse en masse, when directed by an official, to avoid chaos.

One simple way to coordinate the reversal of a race is to have an official blow a whistle at the end of each half hour period. At this signal, the runners complete the present lap, then turn around when they reach the starting point. Runners who have not yet reversed stay on the inside lane, while those who have just turned around run a bit wide. In this way the switch can be completed in a minute or two without collisions or confusion.

Last year I raced 100 miles over a track on which reversing was not possible because a twenty-four hour relay was also in progress. At about seventy miles I began to have trouble with my left ankle. After the race the ankle became swollen and remained so for over a week. In contrast, I have finished three twenty-four hour runs and one twelve-hour run in which the runners reversed each half hour. I had no difficulty at all with my ankles in these races. For some reason, reversing seems necessary only in the longest races. I never had difficulty in fifty-milers on a track where reversing is never considered.

Nick Marshall, who has the fifth best American time for one hundred miles
(Ed Dodd photo)

Lap Counting

In races of many laps, counting can be a major problem. At times the race officials will miscount, and unless you are alert and can verify their counts, you will lose valuable distance. Few runners can count their own laps; it is too easy to become confused. Small, hand-held counters can make this task easier. The runner carrying such a counter can click it each time a lap is completed. While this method is not 100 percent reliable, it does allow the runner to check the official lap count periodically. Metal counters are sturdier than those made of plastic and thus are a better value.

Resting, Exercising, Sleeping

Besides walking, the runner can also take brief rest periods during which he leaves the track and sits or lies down. When I established my personal record at 100 miles, I stopped every ten miles and rested for a few minutes. Then I lifted my feet above my head for several minutes more. On returning to the track, I always felt refreshed by this respite.

Some runners have found that various stretching exercises are invigorating during these stops. In case of fatigue, the runner might even consider a brief nap. I have watched runners grow stiff and weary during twenty-four hour races, only to return from a thirty minute nap looking like they just began running. These techniques sound strange to the uninitiated, but they are part of the sport of ultramarathoning, and they make it possible for ordinary runners to cover surprisingly large distances.

In addition to rests and naps, other methods, including massage, can be used to revive the runners. The great Rhodesian Arthur Newton, who held many world records from fifty miles to twenty-four hours in the 1930s, chose to stop during his twenty-four hour record race to take a hot bath and have a complete dinner, immediately upon completing one hundred miles. He then returned to the track and ran over fifty miles more!

Psychological Preparation

The runner's attitude towards racing should become more casual as the distance increases. Marathons can be run with a certain intensity, but such intensity must be tempered considerably if fifty miles is to be completed. In races of 100 miles the approach is so casual that the scene resembles a workout rather than a race. This is true for all but a handful of world-class runners who can actually run all day long.

The thought of entering a twenty-four hour track race can be very frightening. For this reason I always promise myself that I will be especially timid in my approach to such a race. Unlike my policy for a fifty-miler, I won't "engage" other runners in direct competition in a race of 100 miles. In fact, I promise myself that this will be a day of fun. After all, I'll be free of work and family cares. Nothing more serious than gently walking and running around an oval need concern me. If I get tired, I sit down. If I get hungry, I eat. If I get weary, I sleep. What could be easier?

I will now describe my first twenty-four hour track run. It will allow the reader to see how different principles we have examined are put into practice.

Wednesday, December 8, 1976

I have been studying the efforts of the great pedestrians of the nineteenth century. I am convinced that the secret of their ability to cover 500 to 600 miles in six days lies in their combination of running and walking. Tomorrow, for the first time, I am going to put this theory to a test. I will circle the track for twenty-four hours, and while my greatest previous distance afoot was sixty miles, I am convinced that I can surpass one hundred miles by using this rediscovered technique.

I will be running alone, but the college and community have taken notice of my trial. Each year the students at Glassboro State sponsor Project Santa, a fundraising drive for needy families at Christmas. My run will help in this effort.

A reporter from the local newspaper visits my home in the afternoon. As I relate my strategy for covering more than 400 laps of the track, I notice that my wife Kathy is growing uneasy. After the interview I ask if anything is wrong. We have been married for eleven years, and she has seen me off to hundreds of races without concern. But now Kathy confesses that she is afraid. "The whole idea sounds crazy, and you're apt to kill yourself!" I try to convince her that I have no plans to be "heroic," and that I will simply come home if I get too tired. I don't think she believes me.

Pat Barrett, a three-hour marathoner herself, has driven from her home in north Jersey to help count laps and be my handler. Pat graduated from Glassboro last June and had been my frequent training partner for three years. I retire to bed at 9 p.m. while Pat and Kathy renew their friendship.

I set the alarm for 4 a.m. for a 5 a.m. start. I try to sleep, but it's impossible. I'm like a child waiting for Christmas. I can't wait to get on that track and start running. Over and over I review my plans. I will start by running seven laps, then walking one, running seven, walk one, and so on. If this becomes too difficult I will switch to running three and walking one. If that in turn is too hard, I will alternately run and walk single laps.

I lay still, but don't sleep. Usually I have no difficulty sleeping, but tonight I keep thinking of the old pedestrians. Tomorrow I will have my first chance to feel what they felt. I will start in darkness, I will watch the sunrise, I will see the day unfold. The sun will set, but I will go on into the night. Great!

The night passes without sleep. I rise at 4 a.m. Bob Zazzali, my training partner, who will be running several miles with me during the day, arrives to drive Pat and me to the track. I think about my lost sleep, but I should be fine even without it. Two nights without sleep would be a disaster, but I can survive one.

The Start (5 a.m.)

There is just enough stray light from the parking lot to light the school's cinder track. It is 20 degrees, with no wind. I am wearing ski pajamas on my legs, two sweat shirts, gloves and a hat to guard against the cold.

A few professors and students are there to run a few miles, and without ceremony we start running at 2 minutes past 5 a.m.

I try to relax, but my legs are bursting with energy. I pass the first lap at a 7:30 mile pace. This is ridiculous! At this rate I will set the world's record. Still, I cannot get control of my nerves. Seven laps pass—time to walk. I've never done this before, and my body resists what seems like a highly unnatural pause.

Finally, after covering six miles in 49:49, I have stilled my nerves and walk my first lap. I should have walked earlier, but I have never run and walked in training, and I found it impossible. In the future I'll know better! After the first hour I have established the proper ratio of seven laps run to one lap walked. At last I am in control of myself. Phase one of this effort will continue until 1 p.m. In phase one running should be effortless and not tiring. While the effort is easy, I cannot relax completely, for the wind is beginning to pick up. I hate cold weather, and twenty degrees with wind is very cold.

My long-time friend Neil Weygandt is running the first fifty

Osler and Zazzali at the finish of the twenty-four hour run at Glassboro State, 1976 (Ed Dodd photo)

miles with me. Neil is a 2:40 marathoner; I assure him that he will succeed by using our technique of strategic walking.

The sun is shining brightly and the cinder track is starting to thaw. When we started, the track was frozen hard. By 10 a.m. it had a pleasant soft sponginess, but by noon portions of the inside lane were under water. Apparently there were ice crystals frozen in the cinders and now they have melted. The track has become so soggy that it is nearly impossible to run comfortably on the inside lane. I was aware before the race that this might happen. The outermost lane of the track is in good shape, and at forty-five miles I begin to run there. I won't be able to return to the inside lane because of its soggy state. Since ten laps on the long outside lane equals eleven on the inside, the conversion to 440-yard laps is easy. After I run ten laps, I give myself a free one!

I have been reversing direction every half hour. Not only does this equalize the strain on my legs, it also provides an opportunity to view the stadium from a slightly different perspective. Every mile I check my hand-held lap counter. I confirm my progress with Pat Barrett, who is also keeping count.

Phase one ends with Neil and me passing 50 miles in 8:08:13. Neil stops and joins Pat to help with the lap counting. I stop and walk to the field house, only 50 yards away, for a bowel movement.

Phase Two

As I return to the track, I feel some slight fatigue. This is surprising, since I felt great when I left just ten minutes earlier. Now phase two has begun, and while I can't expect my legs to trot on without some urging on my part, still I must remain very comfortable or the final eight hours will be wasted.

After running for twelve hours, the sun starts to set. I have anticipated this moment since I tossed and turned sleeplessly last night. My running speed is now about eleven minutes per mile, but I feel reasonably strong and am truly able to enjoy the twilight. I have run seventy miles. Many students and faculty came to the track in the afternoon to run a few miles with me, and as darkness sets in, more arrive.

I pass eighty miles in 14:06:27, but I am no longer comfortable.

I shouldn't be this fatigued until phase three! Twenty miles to go before I reach 100, and at this rate that will take four more hours. I am really finding this unpleasant, but I maintain the seven to one running and walking ratio.

At eighty-five miles, a small musical group arrives on the track. They are somewhat tipsy, but still able to circle with me while playing reasonably well. The carnival atmosphere they generate is just what I need to forget my somber trot. They stay for only ten minutes, but they succeed in rescuing me from self-doubt. I continue on with renewed cheer.

Phase Three

I pass ninety miles in 16:09:39. Phase three is just beginning, but I don't see how I will be able to run much beyond 100 miles. As I near the 100-mile goal, however, my spirits rise. I grow more optimistic and the fatigue slips from my shoulders. A small crowd of friends, students and reporters has gathered for the conclusion of the first one hundred miles.

Much relieved, I reach one hundred miles in 18:19:27. Our college president greets me and I briefly enjoy one of the most fulfilling moments of my running career. I feel a desperate need to leave the track and sit down. Kathy has brought a large bowl of spaghetti, and I retire to the field house to enjoy it. I change my clothes and lie down for fifteen minutes, during which time I actually sleep. I am in the field house for fifty-three minutes before I return to the track for the final five hours of the night.

It is very cold, but the wind is still when I walk back down to the cinders. After sunset, the soft track has frozen again; this time it froze in ruts since so many runners had left footprints during the day. Fortunately, the outside lane remained passable throughout the twenty-four hours.

I try to run a few steps, but my legs feel incredibly heavy. To my horror, running is no longer possible. (In retrospect, I made two mistakes. I should have taken several rest breaks during the day, and I should not have eaten so large a dinner. In addition, a nap of thirty minutes to an hour at this point might have enabled me to begin running again.)

If I could no longer run, I could still walk comfortably at three miles per hour. Students are night people, and many of them joined me as I slowly circled the track. By 5 a.m. I had walked fourteen miles for a total of 114 miles in twenty-four hours.

After a short interview on the college radio station, Neil and Pat drove me home. Kathy was relieved to find me alive, and we all went to the living room to discuss the day's events. I fell asleep quickly while the others chatted, much to their amusement.

While my effort had created interest in Project Santa, it had another effect as well. Pat and Neil met on that icy track for the first time. What they said during the long hours spent counting my laps will never be known. Santa's spirit was at work, though, for they became engaged shortly thereafter and are now married.

Post-Run Recovery

After spending a sleepless night Thursday, followed by running all day and night on Friday, I imagined that I would sleep most of the next day when I returned from the track. While I did take a few brief naps during the day I really felt no need for extended sleep.

Having suffered long recovery periods from prior marathon races, and even longer recovery times after fifty-milers, I also anticipated that bouncing back from the twenty-four hour effort might be even worse. I was delighted to find that this was not so. In particular, there was no leg soreness at all. The following day I tested my legs by running a few steps. They felt a bit heavy, but they produced a smooth, pain-free stride. Nevertheless I thought it best to avoid any real running for three days, and when I did resume training, I only jogged a few miles each day for an additional week.

In subsequent long races which mixed considerable walking with running, I experienced comparable recovery. Leg stiffness, which can be painful for a week following a marathon of fifty-miler, is rarely present. In spite of my feeling of well-being immediately following such efforts, I still believe that it is best to forego normal training for at least a week to insure that no unexpected injury develops.

Statistics

The graph on page 237 shows the number of miles I covered during each of the twenty-four hours. It is interesting to note that the run actually does divide itself into three phases of about eight hours each. During the first phase I averaged about six miles per hour, but during the second this drops to five miles per hour. Since I was reduced to walking for most of phase three, my speed dropped to about 3.5 miles per hour.

A close inspection of the data collected during this run reveals that of the 114 miles I traveled in the twenty-four hour period, 88.5 were run while 25.5 were walked. The time spent running was fourteen hours and twenty minutes, while I walked for seven hours and fifty minutes. Counting all stops I was off the track for one hour and fifty minutes. Thus only fourteen of the twenty-four hours were spent in actual running. While running, my average pace was 9:43 per mile, and while walking it was 18:28.

Many people feel that a steady pace is best for racing at short distances. But is it also best for a twenty-four hour run? True to my novice standing in this ultramarathon, my speed declined without interruption over the day. My goal, still far away, would be to blend running with walking so well that the final eight hours are as productive as the first.

24 HOUR RUN AT GLASSBORO STATE COLLEGE
(CINDER TRACK) DECEMBER 9 - 10, 1976

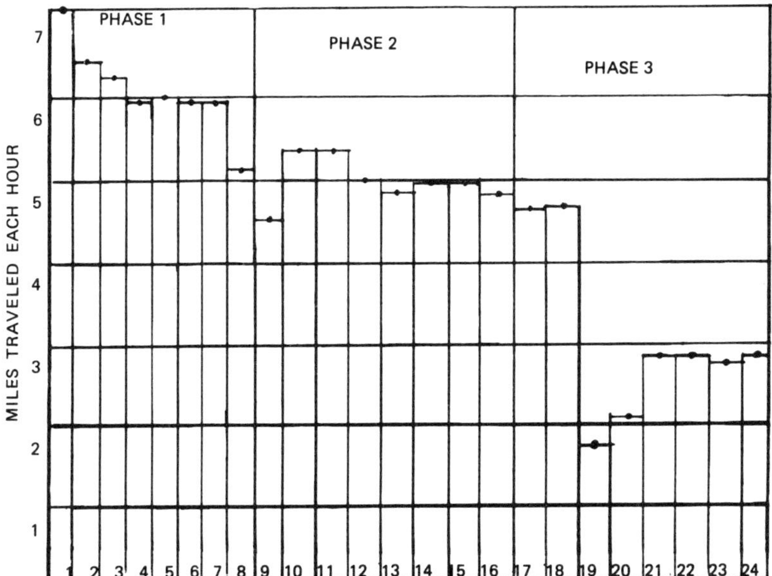

8

Racing for Several Days—Part 1

Very few races in America are scheduled to extend beyond one day. Such races had been popular among professional pedestrians in the nineteenth century but professional long distance walking and running has been dead since the great transcontinental foot races of 1928 and 1929. Should amateur runners attempt such efforts? Park Barner ran a solo 200 miles from Harrisburg to Pittsburgh in 1978 shortly before establishing the American twenty-four hour track record. Recently I ran for three days (200 miles in seventy hours) at Dr. David Costill's Human Performance Laboratory in Muncie, Indiana. Even such demanding runs need not be feared if undertaken properly; they can offer many athletes a chance to explore areas of physical and mental capacity not often tapped.

By the time George Littlewood established the six-day record of 623.75 miles in 1888, the art of the pedestrian had reached great sophistication. Unfortunately that art is now lost. This chapter reports on my own recent three-day trial, and attempts to draw modest conclusions from it.

Sleeping

Sleep is clearly essential in events longer than twenty-four hours. The question really is, how much is enough? Before my three-day trial I was concerned that I would need at least six hours per day. I was surprised to find that I averaged three hours and thirty minutes each day without ever feeling deprived of sleep.

The great pedestrians of the six-day races normally slept only three or four hours per day. (The day before the contest started they would sleep as much as possible.) Newspaper accounts tell us that they would enter their tents, sleep for 30 minutes, awaken, and immediately resume traveling.

Many runners sleep for eight hours each day. How can they hope to get by on half that amount while expending so much energy, shall we say, for several days running? Perhaps the answer is not the total hours of sleep, but the quality of that sleep. Research shows that the deeper kind of sleep, known as REM (rapid eye movement) sleep, is more restful than the earlier, lighter slumber. Runners who can immediately fall into and awaken from REM sleep have a distinct advantage in ultramarathoning.

My sleeping pattern is unusual. I often nap for an hour or two in the afternoon. I go to bed at ten but get up at 1 a.m. for three hours of reading followed by two or three more hours of sleep. I am not recommending this schedule for others, and relate it because it was a factor during my three-day run. Weston had demonstrated that it is best to eat and sleep during a six-day effort at roughly the same times that one would during an ordinary day. A race extending over several days is best approached as a series of ordinary days during which a great deal of running is done at all times other than those reserved for eating and sleeping.

A pattern that emerged during my three-day run was as follows:

1pm - Lunch	1:30pm - Sleep for thirty minutes
7pm - Supper	7:30pm - Sleep for one hour
1am - Snack	1:15pm - Sleep for forty-five minutes
5am - Snack	5:15am - Sleep for seventy-five minutes
7am - Breakfast	

I chose to sleep immediately after eating since it is difficult to run on a full stomach. In each case I fell alseep easily.

It was better to awaken from sleep naturally than to be jolted awake by an alarm; starting to run again is much easier. Only once in three days did I use an alarm clock, and I had a rough time returning to the track.

Eating and Drinking

Unlike races of a day or shorter, three days spent running make solid nutrition essential. In 100-milers or twenty-four hour efforts an athlete can get by on sugared drinks, if he or she has sufficient nutritional reserves. In events lasting three days or more, genuine meals must be eaten.

Earlier I examined how breakfast, lunch and supper might be coordinated with time spent sleeping. It is probably best to eat during the event at approximately the same time of day at which you normally would.

What you eat and drink should also not be too different from foods that you normally prefer. It's likely that a few rich desserts such as pie and cake will help. Large quantities of fluid should be taken continually to avoid dehydration. I have found that fruit juices, coffee, tea and powdered milk mixed with sugar were all effective.

Reviving

It is surprising how quickly runners can revive after a short time spent off their feet. During my efforts at twenty-four hours as well as my recent three-day run I would frequently find myself growing slightly weary while running and walking. After a brief rest, lasting from fifteen minutes for a small snack to two hours for a meal and a nap, I would return to the track. Getting started was always a bit hard, but after about twenty minutes of motion I would begin to feel refreshed and could continue for several hours in good spirits.

As always, the reader must decide upon, through experiment, the effectiveness of these techniques for his or her particular body.

Walking

The longer the run, the greater the importance of walking. While trained runners need not worry about practicing long walks for efforts of twenty-four hours or less, this isn't true for races of three days and up. During my best effort at twenty-four hours I ran eighty-nine miles and walked twenty-five. The walking gave me no problems in spite of the fact that I never walk further than one mile on ordinary days. During my 200 mile effort in seventy hours, I walked a full 100 miles in short segments; here the walking gave me great difficulty. Perhaps I made a mistake in choosing to walk so much. Nevertheless, I believe that I must now practice long walks if I am to attempt such trials again.

Why should training in walking be necessary for the trained runner? If an athlete wants to cover one hundred miles or more by using walking in a race of several days duration, then he or she had best become efficient in his walking style. I soon found that my walk was very energy consuming. In addition, walking places different stresses on the feet. I never get blisters while running, but I did get bad ones from prolonged walking. I need to toughen my feet so that they can also handle walking many miles.

I have outlined my suggestions for sleeping, eating, reviving and walking during pedestrian efforts lasting several days. I will now briefly describe my own three-day trial in order to put these theories in a practical setting.

A THREE DAY TRIAL

Wednesday, April 28, 1979

I am flying into Muncie, Indiana. Tomorrow at 7 a.m. I shall begin my first run longer than one day, a three-day trial. Through the winter, as usual, my training mileage has been low. I have averaged fifty-five miles per week since December; worse, my weight is up twelve pounds. I have no special schedule of when to eat, sleep, rest, walk, or run, but I will decide these things as the event progresses.

At the airport I am met by Dr. David Costill, Director of the Human Performance Laboratory at Ball State University. This laboratory is well-known for its studies of runners. The world's greatest athletes have come here for scientific analysis, and I am delighted that Costill wants to have my trial here. He informs me that he has a crew of twelve graduate assistants to record data during the run. They will analyze blood samples, oxygen, urine, and weight as well as record distances, times and psychological impressions.

Costill drives me to the lab and shows me his equipment. The lab is impressive, but I'm particularly interested in the track. There is a half-mile macadam oval passing through a park-like area of the campus that I can use during the daylight hours. A field house containing an indoor eight-lap-to-the-mile dirt track will be used at night. Both are within a few seconds walk of the laboratory.

At 7 p.m. Costill and I meet with the support crew. After he reviews their schedule of experiments, I explain to them my reasons for attempting this run. I relate briefly the story of the great pedestrians of the past, with emphasis on my hero Weston. I confess that at present I know nothing about how such efforts are best negotiated, but I will learn and this is my school. Ultimately I want to try six days, in an attempt to cover 500 miles. The crew is enthusiastic; most are distance runners themselves. Without their help such a trial would be impossible.

Costill shows me the remaining preparations. There is a complete kitchen as well as a small private room for sleeping right in the lab. Everything I need is here.

I go to bed at 9 p.m. and sleep soundly for eight hours at Costill's home. Unlike my twenty-four hour run described above prior to which I did not sleep at all, I now have the advantage of a full night's sleep. Sleep lost before a twenty-four hour effort is of little consequence, but sleep missed before a three-day effort would certainly be reflected in a reduced performance.

After a breakfast of yogurt and coffee we drive to the lab. It is 6:30 a.m. and I am amazed to find everyone working so hard. Preliminary tests delay the start and I begin at 7:25 a.m.

The First Day—Thursday April 26, 1979

I walk out the lab door to greet a partly overcast breezy morning. It is 64 degrees, delightful weather were it not for the wind. I walk the first mile in fifteen minutes, then I begin alternately running and walking the half-mile laps. My walking style is excessive; I lean forward and come down with my leg straight, like a modified "goose step." In contrast, my running form is smooth and easy. Dave Elgar, a 2:25 marathoner himself, is timing my laps. I am running at ten minutes per mile and walking at fourteen. I am surprised that I can walk that fast.

As I circle the little oval, I enjoy looking at the budding spring landscape. Fresh grass and blossoming trees are everywhere. The path is crowded with students and faculty running in both directions. I always enjoy watching others run. I can study their style in relation to their build and weight. Watching the women run is an extra treat.

At twenty miles I begin to feel a strange sensation on the callus beneath the ball of my right foot. It doesn't hurt, but I am alert to any possible problem. Little do I know that this is the start of a deep blister that will be my greatest concern in the final stages of the run.

After completing twenty-three miles I break for lunch. My bowel movement is very loose, probably due to the grape juice which I am drinking every mile. I have to correct this stomach problem if I am to get needed nutrition from my food.

I had mentioned to Costill last night that today is my thirty-ninth birthday, and the lab assistants now appear with a huge cake. One quarter of it was reserved for me, and I managed to eat it all before the day was over. A tough stomach is a real friend in ultramarathons, and my stomach is my greatest asset. I head for my private room where I fall asleep for twenty-five minutes. When I return to the track, I find that lunch and sleep have taken only fifty-two minutes.

I continue to alternate running and walking half-mile laps. I am now running faster, and walking slower than I did in the morning; I run at eight minutes per mile speed and walk at sixteen. Pete Watson, himself a swimmer and marathoner and a member of my support crew, begins to walk with me. I tell him that the walking is starting to feel harder than the running. Pete reveals that the entire crew has been concerned about my walking stride. It looked excessive to them, but they chose to remain silent. How right they were! My thighs were beginning to stiffen and I had not yet travelled thirty miles. I notice that the thighs are stiff when I walk, but not when I run. This is terrible! Thigh stiffness is usually a severe sign of fatigue. In desperation I try to alter my walking stride. By bending my knee as my foot makes contact and by walking more erect, the stiffness starts to disappear. Blessed relief!

Since lunch I have been drinking powdered milk with extra sugar. This delightful drink tastes like a milkshake. I have never tried it before, and Costill is worried that the milk will be difficult to digest. It isn't, and more importantly, it is helping to tighten my bowels.

By 5 p.m. I am growing weary from so much walking. Perhaps I have erred in choosing to run and walk equal distances. I thought walking would be restful, but it is in fact more tiring than running. I decide to change my ratio to three laps running for each lap walking. This feels much better.

By 7:30 p.m. I reach fifty miles and gladly stop for dinner. Mrs. Costill has prepared a delicious hot meal, and I devour it with delight. After dinner I take a forty-five minute nap from which I awaken very refreshed. This whole break took one hour and forty minutes.

It is 9 p.m.—too dark to run on the outdoor half mile oval. But the indoor facility is dreary. There is nothing cheerful about this giant quonset hut. The track is made of dirt, is very dusty, and measures eight laps to the mile, just like the original Madison Square Garden. At least I have something in common with Weston; I am now on a track similar to those that he made famous.

I am surprised at how quickly I get into motion again. I walk the first mile as a warm-up, then begin running 1.5 miles and walking 0.5 miles in a repetitive run-walk mixture. This feels very comfortable, and I continue in this way for an additional twenty miles.

At 1:30 a.m. I leave the track and take another nap. Fearing that I might sleep until morning, I ask to be awakened within an hour. I awoke from my previous naps without assistance, but this time I must be stirred.

On returning to the track I have great difficulty starting. Why did I get up? I want to sleep. I feel depressed for the first time. I promise myself that I'll never try this again. Perhaps I should quit at forty-eight hours and return to my family.

I share these thoughts with my assistants, and we agree that I must have been awakened during a deep segment of sleep. In the future I will allow myself to sleep until I am ready to get up. After thirty minutes, energy begins to return to my body and my stride becomes easy, but now the pain in the ball of my right foot is growing more noticeable. Costill examined it earlier and suspected that a deep blister was forming under the callus. Since

I have never before had blisters in this location, I was a bit skeptical of his diagnosis. However, I had already walked thirty-five miles. I've never before walked that far in one day, and I believe that this has caused the problem.

At 5:30 a.m. I leave the track, having completed eighty-two miles. This time I'll sleep as long as I like!

The Second Day

I arise at 7 a.m. after sleeping for ninety minutes. In the lab Costill and his crew are busy at work. They seem surprised that I appear fresh, and frankly, I am too. I thought I would want more sleep. A few hours ago I was looking for an excuse to quit, but now I'm eager to get started.

When I leave the lab at 7:30 a.m. I am greeted by warm sunshine. The morning is beautiful, and for once there is no wind. Convinced that I walked too much yesterday, I select a run-walk rhythm of 1.5 running miles to 0.5 walking. I feel great; even better than I did yesterday. The lab assistants continue to take periodic blood samples and every hour they also tap my "exhaust" by having me breathe into a large bag for two minutes as I walk and run. Besides the four major rest periods during which I eat and sleep, there are approximately ten short "stops" during which I change clothes, record my body weight and relieve my bowels if necessary.

I pass 100 miles at 11:30 and decide to celebrate by lying down in Costill's office for twenty-one minutes. One of the assistants is busy working at the newly purchased microcomputer. I own a similar computer and keep it in my office at home. For a few moments I forget the run as we discuss his programming problems.

I enjoy lunch and a short nap as I did yesterday, but when I return to the track in the afternoon the ball of my right foot is mildly uncomfortable. At 4:30 p.m. I ask Costill to examine it again, and now he is sure that it's a blister. He places two small pieces of mole foam on either side of the blister to remove the pressure. When I return to the track I am amazed to find that the discomfort is entirely gone! I can't even tell which foot is giving me trouble. I do have one reservation. Will the mole foam itself cause trouble later? It is always dangerous to change things inside a shoe.

I quit for dinner at 6:30 p.m. having completed 122 miles. If I maintain this pace, I could complete 250 miles in three days, the pace required for finishing 500 miles in six days. On paper it looks easy, but on the track it's proving harder than I had anticipated. I sit down to a large dinner of yogurt, cheese, bread, lettuce, pie and ice cream, and then sleep for one hour.

I resume running at 9 p.m. on the little indoor track. Pete Watson arrives with his stereo, and the air is filled with the sounds of his favorite rock albums. I love music of all types, opera, classical, rock, disco, you name it. I find that running to the beat of the records is very enjoyable. In the old Madison Square Garden pedestrian contests a band played all day long. How this must have helped the pros!

I am still running 1.5 miles, then walking 0.5, but my legs are growing stiff. I'm not really concerned, though I am well into phase two of the trial, and I should be feeling some effort.

Suddenly at 11 p.m. I feel tremondous pain in the little toe of my right foot. We head for the lab and examine the foot. The mole foam that so effectively solved the problem on the ball of my foot has itself created a blister on the little toe. That blister broke while running and has left the skin really raw. Jeff Miller, Pete Watson and Dave Elger work at devising various pads for the toe. All fail. It looks like I'm going to quit, for I can't even walk slowly on this foot without a severe limp. As a last measure, I pull off the mole foam and place a band aid over the toe. Amazingly, the pain is gone.

I return to the track and run for only five more minutes. I solved the toe problem, but with the mole foam gone, the original blister is again bothersome. I feel weary but am convinced that I will be able to continue. I decide to sleep.

We worked on the blister for an hour, and I now sleep for an additional ninety minutes. When I return to the track at 3 a.m., my foot feels better running than it does walking. Why didn't I take long walks in training?

My body is reasonably fresh and willing to work. If only this foot would snap back! By 5 a.m. I have completed 144 miles. I retire again for 90 minutes sleep, hoping that I will awaken with renewed freshness as I did yesterday morning.

The Third Day

I return to the track at 7 a.m. I feel good, but my legs are noticeably weaker. The weather has also turned blustery and overcast with an occasional drizzle. I have to dress warmly.

For the first time, running is no longer comfortable. I decide to run the half lap into the wind, and walk the other half with the wind. In this way I will be warm when I walk.

By 11 a.m. I have reached 160 miles, but my foot is deteriorating rapidly. I stop for thirty minutes and try to alter the shoe so that the ball of my foot doesn't hurt, but nothing really helps. I could travel well if only I didn't have this blister. I begin to calculate how far I can go if I stop running and only walk. There are twenty hours left, and if I walk two miles per hour I will reach 200 miles. It is clear that I cannot cover 250 miles as I had hoped.

By 1 p.m. I have managed 165 miles. I stop for lunch and a nap of forty-five minutes. As always I return to the track feeling refreshed. It is amazing how quickly the body can revive after a good meal and a nap.

By 3 p.m. my run has become an eleven minutes per mile shuffle. I hate running this slowly, and decide to continue with walking only. My foot severely reduces the otherwise pleasant pedestrian stroll. My path takes me past a ten-story dormatory. In one of the upper windows someone has placed a sign in letters four feet high reading, "Go Tom." That sign sure helps lighten my steps. I have circled this path so many times that I was bound to attract some attention. Occasionally as a student passes by, I hear an encouraging "you can do it!" I still think I can cover 200 miles, but I had hoped to do it more pleasantly.

I eat dinner at 7:30 p.m., and I am desperate to relieve the pain in my right foot. I have covered 178 miles, and have twelve hours left in which to cover only twenty-two miles. I take a safety pin and begin to probe the callus under the ball of my foot. If there really is a blister there, letting the fluid out should reduce the pain. Sure enough, a small quantity of clear fluid oozes out. But when I try walking, I discover that I have made the problem worse; I now feel a burning sensation. I rub vaseline into the blister and cover the area with mole skin.

I return to the indoor track and begin walking at 8:20 p.m. A small band of students arrives to watch my progress. There is almost a party atmosphere as Pete's records are blasting and a game of frisbee is begun. I feel embarrassed that I cannot run with so many people watching. At 10 a.m. Dave arrives carrying half a warm cherry pie on an aluminum plate. He holds the plate for me as I circle the track while gorging myself. What a sight I must be!

By 11:30 p.m. I have covered 189 miles and I decide to take my last nap. When I lie down the balls of my feet itch terribly. I rip off the mole skin protection and rub them furiously. How *good* that feels.

I sleep for only twenty-five minutes. I'm excited by the thought of finishing those last eleven miles.

On returning to the track I find that the blister really begins to hurt so I decide to walk very slowly. Soon the pain subsides to the level of discomfort; to keep the pain away, I stop after each mile and lift my feet over my head for five minutes. By 5:25 a.m. seventy hours after starting, I have completed 200 miles. Two hours remain in the three-day period, but I have no stomach for more walking.

I walk back into the lab. What a filthy mess I am! I shower and shave for the first time in three days, and cannot help but laugh as I retire for a few hours sleep. This has been harder than I expected. I never thought that walking would undo a trained runner, but I now know that my lack of experience in walking caused the blister. Nevertheless, I'm happy. I now know that sleep is no real problem in these trials; I need only three or four hours per day. In spite of the uncomfortable blister I feel fresh, and wonder when I can try this again!

Post Trial Recovery

In the days following this run I did not require any additional sleep. I was, however, more accident prone. I was especially careful while driving, for fatigue had caused my reactions to slow. I did very little running for ten days, as is my practice following ultramarathons. The blister slowly healed and there was no problem with leg soreness.

Statistics

I have given a narrative description of my three-day trial. For

TABLE 1

TOM OSLER'S 3 DAY PEDESTRIAN TRIAL
BALL STATE UNIVERSITY, MUNCIE, INDIANA
April 26-29, 1979

TIME OF DAY START OF EACH HOUR		HOUR	DAY ONE TOTAL DISTANCE	DAY ONE MILES PER HOUR	DAY TWO TOTAL DISTANCE	DAY TWO MILES PER HOUR	DAY THREE TOTAL DISTANCE	DAY THREE MILES PER HOUR
A.M.	7:25	1	4.75	4.75	86	4	149.75	4.25
	8:25	2	9.75	5	91	5	153.5	3.75
	9:25	3	14.25	4.5	96.25	5.25	157	3.5
	10:25	4	18.5	3.75	100	3.75	160	3
	11:25	5	23	4.5	102	2	162.75	2.75
P.M.	12:25	6	23.5	0.5	102.25	0.25	165	2.25
	1:25	7	28	4.5	106.5	4.25	165	0
	2:25	8	32.75	4.75	110.25	3.75	167.5	2.5
	3:25	9	37.25	4.5	115	4.75	171	3.5
	4:25	10	40.5	3.25	117	2	174.5	3.5
	5:25	11	45	4.5	121.75	4.75	177	2.5
	6:25	12	49.5	4.5	121.75	0	178.5	1.5

(Table 1 continued on page 250.)

TABLE 1 Continued

TIME OF DAY START OF EACH HOUR	HOUR	DAY ONE		DAY TWO		DAY THREE	
		TOTAL DISTANCE	MILES PER HOUR	TOTAL DISTANCE	MILES PER HOUR	TOTAL DISTANCE	MILES PER HOUR
7:25	13	49.5	0	121.75	0	179	0.5
8:25	14	50.75	1.25	124.25	2.5	182.25	3.25
9:25	15	55.5	4.75	129.5	5.25	185	2.75
10:25	16	60	4.5	133	3.5	188	3
11:25	17	65	5	134	1.0	188.5	0.5
A.M. 12:25	18	69.75	4.75	135	1.0	190.5	2
1:25	19	69.75	0	135	0	192.5	2
2:25	20	72	2.25	136.75	1.75	195.5	3
3:25	21	77	5	140.75	4	197.5	2
4:25	22	82	5	144	3.25	200	2.5
5:25	23	82	0	144	0	200	0
6:25	24	82	0	145.5	1.5	200	0

TABLE 2

TOM OSLER'S 3 DAY PEDESTRIAN TRIAL
BALL STATE UNIVERSITY, MUNCIE, INDIANA
April 26-29, 1979

DAY 1			DAY 2			DAY 3		
TIME OF DAY	REST LENGTH	COMMENT	TIME OF DAY	REST LENGTH	COMMENT	TIME OF DAY	REST LENGTH	COMMENT
9:33 a.m.	6		7:54 a.m.	7	overdressed	8:41 a.m.	4	
10:51	12	rain	11:09	21	lay down	9:15	13	
11:12	3		11:59	89	lunch sleep 30	11:14	26	
11:37	6		1:39 p.m.	2		1:05 p.m.	97	lunch sleep 45
12:23 p.m.	52	lunch sleep 25	2:48	13		5:57	9	snack
2:48	2		4:27	28	fix foot	6:47	31	
5:03	16		6:28	139	dinner sleep 60	7:27	51	dinner sleep 20
6:14	6		11:06	6		10:11	2	
7:32	100	dinner sleep 45	11:34	55	work on blister	10:22	4	
11:18	10		12:44 a.m.	132	sleep 90	11:24	3	

(Table 2 continued on page 252.)

TABLE 2 Continued

DAY 1			DAY 2			DAY 3		
TIME OF DAY	REST LENGTH	COMMENT	TIME OF DAY	REST LENGTH	COMMENT	TIME OF DAY	REST LENGTH	COMMENT
1:27 a.m.	87	sleep 50	3:16	5		11:36	55	sleep 25
4:57	6		3:22	5		1:14 a.m.	2	
5:27	119	sleep 90	5:01	116	sleep 90	1:40	6	
			7:12	6	rain	2:34	7	
						3:21	5	
						3:45	6	
						4:09	5	
						4:32	8	
						4:58	7	
						5:25	120	sleep 90
TOTAL	7:02	sleep 3:30	TOTAL	10:24	sleep 4:00	TOTAL	7:41	sleep 3:00

TABLE 3

TOM OSLER'S 3 DAY PEDESTRIAN TRIAL
BALL STATE UNIVERSITY, MUNCIE, INDIANA
April 26-29, 1979

	DAY 1	DAY 2	DAY 3	TOTAL
TOTAL MILES TRAVELED	82	63.5	54.5	200
MILES RUNNING	47	40.5	12	99.5
MILES WALKING	35	23	42.5	100.5
TIME TRAVELING	16:58	13:36	16:19	46:53
TIME RUNNING	7:32	6:42	2:12	16:26
TIME WALKING	9:26	6:54	14:07	30:27
TIME OFF TRACK	7:02	10:24	7:41	25:07
TIME SLEEPING	3:30	4:00	3:00	10:30
AVERAGE SPEED MPH	4.83	4.67	3.34	4.27
AVERAGE RUNNING SPEED MPH	6.24	6.04	5.45	6.05
AVERAGE WALKING SPEED MPH	3.71	3.33	3.01	3.03
NUMBER OF STOPS	13	14	20	47
NUMBER OF TIMES SLEEPING	4	4	4	12

readers who wish to examine the run in minute detail, three tables (see Appendix, pp. 279) provide a complete picture of miles covered, times taken for rests and sleep, speed walking and running, and more.

Table 1 gives a detailed picture of how the mileage progressed each hour as well as the number of miles traveled within each hour. The careful observer can see how I revived after each meal and nap. For example, on the first day I had lunch and slept during the sixth hour; the mileage covered during the next three hours is greater than in the three hours before lunch. This pattern also holds following dinner.

In Table 2 we record the length of each rest period and note periods of sleep. We can see that little time was required for sleep, while much time was spent trying to relieve blisters and alter my shoes.

Table 3 summarizes the important activities of each day. When I first made these computations I was startled to see the comparative number of hours spent running, walking, and off the track. They are:

Hours Running = 16:26
Hours Walking = 30:27
Hours Off Track = 25:07

Over one day was wasted in not moving at all! There is clearly plenty of room for improvement.

9

Racing for Several Days—Part 2

In the previous chapter we examined my own three-day trial at the Human Performance Laboratory in Muncie, Indiana. The three tables provide a detailed breakdown and summation of exactly how the time was allocated during this run. In this chapter we will examine the schedules of two men who had vast experience at such events. First we will look at a pre-race schedule written by Edward Payson Weston, prior to an attempt to walk 500 miles in six days. This plan will be contrasted with observations made by a team of doctors who witnessed a similar trial by Weston. Finally, we will review the six day run by Henry "Blower" Brown of England in 1880, which established a new world's record.

WESTON'S SCHEDULE

Two months before becoming the first person to walk 500 miles in six days, Weston tried the same feat unsuccessfully at New York City's Madison Square Garden, known then as Barnum's Roman Hippodrome. Before this attempt Weston had printed and circulated his pretrial schedule, a fascinating mix of athletic strategy and self-promotion. He announced a goal of 115 miles of the first day and another 400 miles over the remaining five days. This was to be achieved by starting out with twenty-five miles, resting for five minutes, then falling into a steady rhythm of ten miles walking and five minutes resting until 115 miles were done, which, if all goes according to plan, would be by 11:55 p.m., or just under twenty-four hours after beginning. The second day would add eighty-five miles to the total, the next three days eighty each, and on the sixth day Weston would cover seventy-five miles for his total of 515. The small pamphlet containing this schedule had an introduction which ended as follows:

> You will observe that this calculation allows for an extra distance of fifteen miles, which can be dropped on the first day; as walking 100 miles within the first twenty-four hours will, under ordinary circumstances, insure success.
>
> While I am unwilling in any way to prostitute the powers of endurance with which my Maker has endowed me, yet I assure you, on this occasion, I shall use my best efforts to more than meet your most sanguine expectations, and shall ever remain
>
> Faithfully and gratefully yours,
> Edward Payson Weston

Weston was never one to "prostitute" his powers of endurance. He managed only 346 miles in this effort.

Table 1 shows a summary of Weston's approach to the first day. The trial begins at midnight on Monday morning as was the custom. Weston then proposed to walk twenty-five miles without a rest at about five mph. While it's not shown on this table, the actual schedule shows that the first mile of every walking segment is the slowest. Most often he walked the first mile in thirteen to fifteen minutes, but he would begin as slowly as twenty minutes per mile after rising from a night's sleep. Most of the miles on the schedule are to be walked in twelve minutes. After the first twenty-five miles, the schedule is simplicity in itself. He simply walks ten miles, then rests for five minutes; walks ten miles, rests five minutes, etc. Notice that no lengthy meals are eaten! An observer of Weston once wrote:

> During the walk, Mr. Weston took but few regular meals, a great part of his nourishment being taken while actually walking. In this way he took his beef-essence, soft-boiled eggs, gruel, tea, coffee, and all other drinks.

Also note that no sleeping is planned for the first day.

In Table 2 we see Weston's second day effort. Notice that he allows for plenty of sleep at the usual sleeping hours. Most rest periods continue to be only five minutes, but now longer periods are allowed for the usual three meals. It appears that Weston is trying to stay close to his daily habits. He walks eighty-five miles on the second day.

Table 3 shows that days three through six are identical except that he stops one hour early at the end of the last day.

Over the six day period he allows twenty-nine hours and twenty minutes for sleeping, five hours fifty minutes for meals, and two hours twenty minutes for short rests. His actual traveling time is 105 hours twenty minutes and he averages 12:15 per mile pace.

E. P. Weston's Pretrial Schedule
Six Day Solo Walk-Madison Square Garden
October 5-10, 1874

Table 1
THE FIRST DAY

TIME OF DAY	COMMENTS
12:05 a.m.	Start
12:05 to 5:00 a.m.	Walk 25 miles
5:00 a.m.	Rest 5 minutes
5:05 to 7:05 a.m.	Walk 10 miles
7:05 a.m.	Rest 5 minutes
7:10 to 9:11 a.m.	Walk 10 miles
9:11 a.m.	Rest 5 minutes
9:16 to 11:17 a.m.	Walk 10 miles
11:17 a.m.	Rest 5 minutes
11:22 a.m. to 1:24 p.m.	Walk 10 miles
1:24 p.m	Rest 5 minutes
1:29 to 3:30 p.m.	Walk 10 miles
3:30 p.m.	Rest 5 minutes
3:35 to 5:36 p.m.	Walk 10 miles
5:36 p.m.	Rest 5 minutes
5:41 to 7:43 p.m.	Walk 10 miles
7:43 p.m.	Rest 5 minutes
7:48 to 9:49 p.m.	Walk 10 miles
9:49 p.m.	Rest 5 minutes
9:54 to 11:55 p.m.	Walk 10 miles
11:55 p.m.	Retire for sleep.

Table 2
THE SECOND DAY

TIME OF DAY	COMMENTS
11:55 p.m. to 5:15 a.m.	Sleep 5 hrs. 20 mins.
5:15 to 6:21 a.m.	Walk 5 miles
6:21 to 6:51 a.m.	Breakfast (30 mins.)
6:51 to 9:52 a.m.	Walk 15 miles
9:52 a.m.	Rest 5 minutes
9:57 to 11:58 a.m.	Walk 10 miles
11:58 a.m. to 12:18 p.m.	Lunch (20 minutes)
12:18 to 3:21 p.m.	Walk 15 miles
3:21 p.m.	Rest 5 minutes
3:26 to 5:27 p.m.	Walk 10 miles
5:27 to 5:47 p.m.	Supper (20 minutes)
5:47 to 7:48 p.m.	Walk 10 miles
7:48 p.m.	Rest 5 minutes
7:53 to 9:54 p.m.	Walk 10 miles
9:54 p.m.	Rest 5 minutes
9:59 p.m. to 12:00 a.m.	Walk 10 miles
12:00 a.m.	Retire for sleep.

Table 3
DAYS THREE THROUGH SIX

TIME OF DAY	COMMENTS
12:00 to 5:55 a.m.	Sleep 6 hours
5:55 to 7:03 a.m.	Walk 5 miles
7:03 to 7:23 a.m.	Breakfast (20 mins.)
7:23 to 10:26 a.m.	Walk 15 miles
10:26 a.m.	Rest 5 minutes
10:31 to 12:34 p.m.	Walk 10 miles
12:34 to 12:54 p.m.	Lunch (20 minutes)
12:54 to 2:57 p.m.	Walk 10 miles
2:57 p.m.	Rest 5 minutes
3:02 to 5:05 p.m.	Walk 10 miles
5:05 p.m.	Rest 5 minutes
5:10 to 7:16 p.m.	Walk 10 miles
7:16 to 7:46 p.m.	Supper (30 minutes)
7:46 to 9:49 p.m.	Walk 10 miles
9:49 p.m.	Rest 5 minutes
9:54 to 11:55 p.m.	Walk 10 miles*
11:55 p.m.	Retire for sleep.

*On the last day Weston stopped at 10:55 covering only 55 miles.

AN EYEWITNESS ACCOUNT

We have seen Weston's proposed schedule. This is Weston in "theory". What of Weston in "reality"? Fortunately, an extensive eyewitness account of one of Weston's early performances has been preserved. In 1870 Dr. Austin Flint, Professor of Physiology at Bellevue Hospital Medical College in New York City, together with a team of assistants, studied Weston for a scientific project. Weston agreed to a fifteen day study. During the first five days he rested, but had his every action observed and recorded. All his food as well as his excrement was weighed and analyzed. During the next five days he gave a pedestrian exhibition during which he attempted to achieve two goals: 400 miles in the five days, and 112 miles on one of the five days. On the final five days, Weston was observed extensively as on the first five days.

Dr. Flint's work was published in the *New York Medical Journal* of June, 1871. We will simply relate Dr. Flint's observations of one of the days during which Weston walked for science.

The walk began on November 21, 1870 in the Empire Skating Rink in New York City. The track was made of boards covered with dirt and shavings and laid out in the form of a rectangle. It measured just over seven laps to the mile.

On the first day Weston managed eighty miles. He felt well and walked with great ease, even though he suffered a little nausea. This, he related, was common on the first day of such an effort. On the second day he managed only forty-eight miles, but he was resting for a big "push" for 112 miles on the third day. Dr. Flint writes:

> At 4:05 p.m. he was undressed, and wrapped in a long red flannel gown and a blanket, carried to a vehicle, and driven about five blocks to a private house to sleep. He states that he did not sleep, but dozed and got no rest. About 9:30 p.m. he was brought back to the rink in the same way that he was taken out, ate supper, and began at 10:24 p.m. his first attempt to walk one hundred and twelve miles in twenty-four consecutive hours. He seemed cheerful and confident during the entire day.

The following is Dr. Flint's detailed account of the third day:

12:00 to 6:06 a.m.	6 h. and 6 m. walking 27 4/7 miles, with one stop of 4 m. 30 sec. for rest, and 4 stops for urination, averaging 30½ sec. each.

6:06 to 6:14 a.m.	8 minutes' rest, sitting on the track.
6:14 to 1:31 p.m.	7 h. and 17 m. walking 33 miles, with 4 stops for urination, averaging 31¼ sec. each.
1:31 to 1:37 p.m.	6 minutes' rest, sitting on the track.
1:37 to 2:24 p.m.	47 m. walking 3 3/7 miles, with one stop of 34 sec. for urination.
2:24 to 2:31 p.m.	7 minutes' rest, sitting on the track.
2:31 to 3:05 p.m.	34 m. walking 2¾ miles.
3:05 to 3:32 p.m.	27 minutes' rest, sitting on the track.
3:32 to 4:46 p.m.	1 h. 14 m. walking 5¼ miles, including 2 stops for urination, averaging 27½ sec. each.
4:46 to 5:16 p.m.	30 minutes' rest, sitting on the track.
5:16 to 5:46 p.m.	30 m. walking 2 miles, with one stop of 58 sec. for urination.
5:46 to 6:49 p.m.	1 h. and 3 m. rest in his room (supper).
6:49 to 9:11 p.m.	2 h. and 22 m. walking 11 miles, with one stop of 30 sec. for urination.
9:11 to 9:21 p.m.	10 minutes' rest, sitting on the track.
9:21 to 10:52 p.m.	1 hr. and 31 m. walking 7 miles, with one stop of 43 sec. for urination.
10:52 to 12:00 a.m.	1 h. and 8 m. rest, continued into November 24th.

Walking 92 miles	20 h.	8 m.	43 sec.	
Urination		7 m.	47 sec.	
Rest on the track	1 h.	32 m.	30 sec.	
Rest off the track	2 h.	11 m.		
	23 h.	58 m.	120 sec.	= 24 hours

Thus Weston only managed ninety-two miles on the third day and failed in his push for 112. On the next two days he walked only fifty-seven and forty and one-half miles for a total of 317.5 for the five days. As usual, Weston fell short of his goals.

Upon the conclusion of the walk Dr. Flint observed:

> Notwithstanding the immense muscular and nervous strain to which Mr. Weston had subjected himself for the past five days, culminating on the fourth day in complete prostration of the nervous system, he sat up, talked and joked with his friends until 1:40 a.m., November 26th, then went to bed and slept well until 10 a.m. He then got up, feeling splendidly; wakening his attendants, who are almost exhausted by the five days' labor and watching, and called for his breakfast, which he ate at 11:45, with excellent appetite. For the succeeding five days, he felt as well as ever. During these five days, he did absolutely nothing but eat, sleep, and amuse himself, attending to no business. He took no exercise, walking only about two miles a day, though he said he felt as if he could walk one hundred miles any day without difficulty.

Finally, we are told that on the day following the conclusion of the walk, Weston "smoked six cigars during the day."

"BLOWER" BROWN'S RECORD

Henry "Blower" Brown was born in Paltham, England and was thirty-seven years old in 1880 when he broke Edward Payson Weston's year old record of 550 miles for six days "go as you please" pedestrian match. Brown managed a brilliant 553 miles to become the "champion pedestrian of the world."

Table 4 shows Brown's total mileage as recorded at the end of each hour. It is measured in miles and remaining laps. The track apparently measured eight laps to the mile. The figures are truly impressive. In the first day he covered 125 miles and 225 by the end of the second!

In Table 5 we have a summary of each day's activities. Notice that Brown's average speed was faster on the sixth than the fifth day.

Table 6 gives the number of miles run in each hour. From these figures we can surmise that Brown did most of his sleeping at night, as did Weston.

Sir John Dugdale Astley who promoted these contests left us a vivid picture of Brown and his trainer John Smith. The following is from his autobiography *Fifty Years of My Life - In the World of Sport at Home and Abroad,* published in 1894.

> I must say a word about that peculiar brick-maker, Blower Brown, and his backer, one of the quaintest of old peds, John Smith, whose *soubriquet* when in his prime was the "Regent Street Pet."
>
> Brown had early distingished himself by the rapid manner he trundled his barrow of bricks to the kiln, and back again for another load, and, like all brick-makers (I have ever heard of), he was wonderfully fond of beer; therefore, when old Jack Smith wished to get an extra spurt out of his *protege*, he used to yell at him on the track, and the same exhortation and promise was enumerated whenever his instinct told him encouragement was needed: "Well done, Blower! go it, Blower! you have got 'em beat, my beauty! Yes! Blower shall have a barrel of beer all to himself if he wins; go it, Blower!" One day Blower showed signs of shutting up, and as he was more an animal than an angel, Smith and I agreed that it would be a good thing to wake him up a bit by putting him in a hot bath–quite a new sensation for him–so we took him to my lodgings hard by, and I ordered two chops

TABLE 4

HENRY "BLOWER" BROWN
AGRICULTURAL HALL, LONDON
February 16 - 21, 1880
Six Day Pedestrian Contest

CUMULATIVE DISTANCE (MILES, LAPS)

	MONDAY		TUESDAY		WEDNESDAY		THURSDAY		FRIDAY		SATURDAY	
HOUR	MILES	LAPS	MILES	LAPS	MILES	LAPS	MILES	LAPS	MILES	LAPS	MILES	LAPS
1	8	2.75	125	.75	225	.75	315	.75	405	.75	481	.75
2	16	2.5	125	3.25	225	.75	315	2.5	405	.75	482	0
3	22	5.5	130	7	228	7	319	6.5	408	1	488	0
4	29	1.5	136	4.75	233	3.5	324	2	412	4.25	493	7.75
5	35	2.75	141	.75	238	1.75	328	6.75	414	.75	499	3
6	42	5.5	145	5.5	242	7.5	334	2.5	415	4.25	500	1.75
7	49	1.5	150	6.25	247	.75	339	7	420	2.75	504	2.75
8	53	7	156	6	251	7	345	4	425	3.75	508	5
9	59	7.5	161	5	257	3.5	350	.75	430	2.25	510	.75
10	65	2.75	165	5.5	262	2.75	353	7.5	433	5	513	6.75
11	71	1.5	171	6.5	267	1.5	359	4.75	437	3.5	518	.75
12	75	6	177	0	269	5.5	359	4.75	442	.5	522	5

CUMULATIVE DISTANCE (MILES, LAPS)

HOUR	MONDAY MILES	MONDAY LAPS	TUESDAY MILES	TUESDAY LAPS	WEDNESDAY MILES	WEDNESDAY LAPS	THURSDAY MILES	THURSDAY LAPS	FRIDAY MILES	FRIDAY LAPS	SATURDAY MILES	SATURDAY LAPS
13	80	2	180	3.75	275	2.25	363	7.5	446	5.75	526	.75
14	85	3.5	185	5.25	279	6.5	367	6	450	.75	527	.75
15	90	.25	191	1.5	285	.75	372	6	452	1.75	531	7.5
16	96	.50	196	4.75	289	6	377	5.5	456	.75	536	3
17	100	.75	200	.75	290	5	378	7.5	460	3.75	540	5.75
18	102	7	202	3.75	292	.75	383	3.75	464	7	545	1.5
19	107	2	207	.50	302	6.75	388	1.25	466	7.5	550	1.75
20	112	.75	212	3.75	305	7.75	392	6	471	8	552	7.75
21	117	2	215	6.50	310	1.75	397	4.5	476	1.5	553	0.13
22	121	8	220	6	314	3.5	402	.75	479	3.75	–	
23	125	.75	225	.75	315	.75	405	.75	481	.75	–	
24	125	.75	225	.75	315	.75	405	.75	481	.75	–	

TABLE 5

HENRY "BLOWER" BROWN
AGRICULTURAL HALL, LONDON
February 16 - 21, 1880
Six Day Pedestrian Contest

	MONDAY	TUESDAY	WEDNESDAY	THURSDAY	FRIDAY	SATURDAY
Distance Covered	125 Miles 170 Yards	100 M	90 M	90 M	76 M	72 M
Time on Track	20:02:42	18:39:26	18:07:23	18:05:20	17:21:43	14:57:09
Time Resting	2:57:18	5:20:34	5:52:37	5:54:40	6:38:17	6:22:51
Number of Rests	13	11	9	8	8	9
Average Pace (Mins/Mile)	9:37	11:12	12:05	12:04	13:43	12:28
Average Speed MPH	6.24	5.36	4.97	4.98	4.38	4.82

Total Time on Track = 4 days 11 hours 13 minutes 43 seconds.

Total Time Resting = 1 day 9 hours 6 minutes 17 seconds.

TABLE 6

HENRY "BLOWER" BROWN
AGRICULTURAL HALL, LONDON
February 16 - 21, 1880
Six Day Pedestrian Contest

MILES RUN EACH HOUR

HOUR	MONDAY	TUESDAY	WEDNESDAY	THURSDAY	FRIDAY	SATURDAY
1	8.34	0	0	0	0	0
2	7.97	0.3	0	.22	0	.91
3	6.38	5.47	3.78	4.5	3.03	6
4	6.5	5.72	4.56	4.44	4.41	5.97
5	6.16	4.5	4.78	4.59	1.56	5.41
6	7.34	4.59	4.72	5.47	1.44	.84
7	6.5	5.09	4.16	5.56	4.81	4.13
8	4.69	5.97	4.78	5.63	5.13	4.28
9	6.06	4.88	5.56	4.59	4.81	1.47
10	5.40	4.06	4.91	3.84	3.34	3.75
11	5.84	6.13	4.84	5.66	3.81	4.25
12	4.56	5.19	2.5	0	4.63	4.53
13	4.5	3.47	5.59	4.34	4.66	3.47
14	5.19	5.19	4.53	3.81	3.38	1

(Table 6 continued on page 266.)

TABLE 6 Continued

MILES RUN EACH HOUR

HOUR	MONDAY	TUESDAY	WEDNESDAY	THURSDAY	FRIDAY	SATURDAY
15	4.56	5.53	5.28	5	2.06	4.84
16	6.06	5.41	4.66	4.94	3.94	4.44
17	4.03	3.5	.88	1.25	4.31	4.34
18	2.79	2.38	1.47	4.53	4.47	4.47
19	4.38	4.59	10.75	4.69	2.06	5.03
20	4.84	5.40	3.13	4.59	4.44	2.75
21	5.16	3.34	4.25	4.81	3.81	.13
22	4.125	4.94	2.22	4.53	4.28	0
23	3.72	4.34	2.26	3	1.63	0
24	0	0	0	0	0	0

> to be got ready for him, and then put him into a hip bath of *real hot* water, which livened him up considerably, fairly making him sing out. When he had got him nicely dried, the chops appeared, and whilst I was helping Blower into his running-suit I was horrified to observe old Smith busily employed gobbling up all the best parts of the chops, leaving only the bone, gristle, and fat, and when I expostulated with him on his greediness and cruelty to his man, he replied: "Bless yer, Colonel! Blower has never had the chance of eating the inside, he likes the outside," and, sure enough, the brick-maker cleaned up the dish, with the result that he won first prize, doing 542 miles, a grand performance, and, what is more, his appetite and thirst were in no way impaired.

Four years after setting the world's record, "Blower" Brown was dead at the age of forty-one. The cause of his death was not reported.

10

Race Organization

Ultramarathon races are not easy to organize and direct. Officials spend long hours counting laps, recording times, giving directions, passing out drinks and monitoring traffic. A fifty mile race usually lasts at least eight hours, and a hundred miler spans twenty hours. The officials can become as exhausted as the contestants, but they get no glory. It's understandable that so few ultramarathons are scheduled.

In most cases, ultramarathoners themselves are aware of the great sacrifice that is made by directors of these races, and have been very appreciative of their efforts. In short races, it is common to see athletes badgering the race director with trite complaints. By contrast, ultramarathoners have endured numerous kinds of mismanagement of their races with stoicism. Having directed four such races in the past three years myself and having made many errors, I saw that in most cases the runners never complained, but were quick to thank me for at least trying.

Ultramarathoning has been the stepchild of track and road racing. Sponsors have been reluctant to support such races because so few runners have been willing to enter. Now it appears that this situation may change. Races that a few years ago drew ten runners are now run by more than one hundred. In this chapter I will outline my recommendations for successful organization of these events based on my own experience in both racing and directing them. First I will review guidelines for organization that apply to both road and track races. I will then consider the particular needs of each type of ultramarathon.

General Considerations

A primary requirement for a successful ultramarathon is the availability of competent volunteers to assist in timing, handling and numerous other details. A low-key race can be run with two or three expert officials when the field is small, but a more formal race calls for considerable help.

Once the race director has made arrangements for the necessary assistance he must decide upon the following:

Road or Track?

Track races allow the director to have effective control over the event. Problems of traffic safety, handling stations, toilet facilities and course direction are all trivial on a track. However, on the track the number of runners must be small. There will be so much lapping that the front runners will be seriously hindered if more than thirty contestants are allowed to enter.

On the other hand, road courses allow for very large fields of runners. Lap counting problems are minimal, but traffic is a major concern. Are safe roads available? Can frequent aid stations be manned? Can you obtain official AAU certification that the distance run is accurate?

As a compromise, a road course run over a small loop of two to five miles is often best, because it combines the advantages of both road and track.

Length

If the race is to be run on the road, one of the standard distances—fifty miles, one hundred miles, or one hundred kilometers—is best. The shorter the race, the larger the number of entrants will be.

In track races, it is best to organize the race by time rather than distance. Races lasting twelve or twenty-four hours are most common.Why time as opposed to distance? So that all the runners will finish simultaneously.

This allows every contestant to enjoy the approval of the spectators. It allows the spectators to know exactly when the race will end and to arrange their affairs so they can witness the finish. Also, an awards ceremony can be made immediately at the conclusion of the race, and all finishers will be there to enjoy it.

Physical Facilities

Are suitable dresssing and showering facilities available? Adequate toilet facilities are a must in ultramarathons at the start and at frequent locations along the course.

Time Limit

In every race a time limit, after which all runners on the course are disqualified, should be set. This enables both runners and officials to know when the race will end, and should be clearly advertised on the entry form with the statement that it will be strictly enforced. A time limit permits the would-be entrant to consider his or her ability to meet your standard before entering.

Age Limitations

Ultramarathoning is a very demanding sport appropriate only only for mature, experienced athletes. It is not for children; the young need the protection of those with experience. For this reason I strongly recommend that a minimum age be required for entry. Eighteen probably is a reasonable age, although it could be argued that this is still too young and that twenty-one is better. In any case, the sight of children running in these events harms not only the youngsters but the whole sport as well. In many instances their participation is anything but voluntary, and is due to pressure from an adult. Race directors who permit the entry of children are indirectly participating in child abuse.

Other Qualifications

Frequently race directors require that entrants in ultramarathons provide proof of their fitness to undertake the trial. For entry in a fifty-miler, completion of the marathon in 3:30 is sometimes required. For entry in a 100-miler, completion of a fifty-miler is often required.

Starting Time

Because of their great duration, ultramarathons frequently

begin early in the morning. Many fifty-mile races start between 6 a.m. and 9 a.m. The avoidance of extremely warm weather should be a primary consideration in scheduling ultramarathons.

The starting time should also be arranged so that spectators can easily witness the finish. One twelve hour track race in which I competed started at midnight and terminated at noon. A large group of rooters was on hand to enjoy the finish and encourage the runners.

Late Starters

It is very crucial that every effort be made to start the race at exactly the advertised time. Many runners have elaborate pre-race preparations that are easily upset by a delayed start. The race director who starts his event promptly always earns the approval of the entrants.

At times, a runner or two will arrive late through no fault of his or her own. In this case the race director can either forbid them to start, or allow them to start late, with their time recorded as though they started when everyone else left the line. Thus a runner who starts one hour late and actually runs a fifty mile race in 6:10 will have it officially recorded as 7:10, for that is what the watch reads when the runner crosses the finish line. No special mention should be made of this self-imposed handicap. Likewise, his finishing position should not be moved up in any way to compensate for a late start. In addition, to be fair to all contestants, the race director should let all runners know that this particular entrant started late. In head-to-head competition, the runners in front have the right to know who is or is not catching them from the rear.

Timing

Digital watches are now inexpensive and usually more accurate than mechanical ones. At least three such watches should be available with fresh batteries that will last the entire race. In the longest races, I like to synchronize the watches used to time the race with official standard time. The exact time of day can be determined by a simple phone call. For example, the timer might phone one-half hour before the race starts and set his watch accordingly. In this way if the time pieces fail during the race, the exact time can be obtained again by making a simple phone call.

Aid Stations

The race director should make arrangements for numerous aid stations to provide both refreshment and the opportunity to quit and obtain a car ride to the finish. Runners prefer water, fruit juices, soda, and tea with sugar. In hot weather these stations should ideally be one-half mile apart, but certainly no further than two miles apart. In cold weather, they can be three miles apart.

Handlers

All contestants should be encouraged to provide their own handlers. Before the event starts, the race director should speak to the handlers and inform them of their limitations. In particular, they must not hinder traffic by driving alongside their runner continuously. Rather, handlers should drive ahead and park off the road to wait until their runner arrives.

Disqualifying Runners in Distress

On the entry form, and also before the race starts, runners should be told that they will be required to leave the course if they appear to be in severe distress. Runners who ignore an official's instructions in such cases are automatically disqualified. At times, such runners are semiconscious and must be carried from the road for their own good.

Also, race entrants should be told unmistakably that they are a detriment to the sport if they do not at least appear to be moving well. A runner who begins to stagger down the road is not "heroic", but is occupying the attention of officials who are concerned for his or her health.

Entry Forms

Entry forms should contain all the important items mentioned above such as time limit, age limit, qualifying requirements, as well as the date, starting time and place, distance and course description, and entry fee if any.

Entry Fee

It is best to obtain a sponsor who can provide all necessary funds for the conduct of the race. Often, such a sponsor is not available and part or all of the director's expenses must be paid through entry fees.

Pre-Race Information Sheet

The director should send each official entrant detailed instructions to enable runners to provide for personal care. Maps of the course, guidelines for the conduct of handlers, and other relevant details should be explained. In short, all that the runner can expect from the race officials and all that is expected of the runner should be clarified.

Finish Line

As soon after crossing the finish line as possible, each runner should be informed of his position and time. If he has earned a prize, it is best to award it at that time also.

Mailing Race Results

Besides sending the complete results of the race to newspapers and the running press, this information should be sent as soon as possible to each contestant. For most runners this prompt service is valued far more than trophies and medals.

SPECIAL CONCERNS OF ROAD RACES

There are several types of road race courses which the race director can consider:

Point-to-Point

Races which start in one city and proceed directly to another city that is fifty or 100 miles away are best if you want to attract the interest of the general public. The prospect of runners covering on foot a distance that requires hours to travel by car can spark enthusiasm among both contestants and spectators. Unfortunately, these races are the most difficult to direct. Each aid station is used only once by the runners, whereas on a course consisting of ten loops each would be used ten times. Many support vehicles are required to monitor the point-to-point race, and accurate course measurement is very time consuming. In brief, it can be very difficult to find fifty miles of road sufficiently safe for racing.

The two most famous point-to-point ultramarathons are the London to Brighton race and the Comrades Marathon in South Africa. No race director should undertake to organize such a race unless he or she has sufficient manpower and funds to do the job properly.

One Large Loop

A course run over one large loop has all the disadvantages of a point-to-point race except one. Since the start and finish are identical, the dressing facility can be used both before and after the race. However, races run over a large circle do not enjoy one big advantage of point-to-point races, for the general public does not find the idea as captivating.

Out-and-Back Course

Here the runners go straight out for half the distance, make a U-turn, and return over the same route. The out-and-back course is easier to monitor than the single large loop; each aid station is used twice.The course can also be measured with half the effort required for a point-to-point run or a run over one loop.

Repeated Loops

Courses that consist of one small loop that is repeated many times are the easiest to direct and therefore the most commonly used. I prefer running in such a race, for I know that I will not need to rely on others to help me if I get in difficulty. Loops measuring two to five miles are very common. These allow each aid station to be used numerous times. If a runner must retire, he has little difficulty returning to the dressing room. With courses this small, very pleasant parks which permit the runner to compete in a traffic-free environment are frequently used. When timing a race of this type, the officials should take care to *record every lap time* for every runner. In this way, disputes concerning how many laps a runner has actually completed can usually be resolved easily.

For most races the director should select a course of the small loop type to insure that difficulties are kept to a minimum.

Road Safety

Perhaps the director's greatest concern is the safety of the competitors. Any race which takes place on the open road has the potential for a tragic automobile accident. Every effort should be made to select a course on which there is no vehicular traffic. For example, Central Park in New York City is closed to vehicular traffic on the week-ends and racing becomes very appropriate there. If traffic cannot be eliminated entirely, a director can ask to have the police block an entire lane of traffic so that runners will have a clear path to themselves. If the authorities will not allow blocking a lane, then the course should be abandoned unless there is very little traffic expected. Many country roads are largely traffic-free and are suitable.

Intersections and railroad crossings are important; dangerous intersections should have authorized traffic directors to allow runners the right of way. No course should cross a railroad track before the director has checked the train schedule.

Road Surface

If the runner must share the road with traffic, then a wide shoulder with a suitable surface for racing should be available. If the road's shoulder is poor, competitors will be jumping back and forth off the main road onto the shoulder as cars approach. The director should ride over the course being considered with an experienced runner to ascertain how suitable the surface is for racing. The crown of the road should also be checked. Runners do not enjoy traveling fifty or more miles with one foot landing slightly higher than the other. If the road surface is not free of a severe crown, then another route should be selected.

Run Facing Traffic

Where the runner must share the road with motor vehicles, he must always face oncoming traffic. In this way he will be able to "jump for his life" should it be necessary.

Course Length Certification

The National AAU and RRCA jointly sponsor a Committee on Course Certification. This committee publishes methods of accurately measuring courses and provides assistance (through the mail) to race directors who cooperate in following these methods. The calibrated bicycle technique is probably the easiest and most accurate way to map out a course, but the calibrated surveyor's wheel is also recommended. Once the race director has measured his course *twice,* he files a detailed report of his technique with the Chairman of the AAU-RRCA Committee on Standards. This committee carefully reviews the measuring technique and awards certification to those courses which meet its standards of accuracy. The director can then include on his entry form the statement "AAU Certified Course." The Standards Committee is very careful in awarding certification. If they have any doubts concerning the accuracy of the measuring technique, the director will be required to remeasure the course. In this way runners have learned to have confidence in courses designated as certified.

No runner wants to complete fifty miles only to wonder whether it was in fact forty-eight or fifty-one. Every effort to obtain AAU Certification of the course length should be made by the director.

Course Directions

All too frequently, courses are complicated and a runner will unknowingly go off the required route. The race director should provide the competitors with maps and the opportunity to see the course before it is run. The route should be clearly marked with arrows painted on the road surface and monitors at each turn to show the runners the proper path.

SPECIAL CONCERNS OF TRACK RACES

Another major function of the track race director is the task of counting laps. We will discuss this matter in detail shortly.

Lap Counting for Records

In serious track races, in which athletes are attempting to establish records, every effort must be made to insure that lap counting is performed accurately. A track record will not be accepted as "certified" unless *each lap time is recorded.* This is a very tedious task, but it is the only way to insure that the correct distance was run. If a counter neglects to record a particular lap time, then the runner must lose that lap from his total count. In addition, those who record laps cannot be affiliated in any special way with the runner, in order to avoid any possible suspicion of conspiracy to miscount the laps. When counters are assigned to individual runners, the assignments should be made at random.

Perhaps electronic lap counting devices will be available soon that will not only detect that a runner has crossed the finish line, but will record that runner's name and time. Until that time, teams of human volunteers will be necessary.

Note also that at least two men should be working in shifts counting laps for a particular runner. When one counter is recording, the other can be resting. When they are fatigued, counters like runners, become more error-prone.

Lap Counting in Low Key Races

While it will not always be possible to secure volunteers to record the times of every lap, this should not discourage promoters from arranging "low key" track races in which a less formal method of lap counting is employed. In this way runners will gain valuable experience in running such races. When no assistance is available for lap counting, runners could count their own laps by carrying a small hand-held counter. They simply click the counter at the conclusion of each lap. At the end of each half-hour period the runners can inform the director of their lap count, and he can record this information. Each runner's total distance covered can then be posted on a large bulletin board or blackboard for the spectators.

While lap counting by this method remains unsuitable for certified records, the accuracy of the distance covered should be reasonably correct and the performance listed as "uncertified."

In such cases, a respected AAU or RRCA official should be

present to oversee the contest and attest that every effort was made to insure that the counting was accurate under the severe limitations in manpower.

Reversing Direction

When running a very long distance over a track, the fact that the runner is always turning in the same direction can place strain on the ankle and other areas of the runner's legs. It is simple enough to avoid this difficulty by requiring the runners to reverse direction simultaneously at the end of each half-hour interval. The following procedure can be used to avoid difficulties:

At the conclusion of each half-hour period the race director signals the contestants by blowing a whistle or similar alarm. The runners then proceed to the starting line and reverse the direction in which they had been circling the track. To avoid running into each other, the runner who has not yet reversed assumes the "right of way" and remains on the inside lane. Runners who have just reversed run a bit "wide" until all contestants have reversed.

In the great pedestrian races of the past century, reversing was assumed to be natural, and was always allowed. We have largely forgotten this important technique today, and its use should be encouraged. Reversing is probably not necessary in track races of fifty miles or less; in races of twelve hours or longer reversing is recommended.

Passing Runners

In general, runners should be required to stay on the inside lane whether walking or running; the runner who wishes to pass must move to the outside. In short track races, runners who are being lapped are usually asked to allow the faster athletes overtaking them to pass on the inside. There is so much lapping in ultramarathon races that this courtesy becomes entirely unreasonable. The runners should simply stay on the inside.

When two runners are moving at the same speed and conversing, they habitually run side by side. This practice should be discouraged in track races for it makes the job of overtaking them even more difficult for the faster runners. The director should instruct the contestants to run "single file."

Appendix

Appendix I

Ultramarathon Records

The International Amateur Athletic Federation (IAAF) certifies track records for men at distances up to thirty kilometers. There is at present no recognized international body to authenticate record performances at the ultramarathon distances. The English Road Runner's Club (RRC) recognizes what it terms "World Best Performances" for track records at twenty, twenty-five, thirty, forty, fifty, and one hundred miles; fifty, one hundred and 150 kilometers; two and twenty-four hours. The RRC rules are nearly identical to the IAAF rules for determining the accuracy of a proposed record. In the absence of international agreement on these matters, it would appear that the RRC "Best Performances" are the most reliable records and race directors would do well to follow their guidelines which are included in Appendix 2.

In compiling the following list of records, I did not distinguish between those records which are recognized by the RRC and others which seemed to be noteworthy. Thus I have included professional pedestrian records for races lasting more than one day along with performances recognized by the British RRC.

In compiling these lists I am grateful to acknowledge the help of Andy Milroy, who compiles the records for the booklet "Distance Running Progressive Bests" published by the British RRC, and Nick Marshall who compiles records for the National Running Data Center. I make no claim that the present lists are complete. In some cases (where not specified), both road and track performances are included in the same list without distinction.

WORLD'S BEST TRACK PERFORMANCES

Distances in Miles

Miles	Name (Country)	Time	Date
30	Cavin Woodward (GB)	2:43:52	04/26/1975
40	Joe Keating (GB)	3:49:32	04/28/1973
50	Don Ritchie (GB)	4:53:28	10/28/1978
100	Don Ritchie (GB)	11:30:51	10/15/1977
200	Charles Rowell (GB)	35:09:28	02/28/1882
300	Charles Rowell (GB)	58:17:06	02/28/1882
400	James Albert (US)	84:31:18	02/09/1882
500	Patrick Fitzgerald (US)	109:18:20	05/03/1884
600	George Littlewood (GB)	135:00:00	12/08/1888

Distances in Kilometers

Kilos	Name (Country)	Time	Date
50	Don Ritchie (GB)	2:50:30	03/10/1979
100	Don Ritchie (GB)	6:10:20	10/28/1978
150	Don Ritchie (GB)	10:36:42	10/15/1977
200	Ron Bentley (GB)	16:53:00	11/3-4/1973

Greatest Distances Run in Stated Periods

Hours	Name (Country)	Distance (miles, yards)	Date
24	Ron Bentley (GB)	161m 545y*	11/3-4/1973
48	Charles Rowell (GB)	258m 220y	02/28/1882
72	Charles Rowell (GB)	353m 220y	03/02/1882
96	James Albert (US)	450m 000y	2/9-10/1888
120	James Albert (GB)	544m 000y	
144	George Littlewood (GB)	623m 1320y	12/3-8/1888

50 KILOMETERS - GREATEST PERFORMANCES

World's Best Performances - Track (50 kilometers)

1. Don Ritchie (GB)	2:50:30	1979
2. Joe Keating (GB)	2:54:54	1977

*World's Best Performance" as recognized by the British RRC.

3. Cavin Woodward (GB)	2:55:24	1979
4. Jim Mouat (GB)	2:56:06	1977
5. Tom O'Reilly (GB)	2:56:34	1979

Best US Performances - Men - Track (50 kilometers)

1. Frank Bozanich (32,Cal.)	3:03:36	1977
2. Ken Young (31, Ill)	3:08:49	1972

Best US Performances - Men - Road (50 kilometers)

1. Chuck Smead (24, Cal.)	2:50:45	1976
2. Bill Scobey (27, Cal.)	2:52:24	1973
3. Carl Swift (21, Cal.)	2:53:54	1975
4. Steve Dean (24, Cal.)	2:56:06	1973
5. Kaj Johansen (29, Cal.)	2:57:00	1979

Best US Performances - Women - Track (50 kilometers)

1. Jacqueline Hansen (29, Cal.)	3:51:01	1978
2. Judy Ikenberry (35, Cal.)	4:01:12	1977
3. Donna Gookin (40, Cal.)	4:08:09	1977

Best US Performances - Women - Road (50 kilometers)

1. Sandra Kiddy (42, Cal.)	3:37:08	1979
2. Sue Krenn (28, Cal.)	3:40:52	1978
3. Penny DeMoss (26, Cal.)	3:48:27	1976
4. Sue Medaglia (43, NY)	4:02:13	1978
5. Caron Schaumberg (36, Cal.)	4:03:09	1978

50 MILES - GREATEST PERFORMANCES

World's Best Performances - Men - Track (50 miles)

1. Don Ritchie (GB)	4:53:28	1978
2. Cavin Woodward (GB)	4:58:53	1975
3. Phil Hampton (GB)	5:01:01	1971
4. Tom O'Reilly (GB)	5:05:30	1976
5. Alan Phillips (GB)	5:12:40	1966

Evolution of World's Record (50 miles)

F. W. Firminger (GB)	6h38m41.0s	12/26/1879
John Fowler-Dixon (GB)	6h20m47.25s	12/29/1884
Fowler-Dixon	6h18m26.2s	04/11/1885
Edgar Lloyd (GB)	6h13m58.0s	05/12/1913
Derek Reynolds (GB)	5h30m22.4s	12/13/1952
Jackie Mekler (SA)	5h24m27.4s	09/05/1954
Gerald Walsh (SA)	5h16m07.0s	10/19/1957
Alan Phillips (GB)	5h12m40.0s	10/15/1966
Phil Hampton (GB)	5h01m01.0s	07/10/1971
Cavin Woodward (GB)	4h58m53.0s	10/25/1975
Don Ritchie (GB)	4h53m28.0s	10/28/1978
Noteworthy professional performance		
George Cartwright (GB)	5h55m04.5s	02/21/1887

Best US - Men - Track (50 miles)

1. Ken Moffitt (26, Cal.)	5:21:22	1978
2. Martin Smith (23, Iowa)	5:26:40	1973
3. Jim Czachor (30, NY)	5:26:54	1977
4. Frank Bozanich (32, Cal.)	5:30:31	1976
5. Joe Burgasser (36, Cal.)	5:39:06	1975
6. Nick Marshall (29, Pa.)	5:43:17	1977
7. Bob Cooper (23, Cal.)	5:45:12	1977
8. Tom Osler (35, NJ)	5:49:14	1975
9. George Crandall (42, Cal.)	5:51:04	1975
10. Ted Corbitt (46, NY)	5:54:15	1966

Best US - Men - Road (50 miles)

1. Allan Kirik (35, NY)	5:00:32	1979
2. Jim Pearson (31, Wash.)	5:12:41	1975
3. Frank Bozanich (33, Cal.)	5:14:36	1978
4. Bob Deines (23, Cal.)	5:15:20	1970
5. Skip Houk (28, Nev.)	5:15:22	1970
6. Darryl Beardall (29, Cal.)	5:18:55	1970
7. Chris Hamer (20, Cal.)	5:23:55	1979
8. Max White (22, Mass.)	5:26:26	1973

9. John Garlepp (40, NJ)	5:28:19	1978
10. Jose Cortez (18, Cal.)	5:30:42	1970

Best US - Women - Track (50 miles)

1. Judy Ikenberry (35, Cal.)	6:44:43	1977
2. Eileen Waters (28, Cal.)	6:55:27	1974
3. Donna Gookin (37, Cal.)	7:12:51	1974
4. Jacqueline Hansen (29, Cal.)	7:14:58	1978

Best US - Women - Road (50 miles)

1. Sue Ellen Trapp (33, Fla.)	6:12:12	1979
2. Nina Kuscsik (38, NY)	6:35:54	1977
3. Sue Ellen Trapp (33, Fla.)	6:55:30	1979
4. Candy Hearn (Cal.)	7:11:06	1979
5. Lydi Pallares (40, Fla.)	7:19:50	1979

100 KILOMETERS - GREATEST PERFORMANCES

World's Best Performances - Men - Track (100 kilometers)

1. Don Ritchie (GB)	6:10:20	1978
2. Cavin Woodward (GB)	6:25:28	1975
3. Tom O'Reilly (GB)	6:43:59	1976
4. Mike Newton (GB)	6:44:42	1976
5. Franz Dietzel (W. Ger.)	6:50:19	1976

World's Best Performances - Men - Road (100 kilometers)

1. Don Ritchie (GB)	6:18:00	1978
2. Elvino Gennari (Italy)	6:20:36	1977
3. Vito Melito (Italy)	6:24:18	1977
4. Cavin Woodward (GB)	6:26:05	1978
5. Ryszard Calka (Poland)	6:28:00	1978

World's Best Performances - Women (100 kilometers)

1. Christa Vahlensieck (W. Ger.)	7:50:37	1976
2. Sue Ellen Trapp (US)	8:43:14	1979
3. Edith Holdener (Switz.)	8:50:19	1976

4. Christel Heine (W. Ger.)	8:51:08	1976
5. Marcy Schwam (US)	8:51:09	1979
6. Riet Horber (Switz.)	8:59:40	1978
7. Blaschke (W. Ger.)	9:02:52	1978
8. Lydi Pallares (US)	9:10:39	1979
9. Weilbacher (W. Ger.)	9:18:36	1978
10. Huber (Austria)	9:24:51	1978

Evolution of World's Record - Men - Track (100 kilometers)

Wally Hayward (SA)	7h40m45s*	11/20/1953
Dave Box (SA)	7h29m05s	10/26/1969
Helmut Urbach (WG)	6h59m57s	10/18/1975
Cavin Woodward (GB)	6h25m28s	10/25/1975
Don Ritchie (GB)	6h10m20s	10/28/1978
Noteworthy professional performance		
George Littlewood (GB)	7h52m10s*	11/24/1884

Best US - Men (100 kilometers)

1. Frank Bozanich (34, Cal.)	6:51:21	1979
2. Park Barner (33, Pa.)	7:11:44	1977
3. Jim Person (35, Wash.)	7:15:01	1979
4. Nick Marshall (29, Pa.)	7:17:06	1977
5. Roger Welch (36, Mass.)	7:17:14	1979
6. Don Marvel (36, Md.)	7:22:15	1979
7. Cahit Yeter (43, NY)	7:23:55	1978
8. Warren Finke (37, Ore.)	7:35:14	1979
9. Don Choi (28, Cal.)	7:40:04	1977
10. Jack Bristol (24, Conn.)	7:47:15	1974

Best US - Women

1. Sue Ellen Trapp (33, Fla.)	8:43:14	1979
2. Marcy Schwam (26, Cal.)	8:51:09	1979
3. Lydi Pallares (40, Fla.)	9:10:39	1979
4. Sherry Horner (23, Pa.)	10:55:33	1978
5. Jo Ann Schroeder (28, Haw.)	11:09:00	1978

*estimated

100 MILES - GREATEST PERFORMANCES

World's Best Performances - Men - Track (100 miles)

1. Don Ritchie (GB)	11:30:51	1977
2. Cavin Woodward (GB)	11:38:54	1975
3. Derek Kay (SA)	11:56:56	1972
4. Tom O'Reilly (GB)	12:02:32	1975
5. Dave Box (SA)	12:15:04	1970

World's Best Performances - Men - Road (100 miles)

1. Don Ritchie (GB)	11:51:11	1979
2. Wally Hayward (SA)	12:12:28	1958
3. Ron Hopcroft (GB)	12:18:16	1958
4. George Perdon (Australia)	12:25:09	1970
5. Jose Cortez (US)	12:54:31	1971

World's Best Performances - Women (100 miles)

1. Natalie Cullimore (US)	16:11:00	1971
2. Ruth Anderson (US)	16:50:47	1978
3. Marcy Schwam (US)	19:03:06	1979
4. Miki Gorman (US)	21:05:00	1970
5. Cathy Burgess (SA)	22:00:46	1963

Evolution of World's Record - Men - Track (100 miles)

James Saunders (GB)	17h36m14s	2/21-22/1882
Wally Hayward (SA)	12h46m34s	11/20/1953
Dave Box (SA)	12h40m48.3s	10/11-12/1968
John Tarrant (GB)	12h31m10s	10/26/1969
Box	12h15m09s	7/31-8/1/1970
Derek Kay (SA)	11h56m56s	10/6-7/1972
Cavin Woodward (GB)	11h38m54s	10/25/1975
Don Ritchie (GB)	11h30m51s	10/15/1977
Noteworthy professional performance		
Charles Rowell (GB)	13h26m30s	10/27/1882

*Unratified since no lap times taken

Evolution of World's Record - Men - Road (100 miles)

Sidney Hatch (US)	16h07m43s	07/26/1909
Arthur Newton (Rhod)	14h44m00s	1927
Newton	14h22m10s	01/07/1928
Hardy Ballington (SA)	13h21m19s	07/02/1937
Wally Hayward (SA)	12h20m28s	10/24/1953
Ron Hopcroft (GB)	12h18m16s	10/25/1958
Wally Hayward (SA)	12h12m28s	1958
Don Ritchie (GB)	11h51m11s	06/16/1979
Noteworthy professional performance		
Arthur Newton (Rhod)	14h06m00s	07/20/1934

Best US - Men - Track (100 miles)

1. Ted Corbitt (49, NY)	13:33:06	1969
2. Park Barner (31, Pa.)	13:40:59	1975
3. Don Choi (30, Cal.)	14:45:00	1978
4. Frank Bozanich (33, Cal.)	15:21:56	1977
5. Abe Underwood (40, Cal.)	15:49:41	1978
6. Sidney Hatch (US)	16:07:43	1909
7. Tom Osler (38, NJ)	16:11:15	1978
8. Lu Dosti (43, Cal.)	17:30:00	1970
9. Ray Wieand (19, Cal.)	17:56:53	1978
10. Larry Young (28, Mo.)	18:07:12	1971

Best US - Men - Road (100 miles)

1. Jose Cortez (19, Cal.)	12:54:31	1971
2. Park Barner (34, Pa.)	13:57:36	1978
3. Ken Young (30, Ill.)	14:14:39	1972
4. Cahit Yeter (43, NY)	14:30:05	1978
5. Nick Marshall (30, Pa.)	14:37:05	1978
6. Brian Jones (37, NY)	15:08:43	1978
7. Bill McCray (25, Cal.)	15:13:43	1975
8. Paul Ryan (32, Haw.)	15:31:00	1978
9. Bill Lawder (30, NJ)	15:37:22	1978
10. Darryl Beardall (35, Cal.)	15:38:38	1972

Best US - Women (100 miles)

1. Natalie Cullimore (33, Cal.)	16:11:00	1971
2. Ruth Anderson (48, Cal.)	16:50:47	1978
3. Marcy Schwam (26, Cal.)	19:03:06	1979
4. Miki Gorman (35, Cal.)	21:05:00	1970
5. Elsie McGarvey (49, Mont.)	22:52:31	1978

24 HOURS - GREATEST PERFORMANCES

World's Best Performances - Men - Track (24 hours)

Name (Country)	Distance (miles, yards)	Distance (kilometers)	Year
*1. Park Barner (US)	162m, 537y	261.149km	1979
**2. Ron Bentley (GB)	161m, 545y	259.603km	1973
3. Wally Hayward (SA)	159m, 562y	256.400km	1953
4. Tom Roden (GB)	156m, 439y	251.456km	1977
5. Adriano Piccinali (Italy)	155m, 516y	249.918km	1977
6. Derek Reynolds (GB)	154m, 1226y	248.960km	1953
7. Bretislav Molata (Czech)	152m, 798y	245.350km	1977
8. Rino Lavelli (Italy)	150m, 1064y	242.374km	1976
9. Derek Funnell (GB)	145m, 1314y	234.557km	1977
10. Carmelo Andreatta (Italy)	140m, 1351y	226.554km	1974

World's Best Performances - Women - Track (24 hours)

1. Marcy Schwam (US)	113m, 1193y	182.908km	1979
2. Mavis Hutchinson (SA)	106m, 736y	171.263km	1971

Evolution of the World's Record

Charles Rowell (GB)	150m 395y	241.762km	***02/27/1882
Arthur Newton (Rhod.)	152m 540y	245.113km	***04/3-4/1931
Wally Hayward (SA)	159m 562y	256.400km	11/20-21/1953
Ron Bentley (GB)	161m 545y	259.603km	11/3-4/1973
Park Barner (US)	162m 537y	261.149km	06/1-2/1979

*Uncertified record performance **Official world's best performance
***Professional indoor performance

Best US Performances - Men - Track

*1.	Park Barner (35, Pa.)	162m, 537y	261.149km	1979
*2.	Don Choi (30, Cal.)	136m, 716y	219.525km	1978
3.	Ted Corbitt (53, NY)	134m, 782y	216.368km	1973
4.	Frank Bozanich (33, Cal.)	128m, 964y	206.877km	1977
5.	Lu Dosti (43, Cal.)	127m, 600y	204.935km	1970
6.	Tom Osler (36, NJ)	114m, 0y	183.465km	1976
7.	Ed Dodd (32, NJ)	111m, 1100y	179.643km	1978

*Unofficial records

PROGRESS OF THE WORLD SIX DAY GO-AS-YOU-PLEASE RECORD

Date	Pedestrian	Mileage	Place of Event
1874, Dec. 14-19	E.P. Weston	500m	Rink, Newark
1875, May	D. O'Leary	500m	West Side Rink, Chicago
1875, Nov. 15-20	D. O'Leary	501m, 384y	Chicago
1876, Oct. 16	D. O'Leary	502m	Toxteth Park, England
1877, April 2-7	D. O'Leary	519m, 1585y	Agricultural Hall London
1878, Mar. 18-24	D. O'Leary	520m, 420y	Agricultural Hall London
1878, Oct. 28-Nov. 2	W. Gentleman	520m, 503y	London, England?
1879, April 21-26	H. Brown	542m, 440y	London, England?
1879, June 15-21	E.P. Weston	550m, 110y	Agricultural Hall, London
1880, Feb. 16	H. Brown	553m	London, England
1880, April 5-10	F. Hart	565m	New York City
1880, Nov. 1-6	C. Rowell	566m, 165y	Agricultural Hall London
1881, May 23-28	R. Vint	578m, 440y	Madison Square Gar. New York City
1881, Dec. 26-31	P. Fitzgerald	582m, 55y	Amer. Insti. Bldg., New York City

1882, Feb. 27-Mar.4	G. Hazael	600m, 220y	Madison Square Gar. New York City
1884, Apr. 28-May 3	P. Fitzgerald	610m	Madison Square Gar. New York City
1888, Feb. 6-11	J. Albert	621m, 1320y	Madison Square Gar. New York City
1888, Nov.27-Dec. 2	G. Littlewood	623¾m	Madison Square Gar. New York City

Index to Part One

Index to Part Two

About the Authors

Ed Dodd was born in Drexel Hill, Pennsylvania, where he began his running career as a high school cross-crountry runner. He has been a runner for nineteen years, and has competed in races ranging from half-mile to twenty-four hours. He holds a Masters degree in Mathematics, and teaches at Haddon Township High School in Westmont, New Jersey as well as at St. Joseph's University in Philadelphia. He now lives in Collingswood, New Jersey with his wife and their three children.

Tom Osler is a veteran of more than 800 races ranging in distance from one mile to 200 miles. He won the AAU 25 Kilometers in 1967, and the RRC 50 mile race in 1967. He has a Doctorate in Mathematics and is an Associate Professor at Glassboro State College in New Jersey. Dr. Osler is the author of *Serious Runner's Handbook*, published in 1978 by World Publications.

Recommended Reading

Marathoning by Manfred Steffny. Offers a systematic plan for becoming a marathoner and gives a logical training progression that will be useful even to runners competing at international levels. Paperback, $5.95.

Serious Runner's Handbook by Tom Osler. A guide to training and racing for the competitive distance runner. Using a question and answer format, Tom Osler gives his views on "Training Smartly," "Staying Healthy," and "Racing Quickly." Paperback. $3.95.

Dr. George Sheehan's Medical Advice for Runners by Dr. George Sheehan. Here's Dr. Sheehan's first book designed to help you stay injury free. Dr. Sheehan feels that many running ailments are self-inflicted and therefore are preventable if we find and eliminate the cause. Hardback, $10.95.

The Complete Woman Runner by the editors of *Runner's World*. Covering everything from getting started to entering competition once the body is properly conditioned, the book also contains a section on the mind and body of the woman runner, her potential and aptitudes. Hardback, $10.95.

Run Farther, Run Faster by Joe Henderson. Organized into thirty easy-to-follow lessons. Each lesson includes charts, training schedules, and a self-test to help the runner gauge his progress. By following Henderson's clear, logical approach, any runner can build his technique and confidence in the area of racing. Paperback, $4.95.

Cures for Common Running Injuries by Dr. Steven I. Subotnick. Required reading for all runners who want to stay healthy and on the roads. Runners at all levels will profit from Dr. Subotnick's well-written and informative book. Paperback, $5.95.

Available in fine bookstores and sport shops, or from:

World Publications, Inc.

Box 366, Mountain View, CA 94042

Include $.45 shipping and handling for each title (Maximum $2.25).